PRAISE FROM THE TRENCHES

"With the number of businesspeople going to China for the first time rising each year, *The Chinese Negotiator* is going to immediately land on many people's want list. It really takes ownership of negotiating, offering a balanced mix of culture and business and a splash of history, with an emphasis on ethical behavior, essential for successful, long-term business dealings in China. March and Wu clear away much of the confusion that assaults first-time businesspeople going into China. If you do business in China this book is a must read before you commence your negotiations."

— **Paul Rohan,** *Managing Director,* **Rohan Group,**
international trader of Asian foods and beverages

"Negotiating in Asia is an exciting and at times frustrating experience. It requires a blend of business, cultural, and psychological knowledge that can usually only be gained from years of experience. Robert March's vast experience and wisdom gained in the region makes him the leading exponent of the art of negotiating in Asia. In *The Chinese Negotiator* March condenses his years of experience in China into easy-to-understand principles and strategies to master the mysteries of dealing with the Chinese, among the most formidable negotiators in the world."

— **Robert Seidler,** *Chairman,* **Hunter Phillip Japan**

"This is a defining book on how to, and how not to, negotiate with we Chinese. Robert March, presently a professor of international business at Nanjing University, together with businesswoman Su-Hua Wu, show how and why Western success or failure in China so often comes down to knowing how to prepare and respond in ways that communicate across the Chinese divide. Through many real-life examples and sharp analyses, the authors map out the best approaches for the modern businessperson or negotiator."

— **Wang Hua,** *diplomat* and *Director General* of
Foreign Affairs, Jiangsu Province, China

"*The Chinese Negotiator* is both comprehensive and enlightening. If you would like to know how to become a good negotiator in the Chinese context, and how to apply the 36 stratagems in business, *The Chinese Negotiator* gives you invaluable lessons."

— **Huang Zhenhua,** *Professor,* **University of International**
Business and Economics, China

THE
CHINESE
NEGOTIATOR

THE
CHINESE
NEGOTIATOR

How to Succeed in the World's Largest Market

ROBERT M. MARCH

SU-HUA WU

KODANSHA INTERNATIONAL
Tokyo • New York • London

NOTE
- All dollar amounts are expressed in U.S. currency unless otherwise noted.
- The surnames of the Chinese and Japanese mentioned in this book are listed in the traditional manner, last name first. However, when the given name is Western in origin, the given name comes first. The name of author Su-Hua Wu is also listed in the Western order.

Distributed in the United States by Kodansha America, Inc., and in the United Kingdom and continental Europe by Kodansha Europe Ltd.

Published by Kodansha International Ltd., 17–14 Otowa 1-chome, Bunkyo-ku, Tokyo 112–8652, and Kodansha America, Inc.

ISBN 978–4–7700–3028–3

Library of Congress Cataloging-in-Publication Data available

First edition, 2007
15 14 13 12 11 10 09 08 07   10 9 8 7 6 5 4 3 2 1

www.kodansha-intl.com

Contents

Introduction

Among the foreign companies that entered China in the 1990s, the only ones to survive were those with small investments in soft drinks or mobile phones. The failures included Pfizer, Novartos, Glaxo Wellcome, GM, Peugeot, AT&T, Maytag, Whirlpool, and numerous others. For private U.S. equity funds, China was a Trojan horse. They went there in the 1990s with nearly $6 billion in funds. By 1999, one-third had cut their losses and dissolved.

Yet, even now, in spite of the clear evidence to the contrary, many foreign businesses continue to believe in what Joe Studwell calls the China Dream—that awesome projection: numbers of consumers and potential profits.

The opportunities for the foreign negotiator to blunder and fail in China are many, though either side can be responsible for failure. This book focuses on the negotiator and two monumental opportunities for success. The first opportunity comes with the negotiator's ability to develop genuinely professional skills to deal with the many types of Chinese. The second derives from the ability to build long-term friendships and relationships with people whose culture is unlike that of many other countries in a multitude of ways.

Learning how to make friends with the Chinese means learning how to give them face, listen more than talk, socialize cheerfully at banquets and lunches, let discussions flow at their own speed, and make that new "you" in a strange land second nature over the long term.

These are the necessities of your social and business existence in China, however senior (or junior) you might be. You need to become accepted as a good guy, Chinese style. In addition, you must prepare for the banquets and meetings, the generally exotic ambience, and the differences among the Chinese you will have to deal with.

China has eight major regions, characterized by distinctive dialects (most mutually unintelligible, such as Cantonese and the Beijing dialect) as well as differences in foods, culture, and leisure pursuits. It bears comparison to western Europe. Moreover, depending on where you go in China, you will find the people sophisticated or simple, dressed tastefully or sloppily. They may be polished or rough, manifestly pro-Western or suspicious and subtly anti-Western, relaxed and at ease with you, or shy and socially awkward.

The study of Chinese etiquette is of some use, but it takes you merely a small step or two. Sweet words and nice smiles alone do not get you far in China, where you face the most strategically minded people in the world. To do business there, it is essential that you have a strategic mind, determination, composure, and your own team of like-minded warriors to accompany you on the journey. Only then—whoever you face, wherever you might be, and however bizarre the challenges (and there will be some!)—can you remain composed and indefatigable, the clever self-manager, accompanied by a team of smart colleagues with whom to take counsel.

The Chinese have tended to receive bad press over the years for their negotiating techniques, and their occasional use of possibly unethical stratagems by a few of them does not improve matters. We do not dispute that some Chinese can be tricky and slippery some of the time. Carolyn Blackman's book, *Negotiating China*, is full of wonderful, gritty anecdotes about slick Chinese and uncomfortable Westerners. But the Chinese and their negotiation style are, overall, steadily improving.

So what the foreign businessperson needs is guidance on how to be professional in managing relationships and negotiations with the increasingly professional Chinese. You need to be adroit and professional with the Chinese who, as we will show, are undoubtedly stratagem masters.

Most Chinese negotiators, when they look you and your accompanying team over, will readily see themselves as less international, sophisticated, experienced, well dressed, rich, and well paid. They will not even regard themselves as skillful as you at managing international business or running an international negotiation. They will accept that their negotiating teams are sometimes disorganized—and occasionally chaotic—and that their members unashamedly play power games among themselves in front of you.

Nonetheless, even a disorganized Chinese team stands a better than even chance of making a deal hugely to its advantage while it is negotiating on its home turf, controlling the agenda, bringing in replacement teams, using time to your disadvantage, and employing tactics with which you are totally unfamiliar (what the Chinese call stratagems, or *ji*, 计). When you read about what foreign companies have done in the past, you will realize that the negotiating success of Chinese teams rests on more than the skills of their team leaders.

CHINESE NEGOTIATING STYLES

Whether it is background on the Chinese, the way they negotiate among themselves, or how they view foreigners, it is important to be properly informed. In chapter 1 we describe the many varieties of Chinese negotiation style based on our own research. Chapter 2 looks at how foreigners and Chinese view one another.

Central to the success of the Chinese is their teamwork at home. Their methods are similar to the twelve-step process and Strategic Negotiation Process (SNP) that we introduce in chapters 11 and 12. The next most important element is the skillful way in which they play their cards, holding them close to the chest.

To counter the strategic approach of the Chinese, at the very least you will need a cohesive team of skillful players with whom to take counsel. The team needs members with experience both in recognizing the strategies put into play by their opponents and in understanding how to counter them.

CASE STUDIES PINPOINT ASPECTS OF PROFESSIONALISM

Chapters 3 through 7 contain cases illustrating real team negotiations involving foreigners and Chinese. Successful case studies are presented featuring foreigners operating as smart teams (or, occasionally, as individuals). They are trusted by the Chinese as people of integrity and their word; they demonstrate that they have what it takes to work as partners with the Chinese over the long term; and they are sometimes even as skillful as the Chinese in responding to or countering Chinese stratagems.

Price bargaining is the central emphasis of cases in chapter 6, while the cases in chapter 7 concern the pivotal role of mutual relationships built on favors, or *guanxi*, in business relationships with the Chinese. We underline the importance of understanding and playing by the rules of guanxi in long-term relationships.

THE THIRTY-SIX STRATAGEMS

Chapter 8, which deals with the thirty-six stratagems, is the longest in the book. For most non-Chinese, the material presented here is the most exotic and least familiar, but it is easy to read and understand. If you are skimming through the book for basic essentials, read this chapter but perhaps leave the study of it to an occasion when there is enough time for you to think it over at leisure.

The challenge of Chinese stratagems is that they are neither easy to translate into action, nor can counterstrategies be quickly devised for them. This chapter will appeal most to the individual who excels at mastering complex strategic ideas. Yet, understanding is one thing; mastering and putting the stratagems into practice is something quite different.

BUILDING TRUST BUILDS RELATIONSHIPS

Chapter 9 deals with the most profound issue for the Chinese: **trust,** and its obverse, **distrust,** and suspicion of foreign negotiators. Why should this be? If you ask businesspeople in any country how they negotiate with people of their own culture, most will say that they do so amicably, misunderstandings are rare, and there is mutual trust. But, they might add, "When it comes to doing business with foreigners, I'm at a loss to know how to negotiate."

With their own people, they share similar values of fair play. When dealing with the Chinese, foreigners find they have little in common, negotiations seem heavily tactical, and they miss the reassurance of a shared culture. From the beginning, therefore, feelings of ambivalence as well as a sense of distance and distrust can color negotiations. We have thus included in the chapter many trust-building behaviors that the Chinese appreciate.

BUILDING PROFESSIONAL NEGOTIATING SKILLS

This section contains six chapters—10 through 15. We believe you should read these after the seventeen case studies in chapters 3 to 7, since they focus on the real-world challenges that can only be met by building professional skills. To be professional, everyone in the preparation and planning team— most notably the manager responsible for the project—needs to have a common understanding of what they will face in negotiations. Most people go in woefully unprepared, while *believing* they are fully prepared. To get some idea of the problems to be surmounted, try this short quiz.

ANSWER "YES" OR "NO" TO EACH OF THE FOLLOWING

1. Negotiating with the Chinese is not essentially different from negotiating with people in my own country.

2. I can easily handle a different business culture in which people take much longer to trust others.

3. Other people make costly mistakes and irritate the Chinese, but not us—we are professionals.

4. I know how to budget adequate time to conclude this project.

5. Reading a book on the plane (or its equivalent) is sufficient preparation for me.

6. I always build trust quickly with foreign partners, so no special preparation is required.

7. Talk about me building a professional negotiating team for China fails to appreciate how good I believe I am.

8. Stratagems are just old-fashioned tactics from ancient China. They aren't relevant to today's China.

9. I know the Chinese for what they are—Third-World people on the move. But they are far less experienced, sophisticated, and educated than us.

10. I don't need to upgrade my negotiating techniques to be successful with the Chinese.

If you answered "yes" to any of these questions, you would be on your way to creating problems for yourself in negotiating with the Chinese.

Experience has taught us that negotiating with the Chinese takes more time, money, energy, patience, and trust-building than negotiating back home, and the financial risks are much higher. A special kind of professionalism is required.

Horror stories of negotiations with the Chinese ending in bitter failure and recrimination are far too common. However things might be done in other parts of the world, no one should ever imagine they can wing it with the Chinese. Being successful in China requires an experienced, insightful, and knowledgeable team[1] that includes—and this is critical—native-born Chinese members experienced in both cultures.

I (March) trained my first international negotiating team in 1979, in Japan. I learned very quickly that *the ability to negotiate across cultures is not an innate skill*. It has to be acquired by learning and by trial and error. Without training or considerable accumulated experience, most teams behave erratically or are totally unprepared. The leader might fancy himself able to negotiate anywhere, off the top of his head; but if he delegates preparation to unprepared lieutenants, sooner or later team members will begin to compete or bicker with one another, or just switch off.

Brainstorming about strategy is useless if it outweighs building an understanding of the context of the subject matter and the main issues. Underprepared foreign teams in China will find themselves out of their depth sooner or later. Functioning like a disparate group of individuals, rather than a team, is virtually the same as being leaderless. This will not show in the honeymoon phase of the relationship, but as soon as the so-called team is put under pressure, cracks will appear—and be especially apparent to the Chinese. It is shortcomings of this kind that underlie many foreign investment failures in China.

"In the hands of a prepared team," says Matt Starr, a management engineer trained in our SNP and twelve-step negotiation planning process, "the SNP establishes a solid framework for the international negotiation process. It ensures a significantly better outcome for us than would otherwise be the case, provides a common approach and perspective that particularly enhance team negotiations, and boosts self-confidence."

We have found that, once seasoned international negotiators see how SNP-trained teams perform, their respect for the approach takes wing. Bob Seidler, one of Australia's leading lawyers who specializes in the Asia region, says:

"I was skeptical about Bob March's method, myself having come through the 'experience' school and bearing all the psychological scars. But it was fascinating and great fun. I am now a convert. Our opposition was the best prepared and most formidable team that I had encountered. However," Seidler concluded, "anyone negotiating with them had better be prepared!"

The SNP provides the foreign team with the techniques, confidence, and muscle to meet the unknowable and unpredictable in China. Peter Benjamin, a master brewery designer and builder who, in the 1990s, successfully negotiated to build China's largest brewery and who has negotiated other international contracts in other countries, says, "I could not have been successful on my own in China. My team was essential. Negotiation is too stressful, too complex in China; I would have been too prone to make poor judgments." Benjamin trained himself and his people to negotiate in a way that was nearly identical in spirit and style to our SNP. His case study, "How Giving Face Can Brew Success," is in chapter 3.

Chapter 13 presents material on an essential topic: *personal composure*. We have not seen it taken up anywhere else in connection with international negotiations, yet it can be critical when dealing with the Chinese, because many foreigners lose composure before the so-called inscrutable Chinese. Chapter 14 looks at another important issue—the ability to adapt to and make friends with the Chinese, a skill that can help you select the right people for your team in China.

Chapter 15 presents a final overview of the book, with emphasis on the central role of the international negotiation team and the benefits of coaching in preparing to negotiate successfully in China. The appendix provides detailed guidelines on using interpreters and translators in China.

CHAPTER 1

HOW THE CHINESE NEGOTIATE

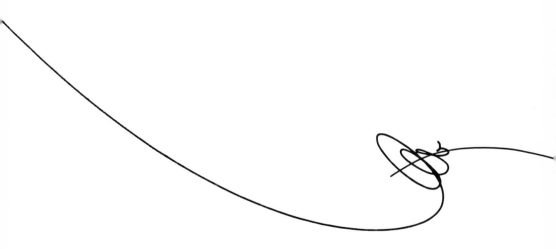

If you are preparing to negotiate with the Chinese and want to do it in a culturally appropriate way, it is helpful to understand first how they negotiate with one another. For them it is common sense to behave in the way they are accustomed to, in the way that is accepted by their fellow Chinese.

The degree to which Chinese trust each other is the key factor dictating the outcome of negotiations between Chinese. Transactions conducted between Chinese parties who completely trust one another show that what one side proposes, the other accepts with little or no adjustment. Dealings between Chinese family or quasi-family members are typically like this as well.

In sharp contrast are transactions involving parties at least one of whom does not trust another. Often marked by dishonest intent, deceit, and bribery, such dealings are generally beyond the scope of negotiations. In the following sections, we examine the extremes before concentrating on the fertile ground of negotiations.

COMPLETE TRUST AT THE BUSINESS AND PERSONAL LEVEL

When there is complete trust in China, the need to negotiate disappears. When one family member (or a friend with similar status) asks another to supply a good or service, the quality, price, and delivery may be specified—but there will be no bargaining. Based on past experience, Chinese will assume that the relative or friend will do everything possible to supply the best-quality good or service at the best-possible price.

Chinese put demands from long-time friends ahead of their own. Moreover, they are reluctant to ask for or accept money from friends for minor services. Genuine friends, most Chinese believe, bind themselves to one another by doing favors or giving small gifts in the spirit of reciprocity, which to many is the essence of Chinese culture. Receiving payment for performing a service for a friend is thought to destroy the basis of the relationship by making it commercial.

NO TRUST—COERCION, FRAUD, BRIBERY, AND CORRUPTION

Since this book focuses on negotiations—situations in which each party uses persuasion and financial inducements to reach a mutually satisfying agreement, although in some cases mild forms of oral intimidation and oral aggression might come into play—we are not concerned with occasions when parties cease negotiating and try to win by coercion, fraud, bribery, intimidation, or other underhanded means.

In China, a bribe most commonly takes the form of giving a gift—which is usually not illegal. Gifts can include money, a motor car, a package tour, sporting goods, club fees, and scholarships for children. The story is told of an invitation to Motorola, by a well-connected expatriate, to set up a $10 million dollar discretionary slush fund with no questions asked to help Motorola be awarded the new cell phone standard by the Chinese government.

Another aspect of which to be aware in Chinese negotiations is the problem of forged documents, such as forged title deeds for land on which a foreign factory is to be built. Moreover, Chinese governments—national, provincial, and local—will often do what they can to assist their constituents in disputes with strangers, whether the opposing party is from abroad or elsewhere in China. They might be induced to blacklist outsider companies; rules and guidelines might be used to make life in their locality more restrictive. However, companies that toe the Communist Party line and do not criticize China can be applauded for their "constructive engagement," or what has ironically been called Western capitalism with Chinese features. Chinese in dispute with their external partners will often search for loopholes in policies, guidelines, and laws to use against them.

While secrecy on either side does not necessarily vitiate negotiations, the challenge for the non-local or foreign negotiator is how to recognize when Chinese fail to provide all the information needed to make decisions or to understand what they are thinking. Since it is wise to assume that insufficient information is often consciously proffered, strangers should allow their team adequate time to assess what information is still needed. Such an assessment can generally be made by putting the Chinese at their ease and gaining their trust, a move that will provide the basis for eventually drawing out what information is being withheld. Nonetheless, the Chinese are masters at making strangers wait, in expectation that they will get sick of waiting and yield to the local demand.

A TYPICAL CASE OF DECEIT AND TRICKERY

In 1996, China-born Harry Wang, an Australian citizen, established a food manufacturing business in Guangdong with a local partner, Pang Hua-li. Pang had been introduced to Wang by an old school friend, Sun Guo-ai. The business was successful, with an annual turnover of $20 million in 2001.

In 2002, Wang decided to take a long holiday in Australia. While there, he heard from Pang that a local consumer had died from eating one of their pickle products, and that the family of the deceased was demanding $2 million in compensation. Moreover, the Guangdong provincial government had a warrant out for Wang's arrest and planned to take action against the company.

Pang told Wang that, while he could save the company by making appropriate under-the-table payments to government officials, there was nothing he could do to save Wang, whom he advised to stay in Australia where he would be okay.

To check on the story, Wang contacted Pang's school friend Sun. But Pang had already been in touch with Sun, to whom he had shown (forged) official documents concerning the death of the consumer, the subsequent inspection of the factory, the assessment of the plant's hygiene standards, and the letter from the deceased's family demanding $2 million.

When Wang heard that the situation was as reported by Pang, he remained in Australia and soon after sold his share in the company to Pang for a fraction of its value.

NOT AN ISOLATED CASE

Cases such as that involving Wang are not isolated. In China, coercion, bribery, deceit, and corruption are serious problems, and cases of theft and embezzlement are commonplace. In the same week of April 2005, for example, two instances of the misappropriation of funds were reported in the press on the same day. First we read that a junior typist in a Chinese bank had been arrested for embezzling $3 million while in her lowly position. Then, later that day, we read of the arrest of the Chinese president of a soft drink company who, with the assistance of his senior managers, had stolen 160 million yuan (about $16 million).

Moreover, there is a fear—widespread in foreign companies and increasingly in those run by Chinese—that Chinese staff cannot be trusted to handle cash. Even Taiwanese Chinese are targets, as a number of our Taiwanese business friends have discovered when defrauded by staff in their China subsidiaries.

Another story concerns a Taiwanese who built a farm in central China, on a mountain site he had been given (at no cost) by the village council. He was, however, unable to make the enterprise profitable, not because of the cost of building a road and connecting services but, rather, because his eight members of staff would periodically, during his absence, report a pig or sheep "missing," or find the need to "dispose of" a pig or sheep that was "terminally ill." He suspected the employees were stealing and selling off the animals to supplement their modest wages.

Yet another Taiwanese was not only robbed of one million yuan (about $100,000), but suffered a second, related financial assault. One of the accomplices in the robbery, discovering the victim's home address in Taipei, went there to tell the wife a concocted story that her husband had been kidnapped, and that she had to pay one million yuan immediately for his release.

Such incidents are not unusual and occur nationwide. As a result, a number of security companies in China plan to offer new systems to counter the business-related problems of pilfering and petty crime. So it is only natural in this kind of environment that newcomers worry about how their business in China might be affected.

BUSINESS NEGOTIATIONS

Having briefly explored the fringes where transactions are not negotiations—because of either the presence or absence of trust—we can now focus on our central theme, negotiation. The bulk of the people with whom you will negotiate will be members of large companies and government officials, professional people, the well educated, and entrepreneurs. We will call them mainstream society.

Members of the well-educated and cultivated middle and professional classes display many aspects of Confucian morality. They have a sound knowledge of Chinese history, its anecdotes and lessons, as well as the legends illustrating many of the moral maxims of Confucius and other sages. By this we do not mean that they are worshippers of Confucius, but that their core values for living harmoniously are infused with Confucian sensibilities. In contrast, those Chinese who neither respect and obey their parents and elders or their surrogates, nor accept the moral and ethical precepts of Confucian values, will not fit comfortably into mainstream society.

Most Chinese government officials and businesspeople, especially in the coastal regions and cities, recognize that if they are to do business successfully over the long term with other Chinese whom they have not met or with whom they have not done business before, it is first necessary to develop a friendly working relationship in which all parties are comfortable. This, in turn, leads to trust and respect.

These views, in no essential way different from those of Chinese at the highest level of government, are epitomized by great modern Chinese negotiators and diplomats such as Zhou En Lai (1898–1976), who was prime minister of China 1949–76; former Premier Zhu Rongji (1928–); and Deng Xiao Ping (1904–97), one of China's most prominent exponents of economic modernization.

Reciprocity Is Key

The Chinese do business with you as a person, not as an organization: hence the belief that friendship between organizations derives from friendship between individuals. Moreover, as the Confucian ethic bases relationships on reciprocity, the junior's loyalty, filial piety, obedience, and respect for the senior party are expected traits. In turn, the senior individual must be righteous, benevolent, charismatic, and loving; otherwise the junior party can disobey and even choose a better senior.

Mencius, the Confucian philosopher second only to Confucius, wrote: "If a ruler regards his ministers as his hands and feet, then his ministers will regard him as their heart and mind. If a ruler regards his ministers as dogs and horses, his ministers will regard him as any other man. If a ruler regards his ministers as dirt and grass, his ministers will regard him as a bandit and an enemy."

For the Chinese, it is common sense that, from the friendly atmosphere in which all feel comfortable, a new relationship will flower, nurtured by such conditions as:

- Greeting everyone, regardless of their position, with a *Ni hao?* (How are you?) and a smile is a sure-fire beginning to a good social atmosphere. Treating everyone as your equal is essential.

- Friendship. This begins with good first impressions and is best when people have an instinctive liking for one another.

- The mutual giving of face. This skill is critical to making a good impression. The Chinese believe that they look good—acquire face—as a result of having relationships with good people and being praised by others.

- Deference to and respect for senior people, as required by social protocol.

- Participation in the eating and drinking culture. Chinese believe there is no better way of developing friendship.

- Showing your "true personality" to one another—the personality that is ordinarily hidden behind the poker face of everyday business life—is probably essential, and often requires getting drunk with one another. This usually means that new Chinese friends will want to get the other party drunk in order to see the "real" them.

- Lack of pressure to make a deal or sign a contract.

- Acceptance of decisions made by a single leader, who may not participate in meetings or dinners. Chinese decision makers work up to eighteen hours a day and tend to become remote from negotiators.

Team Skill Weaknesses

Since Chinese negotiators are person-oriented, rather than team- or system-oriented, they believe themselves accountable only to their own constituencies or their immediate bosses. Thus they are not good team players. Moreover, although most Chinese think carefully before making or rejecting an offer, the fact that they do not always function well as teams can make them seem unorganized and chaotic, as they play power games while trying to gain personal benefits or recognition from their superiors or the other side. Occasionally even fighting in front of the other party, Chinese negotiators can also be flexible on some matters (such as agenda and documentation) but stubborn on others (firm price offers).

Nearly half the businesspeople living in coastal regions (especially in Beijing, Shanghai, Guangzhou, and Tianjin) see themselves as systematic negotiators who abide by international conventions. The remainder tend to consider their negotiating strategies unsystematic and unplanned. Team design and functioning can thus be problematic when, for example, Communist Party cadres are included in negotiating teams: role allocation is lacking; members confuse their job titles with their negotiating roles; and everyone talks at the same time. The fact that one side's position, or its final decision, is nonnegotiable because it came from the top administrator—who is often not the chief negotiator and not even present at meetings—can intensify discord within the team.

Individual Negotiators

On a positive note, some veteran negotiators maintain that they use rational and principled negotiation strategies. They take the initiative, give in on minor issues without sacrificing their principles, and present justified counter-proposals.

Technology transfer and joint venture negotiations see more professional, expert, and responsible negotiators than do trade talks. The former draw more on systematic strategies and exhibit better business ethics and better teamwork.

The quality of players in business negotiations has changed over the past ten years, and their negotiating competence has improved. Previously, negotiators were often Communist Party cadres, sloppy in appearance, with approaches to negotiating that were clouded by politics and ideology. Today we can see that China's businesspeople are becoming increasingly professional in their dealings with one another, and Communist cadres, when they appear, are better educated and more sophisticated.

Most Chinese consider themselves careful thinkers, patient negotiators, friendly, hospitable, and helpful. At the same time, they also see themselves as tough, clever, confident, profound, wise, and sometimes difficult negotiators. They are, thus, particularly cautious when dealing with other Chinese whom they do not know well, in the knowledge that, should matters not go smoothly, they may have a monumental fight on their hands—something to be avoided at all costs.

Outward Appearance

Chinese negotiators vary widely in their dress, speech, and manners. Those from coastal cities consider their appearance acceptable, while those from inland areas hold a negative view of their own appearance and manners. Coastal people say that many of their associates and buyers from the country lack fashion sense, cannot coordinate clothes, have poor posture, and lack social manners. Some, they say, look like farmers (because of their deeply tanned faces), and indeed many are part-time farmers.

Inland negotiators say of themselves that, lacking social skills, they arrange many ceremonial activities as part of the negotiating process, for example, taking visitors sightseeing and inviting government officials to give speeches at banquets. The implication seems to be that they lack the confidence to develop personal, one-on-one relationships with the more sophisticated people from coastal areas.

Banquets and Friendship

Banquets, which feature in all Chinese relationship building, have deep cultural underpinnings. Eating together has long been considered the best, most civilized way of creating an atmosphere that will foster friendship and good humor. Shared meals are central to Chinese life because they are seen as reinforcing human relationships. In business, they also provide an opportunity to discuss issues that have proved intractable at ordinary meetings.

Banquets can be daily events, organized at the personal, official, governmental, company, and factory level. The Chinese will find any number of reasons to hold a banquet, including birthdays, weddings, promotions, and moving into a new house.

"Getting to Know You"

Groups that are considering doing business together devote their initial meetings to becoming better acquainted. The initial encounters are likely to involve a number of dinners or banquets that are also business meetings. Alcoholic beverages will flow freely—cognac in the largest cities; and inland, beer or *baijiu* (a potent white liquor, with an alcohol content of between fifty-five percent and sixty-five percent, that is sometimes referred to as the national drink). It is regarded as rude to turn down the offer of a drink, so one must be prepared to deal with the consequences of drinking large quantities of liquor. Note that baijiu is not regarded as a drink for women, and those who do drink it may be derided.

Toasting is de rigueur at any banquet or party. All parties will make many small toasts throughout the night, always drinking with others and never alone. When companions' glasses are empty, etiquette requires that one fill them, starting with whoever has the most seniority and always pouring for oneself last. When someone pours one a drink, one should hold one's glass up with both hands (placing one hand on the bottom of the glass) and stand to acknowledge that one is receiving a gift. Even if there is no one to be toasted, there is pleasure to be had in drinking together.

Two sayings in particular epitomize this culture of drinking and conviviality: "The truth [about you] comes out when you drink" (*Jiu hou tu zhen yan*) and, "Don't pretend [be yourself]" (*Tan cheng xiang dui*). Threaded through all convivial drinking scenes will be many occasions when both sides seek mutual opportunities to give face. Such details as hometown, alma mater, successes, and achievements—the focal points of one's identity as a Chinese—will be noted and praised to those assembled.

As the friendship begins to develop, there will probably be a series of parties or banquets with a similar atmosphere of goodwill, and all the while business will be discussed and, perhaps, deals struck. The CEOs—the company decision makers, or vice-mayors of cities who are one-man managers of the local economy—will stay out of sight but may come together at the final dinner, in a private room over cigars and cognac, to reach agreement on future cooperation. They will then pass over to their team of managers the tasks of working out the details and plans. CEOs keep out of sight so that their managers can relax, be themselves, and better enjoy the event.

Communication

Goodwill and good humor greatly depend on harmonious, friction-free, argument-free conversation, which is usually loud and boisterous, cheery and manly. No one will be interrupted; everyone is permitted to finish their remarks and is given due respect. This is possible because there is a definite culture of listening—rather than talking—among the Chinese. The essence is to focus on the speaker, show interest, and never interrupt. The good Chinese listener:

- Does not interrupt the speaker.

- Uses a soft gaze.

- Nods frequently to indicate interest.

- Maintains an erect posture.

- Appears to understand more about the subject than what the speaker is saying.

- Does not point out any mistakes made by the speaker.
- Waits for the speaker to finish before commenting or seeking clarification.
- Keeps smiling and maintains a pleasant expression.

A good listener has the advantage of learning far more from and about the speaker than does someone with an intrusive style intent on having their views heard. When a Chinese speaker avoids saying something so as not to lose face, attentive listening will allow most Chinese to read between the lines

Young businesspeople, or those from inland areas who are older and lack sophistication, will sometimes compensate for being shy by drawing on lists of conversation topics such as the following:[2]

- Food
- One's hometown
- Chinese geography—one's province and its main attractions
- Mutual friends
- The weather
- Hobbies

- News
- Travel
- Family
- Health
- Work
- Clothing

With food and one's hometown or province a sure-fire subject, the double-barreled topic of hometown food is likely to get conversation off to a good start.

Building Mutual Trust [3]

The Chinese will always want to know whether a Chinese they have just met is genuinely friendly or just after profit, and whether he has a heart and will be sympathetic and flexible should things become tough.

The underlying suspicion of business in modern China is aptly expressed in two contemporary sayings that every Chinese knows: "There is no businessman who doesn't hard-sell his customers" (*Wu shang bu jian*); and "The marketplace is a battlefield" (*Shang chang ru zhan chang*).

With Chinese suspicion of business and their aversion to people who are too slick, the term "smooth operator" (*ba mian ling long*) is used to describe businesspeople who are perceived to be sly, reflecting the perceived need among Chinese to prove that they can be trusted.

For most educated Chinese, the worthy man who can be trusted in every way is virtuous (has *de*)[4] and behaves properly (with *li*).[5] Confucian values underlie the Chinese view that the virtuous and well-behaved individual is superior, while the individual who lacks virtue and seeks profit is inferior.

Issues of trust can thus be complex in business relationships involving extremely large companies, and it is at the trust-building stage that a relationship starts—or ends. Negotiation is only feasible when there is mutual trust, and many Chinese believe that if you do not become a friend, you will become an enemy.

Being Loyal, Keeping Promises

Besides proper behavior and integrity, two other important dimensions of trust are loyalty to friends and family, and keeping promises. This can be seen from the behavior of many Chinese who worked as agents for Western companies before 1979, when Deng Xiao Ping–inspired economic reforms began. Many of the former agents renewed contact with foreign companies, much as though they were old friends who had last been in contact only yesterday.

Chinese history and legends are filled with stories of people who have kept promises over many years. One story relates how a high-ranking Tang Dynasty (618–906) government official in Anhui province renounced his daughter, Wang Bao Chuan, for falling in love against his wishes with a poor worker. After marriage, the poor man, Xue Ping Gui, joined the army and went away to fight the barbarians on China's frontiers, returning home eighteen years later. He found Wang still waiting for him. Chinese tell this story as a reminder of the importance of keeping a promise.

THE ART OF BARGAINING

As elsewhere in Asia, bargaining is the prime skill of the small merchant. Moreover, since everyone is a consumer and inevitably in competition with merchants, the competence is widespread.

In the 1990s, the historical drama *Zai Xiang Liu Luo Guo* was a great success on Chinese television. Set inside a government ministry in nineteenth-century Beijing, the production was replete with twists and turns; tension was high between the minister and his advisors, as also between seniors and juniors. At one point, the minister ordered all junior officials to discard their old, worn uniforms for new ones (at their own expense). Then, just a few weeks after the old uniforms had been sold, the minister changed his mind and ordered the officials to again wear their old uniforms.

Obediently, the young men returned to the merchant to whom they had sold their uniforms, asking to buy them back. The merchant offered to sell back the uniforms for one hundred taels each, and when the officials remonstrated that he had only paid each of them two taels, he scornfully pointed out that the articles were now his and the money theirs, so it was up to them to decide what they were willing to pay or if they would rather forget the whole idea.

Chinese regard this kind of situation as typical, since bargaining has few rules save those of supply and demand. Most Chinese understand that merchants will offer goods in demand at some multiple of the price they paid.

In Shanghai, there was a famous marketplace called Xiang Yang (now closed) that was principally for tourists. While few local people shopped there because it was overpriced, tourists considered it to be a bargainers' paradise.

Now and again, innocent tourists from the countryside or abroad would buy goods at the market, only to find later that they had paid three or four times the downtown price. The difference could be hundreds or thousands of yuan. Some would go back to the vendor wanting their money back, but vendors always refused, having done no wrong.

China abounds with anecdotal evidence of shrewd bargaining tactics (or extreme price gouging, depending on one's point of view). A friend, Alex, once went to Xiang Yang to buy a pair of sunglasses. Alex knew what he wanted and how much he was willing to pay. He indicated the sunglasses he wanted, and the vendor entered his price into his calculator—380 yuan—and said inquiringly, "OK?" Alex shook his head. "Your price?" he asked, and handed the calculator to Alex, who typed in 10. The vendor expressed incredulity. "Oh, no, no," but then quickly put in a new price: 330, and gave Alex a big smile. "OK?" Alex shook his head. He asked for Alex's price and he again typed in 10. This ping-pong bargaining went on until the vendor's price had fallen to 90 and Alex's had risen to 25. After various small dramas about not earning enough to feed his family, and Alex walking away, the vendor chased after Alex, and with good humor accepted his 25.

Alex's wife, Jolin, seemed pleased with his "bargain," and proudly told some of their Shanghai friends how smart Alex was. They were scornful of his deal. "We never go there," one said. "It's far too expensive. But if I did

I'd pay no more than 20 yuan for those sunglasses."

"That brought me back to earth," Alex said. "I didn't think there was any 'light' between my 25 and his absolute minimum. But maybe there was. I said to myself, 'I'll be tougher next time.'"

NEGOTIATING WITH STRANGERS

The stranger—whether Chinese or foreign—occupies an ambiguous place in a low-trust society such as that of China. The people closest to you are family and friends; the rest are strangers (*shuren*; literally, "raw" people). Since strangers are thought cold and distant, Chinese are not known for public courtesy to them. Negotiations will not begin until strangers have developed a rapport that allows mutual trust to develop.

Chinese may queue, reluctantly, but when they board a bus or train with no reserved seats, they are known to use fists, elbows, and boots to get a seat. It is not a pretty sight, and few people would say they enjoy this behavior. But this is what one must do to avoid standing in a crowded aisle with strangers during a long journey.

Those who drive in Chinese cities will know what a competitive, dog-eat-dog world the roads have become. In 1990, there were barely one million cars in China; in 2006, there were in excess of eleven million cars, and the figure is expected to continue rising by more than one million a year. While young Chinese aspire to owning a car, the cost to society is calculated in terms of the chaos caused and the death toll on the roads exceeding 100,000 annually. Not only is the average driver young, inexperienced, accident prone, and intensely competitive, but there are few traffic police and it can take them hours to reach an accident scene.

On Chinese roads, there are no gentlemen (*junzi*, Confucian gentlemen). Rules, if they exist, mean nothing. Deference is nonexistent. Every driver aims to gain an advantage, however small. Whatever happens while driving, no one looks at the other driver—unless there is a collision. In that case, they may negotiate unless either party flees the scene—or both parties flee. However, since this would be a negotiation between strangers, the pattern is likely to be one of mutual anger, each party accusing the other of having caused the accident. It is not uncommon for people to come to blows, or at least hold a shouting match.

LESSONS TO BE LEARNED

Business negotiating behavior among members of mainstream Chinese society suggests ways in which you can build trust, friendship, and relationships with the Chinese.

- To negotiate, appoint people who like the Chinese, want to get along well with them, and are partial to the local cuisine.

- Take part in banquets as the Chinese do. Offer toasts to the other party and respond to toasts they make; don't hesitate to open up when modestly inebriated; and if a non-drinker, at least appear to sip at each toast.

- Resolve to get along well with the other party on their own terms. Praise their good points; avoid critical, ironic, or sarcastic remarks; be open, natural, and nice without being offensive or showing off; and be modest, since this is a quality much admired by all Chinese, especially in top managers.

- Be a good listener, Chinese style. In particular, remember to smile, not to interrupt, and to show interest nonverbally.

- Give and preserve face. Make positive statements about China, the other party's company, and the other party as an individual; praise the good points, and ask questions about China and the other party's company that show genuine interest in both.

- Reciprocate every kindness and favor.

- Learn to appreciate Chinese food and gain enough knowledge about it to be able to ask intelligent questions and make interesting conversation. Asking about the other party's hometown, mutual friends, famous places to visit, and so on fosters the rapid development of friendships.

- Begin to negotiate only when both sides are comfortable with one another.

- Recognize that you and your colleagues will need to become good friends with the Chinese and discover much about their psychology, and—as improbable as it may seem—that some of you over time should learn to read their minds.

MAIN POINTS OF CHAPTER 1

❑ Negotiations among the Chinese depend on the degree to which they trust each other. It is standard policy for longtime friends to put the other party's demands ahead of their own. People are reluctant to ask for or accept money from friends for minor services. Friends make binding ties by doing favors or giving small gifts in the spirit of reciprocity, which many believe to be the heart of Chinese culture.

❑ When there is no mutual trust, some may use fraud, bribery, threats, intimidation, and other forms of deception to achieve a goal they would have tried to achieve by negotiation had the other party been a friend.

❑ The Chinese do business with you as a person, not as an organization: hence the belief that friendship between organizations derives from friendship between individuals.

❑ It is most important to be friendly and get along comfortably with others.

❑ The Chinese, who do not always function well as a team, can be unorganized and sometimes chaotic. Be prepared for negotiation with unorganized as well as organized Chinese teams.

❑ Most Chinese regard themselves as careful thinkers, patient negotiators, friendly, hospitable, and helpful. They also see themselves as tough, clever, confident, profound, wise, and sometimes difficult negotiators.

❑ Banquets feature in all Chinese relationship building for cultural reasons. Eating together is considered the best, most civilized way to create an atmosphere conducive to developing trust and friendship.

❑ China is a listening—rather than a talking—culture, in which it is important to focus on the speaker, show interest, and not interrupt.

❑ The Chinese want to know if they can trust someone they have just met, if the individual is genuinely friendly or just after profit, and if he or she would be sympathetic and flexible were things to become tough.

❑ Friendships are long term, and high value is placed on being loyal to friends and family, as well as on keeping promises.

❑ The prime skill of the Chinese small merchant is bargaining, a competence that is widespread as everyone is a consumer and competes with merchants.

CHAPTER
2

CHINESE AND FOREIGN BUSINESSPEOPLE

Mutual Views

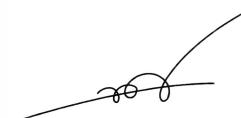

Understand what Chinese and Westerners think of one another when they first enter negotiations, and we begin to understand what happens within negotiations proper. This chapter provides a broad picture of the view each holds of the other, as well as giving a social, psychological, cultural, and ideological backdrop for the case studies of Chinese-Western negotiations that are reviewed in the chapters that follow.

Su-Hua and I present the background on the everyday thinking of both sides of the cultural divide. There is a tapestry of colors that shades our everyday thinking about one another. This is the thinking that most of us first bring to business encounters. It is an intricate tapestry, combining social, cultural, psychological, and ideological factors with opinions, stereotypes, historically anchored prejudices, and, not least, rumors.

FOREIGNERS THROUGH CHINESE EYES

Most Chinese suffer from the curse of their history—as do many foreigners, particularly the British, Americans, and Japanese. These Chinese believe that their country was the victim of an unfair treaty as a result of the first Opium War (1839–42) with Britain that ended with the Treaty of Nanjing. In the 1930s there were also Japanese invasions that victimized and brutalized the Chinese and are most remembered by the Chinese through their persistent emphasis on the atrocities of the 1937 Japanese Rape of Nanjing. And, after World War II, the United States treated China as a pariah communist state from the time of the communist victory over the Kuomintang in 1949 until the friendship treaty signed in the seventies by then-U.S. President Richard Nixon.

The past actions of foreign powers have made many Chinese believe that they are neither accorded respect nor treated as human beings. By extension, they believe they have no face and are nobodies, for whom no one will show consideration. Sometimes the upshot of this is deep hurt and suspicion, with a profound rage simmering close to the surface. The older the individual, the more likely it is that they have a hidden suspicion and resentment of foreigners. Should your behavior suggest that you disrespect them, the Chinese are likely to become indignant or angry and may even extract revenge of one sort or another.

The Chinese can portray themselves as weak and helpless people who are being used by powerful and heartless villains: At times, theirs can be a victim mentality. Absent pressures and intimidation, people are not likely to feel they are victims. However, this can change when a seemingly stronger party—notably British, American, or Japanese—seems to threaten. Chinese psychology will transform that perceived threat into an unfair and incorrigible—but historically predictable—act,[6] requiring compensation. Usually this will take the form of a sincere written apology, but occasionally financial compensation will be required.

Today, many young Chinese take delight in meeting foreign visitors. The CEO of a furniture maker in Shandong told us that his workers always became excited when he told them that "the Americans will visit soon." From other reports, that seems today to be typical of young Chinese, many of whom see Westerners as exotic and on a par with Hollywood stars. A great number hold romantic views of the United States, about which they may say gushingly, "In America even the moon is bigger."

Problems begin when Chinese feel they have been insulted or slighted. One day a Western friend was waiting to pay the cashier in a Shanghai bookshop. An ill-defined line had formed and so, when the cashier indicated a proper queue was required, my friend stepped to his left, in front of a thirty-something Chinese man who stood a half pace behind him. This prompted the Chinese man to say loudly, in good English, "You think you are better than any Chinese. You just pushed in front of me." My friend replied, "No, that's not true," at which the Chinese man turned to a woman behind him saying, "They think they can do what they like." The situation was only defused when my friend's Chinese spouse, who stood nearby, said in Chinese, "My husband is not that sort of man. It's just a misunderstanding. We apologize." It was that simple.

Unfortunately, remarks based on stereotyping, such as those made by the Chinese man, are not uncommon. Further, by making a generalization based on the action of one individual, the Chinese man underscored the considerable psychological distance he felt between "us" and "them." He saw my friend as representing foreigners en masse, rather than as an independent individual.

Sinologist Geremie R. Barmé (1999) is of the opinion that "the new mythology of East Asian material strength and spiritual worth feeds into the century-old Chinese dreams of national revival and supremacy." These attitudes, he continues, "express deeply frustrated and compelling nationalistic aspirations." His analysis of the popular Chinese television series *A Beijing Man in New York*, supports this. The series recounts a "trip by the hero [Wang Qiming] to [New York], where he overcomes adversity, obtains fortune and sires offspring by ravishing [American] beauties." Wang "is forced to give up his wholesome Chinese values to be successful in America." The series is variously a fairy story for modern Chinese and a melodrama with a wholesome Chinese hero and a wicked American villain. Its success lay in Wang's Chinese purity, which helped "him maintain a certain superiority and humanity quite absent from the foreign characters in the story."

Whatever direction China takes this century, the Chinese belief that it is destined to be great again, by virtue of its superior spiritual culture, makes for interesting times ahead for Western businesses in China. The Chinese are very concerned about the moral behavior and ethics of those with whom they do business. The lesson to be drawn from this is that individuals of character and flexibility should head the list of those who represent Western companies in business with China.

It is because of the Chinese concern about foreigners' ethics that we so often hear that Chinese businesspeople feel they have been insulted by a foreigner, at times described as a capitalist exploiter hungry for profit. By such comments, foreigners are stereotyped just as our friend was by the Chinese man in the bookshop queue.

Fortunately, more realistic, positive attitudes prevail among Chinese professional negotiators. Vivian Sheer (2003) found that the Chinese "spoke highly of Western businesspeople's professionalism. First, foreigners are often well prepared. They invest time and money in gathering information prior to negotiating major business deals.... [Their] paperwork [is] detailed and thorough.... [They show] expert product knowledge, [are] familiar with their industry and firm, and [have] good negotiation skills."

Ding Gang, an upper-level manager of *The People's Daily* who has spent time posted to the United States, says that after analyzing years of survey results, "the Chinese have conflicting feelings of both love and hatred towards Americans—or put another way, 'love and fear.'"

Sheer also found that "most Chinese thought Westerners' ideas of China were outdated and came from television. Some Americans bragged about their Chinese connections to show off their knowledge of Chinese business. Patronizing attitudes put Chinese off—some foreigners seemed to exaggerate their own technologies and look down on Chinese.... Some Chinese were not pleased that foreigners, particularly Americans, trusted overseas Chinese more than mainlanders."

FISHING FOR FOREIGNERS

Many Chinese see foreign businesspeople as fish to catch. A commonly used saying reflecting this perception is: "The hook hangs over the water, so the fish must jump to take the bait" (*Jiang tai kong daio yuen zu shang go*). The fish in this maxim is the foreigner, and the jump is the extra one is asked to pay for the product.

Foreigners (especially Taiwanese) are taking money to China in quantities that the Chinese still find hard to imagine. "How could they have so much money?" is a commonly posed question. This is such a temptation! As mentioned in connection with the concept of guanxi (chapter 7), Chinese values require that those who have more should share it with the less fortunate.

But when it comes to some foreign businesspeople, the thinking goes beyond that. It can then strike the Chinese that: "These are also the people who invaded our country, took advantage of us, look down on us, have treated us as less than human for generations. They need to be taught a lesson." Certainly not every, or even most, Chinese are determined to rip off foreigners, but they are all aware of this kind of thinking and that a few Chinese use these ideas to rationalize theft and fraud.

DREAMS OF BEING BOSS

The Chinese do not take pride in their teamwork when they negotiate with foreigners, and they know that their performance sometimes is chaotic.

Chinese negotiators mostly concede that foreigners are more articulate and communicatively competent. Moreover, many Chinese interpreters have said of the Chinese for whom they work that they have been "frequently ambiguous, lost focus of the speech, displayed poor or no logic, and used many unnecessary disclaimers," concluding that they "often had a difficult time figuring out what Chinese negotiators really meant" (Sheer, 2003).

One reason the Chinese are indifferent to teamwork is that they prefer not to work under a boss but, rather, to be their own boss and work for themselves. This sentiment is contained in the Chinese saying "I'd rather be a chicken's head than a bull's tail" (*Ning wei ji shou bu wei niu hou*), which underscores the wish not to work under someone.

I was once shown around the kitchen at one of Guangzhou's biggest restaurants. There were six wok chefs, all of whom had been working for the restaurant for fifteen or more years. Innocently, I asked the general manager, who was showing me around, what he would say should one of his chefs want to leave and set up his own restaurant. I asked because I knew that in Japan the boss would be likely to say: Go with my blessing and put my *noren* (a shop's identifying curtain that hangs at the entrance) outside to show you come from here.

The Chinese situation could not be more different, however. The general manager's answer was to pull a menacing face and draw a finger across his throat. In other words, to leave and start up on one's own would be considered treachery.

It is interesting to note that, when young Chinese first venture out into the world—for instance, to visit someone's home—they will be cautioned to say little and not make fools of themselves. Likewise, when older and going abroad on business for the first time, or meeting foreigners in China for the first time, they receive much the same warnings: Say little, be sure you are well prepared, do not make any mistakes, and do not make a fool of yourself. Without this cultural nugget, foreigners at a party find themselves surprised at how many Chinese have nothing to say.

What surprises the Chinese is the openness and frequent artless spontaneity displayed by foreigners. For instance, a foreigner might say: "Glad to meet you. My name is Bill Smith. I come from [country name]. I'm married with three children. We have three dogs and a cat. I think China is a fantastic country. I want to buy my wife one of those jade Buddhas I see in the shops. She loves stuff like that." Certainly this example is a trifle overdone, but it captures the tone the Chinese pick up from the initial gushing, artless conversation. Members of a foreign negotiating team should not display unguarded artlessness when facing the quiet, alert, observant Chinese.

It takes a long time to become friendly with most Chinese. However, when a friendship is struck, it is not uncommon to find that an individual's true personality is a complete contrast to the quiet, retiring manner first exhibited. We can think of many Chinese friends who are quiet and reserved on the outside, but witty and talkative on the inside.

CHINESE NEGOTIATORS THROUGH FOREIGN EYES

The comments about the Chinese made by foreigners with little international experience tend to be negative and predictable. The Chinese, they will say, waste time, are too formal and ceremonial, are slow to get down to business, have a poker-faced style of communicating, break promises, don't trust anyone, and are themselves hard to trust (especially if they are local government representatives).

Many inexperienced foreigners, particularly from Western countries, are baffled by Chinese etiquette, especially that of high-level Chinese officials. These individuals have the habit of elaborate displays of self-deprecating behavior: They talk down their own person or their surroundings when first meeting foreign visitors. It is an etiquette of humility that is widespread throughout East Asia.

In such circumstances, while the Chinese might believe this self-deprecating official actually to be someone of extraordinary inner qualities, and be even more submissive in return, foreigners often react differently. Thus, should an official apologize for his humble, shabby surroundings, the foreigners would be likely to nod with a bleak smile and say: "You can say that again!"

The more experienced foreign negotiator is likely to notice that the Chinese place little emphasis on Western pricing principles and do not stress quality, provided the price represents a win for them. Further, they expect a lot of time to be taken up with entertainment and eating. Given the same circumstances, the less experienced negotiator is likely to be nervous and suspicious.

One foreign negotiator was briefed that all Chinese are unscrupulous, and they might bug his room or telephone. Nervously, he entered the first meeting alone, to face ten Chinese sitting poker-faced, chain smoking, and continuously drinking tea from large, lidded cups. They listened impassively to his presentation through an interpreter. By the end of the first day, this negotiator was a nervous wreck, and after the second day he was exhausted and slept twenty-four hours straight.

Although some issues may seem formidable, they are not insurmountable if you arrive armed with knowledge and patience. And above all, be flexible in your reaction to what will be, more likely than not, unusual conditions, mentally and physically.

THE CULTURE OF COMMUNICATION

As in all cultures, methods of communication are culture bound. The Chinese tend to look for the real meaning that lies behind what is said. So, should you comment on a matter or ask a question, the Chinese will typically say— or think—"Oh, so this is what you really want."

Reflecting this line of thinking, were a foreigner to say: "That Chinese lady is beautiful," the Chinese would be unlikely to interpret it as a mere expression of admiration but, rather, as indicating that the individual may wish to be introduced to the lady. Or, were one to be taken by a Chinese acquaintance to a shop where one sees a beautiful painting about which one asks "Please tell me about this painting. Who is the painter? Where was it painted?" the typical first response is likely to be not a reply, but a question: "Oh, you want to buy this?"

Sensitivity to the other party's needs stems from the cultural preference for indirect communication and from cultural injunctions against verbalizing demands, desires, emotions, or criticisms. China's culture is one of low-level interpersonal openness, in which personal questions are rarely asked for fear of offending. Thus, Chinese rarely initiate discussions with others (unless there is a strong bond) and tend to be passive during discussions. A part of the cultural background is acquired at school and in college, where teachers are expected to dominate and students learn to be overly anxious and excessively respectful. In such situations, the Chinese easily produce a smile—often a physiognomical indication that they are embarrassed and experiencing some difficulty.

When annoyed or angered by someone, the Chinese almost never express their feelings verbally. Instead, many adult male Chinese are likely to show what appears to be considerable, or even exceptional, pleasure. That they are annoyed will only come out later, in the form of a reluctance or refusal to meet some further request from the party perceived to have caused offence. For instance, Chinese invited to have lunch at an excellent and reputable restaurant might decline to accept, perhaps using the excuse that they are too busy. This is the first sign that something is amiss.

Even among the well educated in China, verbal communication, particularly of concepts and ideas, is far less important than it is in many other cultures. Moreover, with an individual's broken or nonexistent English factored into the equation, it is very difficult for foreigners to assess how smart a particular Chinese might be. One would thus be wise to assume that every Chinese one faces in meetings or at banquets is very smart indeed.

Another difference in communication styles lies in the Chinese belief that there is no need to provide a verbal background briefing before making a request of foreigners, because to do so would give offense. A Chinese given a briefing would probably say, or at least think, "How condescending! I know all that."

Of course, a written brief avoids the problem in part. But, because there is no general practice among Chinese of issuing briefings and context-setting statements, one is wise to assume that one needs to know more about the context and background than appears in any such written document. Moreover, because the Chinese business group will be highly sensitive to political issues affecting the foreigner's business, political demands will color and censor the matter about which the foreigner is briefed.

At times, the Chinese will appoint an individual or team to negotiate with the foreign company on operational details. However, since the appointed Chinese, just like the foreigners, are likely to lack information, they may agree to matters on which they have not been briefed. Thus, even when one *believes* one has reached an agreement, the Chinese operations team may come back and say: "The director will not agree to those matters," or, more likely, deny that an agreement had been reached.

Unless one can exert influence on the Chinese CEO or director, one must either accept the situation and negotiate anew, or, right from the outset, adopt the strategy (particularly disagreeable to the Chinese) of asking questions about everything that seems germane regarding both parties.

We suggest it is best to be suspicious (without showing it) of any positive feedback from Chinese, since it might easily mean the opposite—or nothing at all. In any event, such feedback should be viewed only as a preliminary reply that could easily be overturned.

One of the strangest, yet most important, lessons that foreigners can learn about negotiating with Chinese concerns the expression of discontent or annoyance regarding the people with whom one is dealing. Such displeasure or unhappiness cannot be expressed directly to the Chinese if amicable relations are to be maintained. The Chinese are typically thin-skinned and easily become resentful.

The solution is to speak in an acceptable code for expressing displeasure and annoyance. The following flowery expression of satisfaction generally fulfils social requirements: "Let me first say how grateful we are for the many kindnesses and the assistance we have received from Senior Director Bing Fa and Mr. Sun Zi." Thereafter, the tone should be entirely positive, and the conversation not too detailed. Or, should one be annoyed with Sun for not being organized, one might say: "May we ask Mr. Sun to guide us on the points that remain outstanding in our discussions?" Further, were one concerned with Director Bing's failure to have given detailed direction to Sun, one might say: "May we also ask Mr. Sun to convey to us the remaining issues that Director Bing wishes to have included in our discussions?"

In China, virtually everyone will pick up on what is really displeasing an individual if a letter is written. Moreover, the Chinese applaud the civility of writing a letter, which should be free of criticism. When using such indirect communication, the Chinese depend on the acuteness and sensitivity of the receiving party to pick up the real message, and conflict is thereby avoided.

The Chinese predilection for being indirect and allusive in communication indicates a different attitude to language from that found, for example, in many Western cultures, which have a tradition that places great store on intellectual debate and the search for truth—both of which aspects are ultimately expressed in words.

The Chinese tradition, with roots in meditative Buddhism, Taoism, and Confucianism, leans in the opposite direction. Since ancient times the emphasis has been on what is immediate, rather than such verbalized, intellectual experiences as debating, theorizing, and rhetorical discourse.

The cultural injunctions against excessive verbalizing still affect everyday behavior in China. The culture is rich in proverbs that decry words and talk. "Silence is golden," a meaningful proverb in the West three or four centuries ago, is still considered relevant in China. One also commonly hears the phrase: "Keep your mouth closed and your eyes open," and even the old warrior's saying, "In your speech, honey; in your heart, a sword."

LANGUAGE: A REFLECTION OF SOCIAL VALUES

China's society remains hierarchical, and language is designed to acknowledge the social status of the individual addressed. A central theme in society is the respect of authority.

Even should an individual believe the authority figure is in the wrong, social mores require a search for consensual, indirect ways of bringing about change, to ensure that no one loses face. Debate and argument are seen as threatening the harmony and status quo that hinge at every level on respect for authority.

Unlike in Western countries, creative self-expression in business conversation is neither aspired to nor welcome in China. It is not even recommended in social contexts, since unexpected expressions can be misunderstood, appear to lack courtesy, and seem sarcastic or even disparaging.

There is a plethora of standardized phrases, so in some situations everything that is said follows a standard pattern. Although other cultures also make use of set phrases, they have been finessed to such a level and are so automatically used by the Chinese that many have come to mistakenly believe that what they are hearing springs from the heart. In fact, those "heartfelt" sentences are merely accepted phrases, albeit gracious and often elegant, even in translation.

When Chinese set out to expunge from their conversation all subjects perceived to be controversial, arguable, or challenging, it is common for the only communication to be utterances that, representing harmony-reinforcing stroking, focus on the feel-good factor between people.

Once foreigners learn to appreciate this aspect of communication, they gain an insight into the Chinese perspective on verbal intercourse: namely, what it is like to have no idea, based on what their opposite number says, of what that other party is really thinking and, thus, of what is permissible in public discourse versus what is literally a state secret. This is a major, inevitable consequence of the emphasis on obeying government and party directions, respecting and obeying seniors, as well as being polite, undemanding, flexible, and non-egotistical.

COMMUNICATION PROBLEMS

As do people of other cultures, many Chinese suffer from communication-related interpersonal problems. In everyday life, a major cause is the poor manners[7] of Chinese, indifference to making timely responses, and the tendency to try to cheat others.

Educated Chinese usually try to solve these problems by culturally acceptable, nonverbal means—heart-to-heart connection or touching each other's core. Chinese culture teaches that heart-to-heart communication cannot be achieved logically. Many Chinese find that first meetings with foreigners are dry and logical. This seems almost inhuman, the Chinese believe, and think secretly to themselves: "Why doesn't this person realize that the process of getting comfortable with others begins with the heart and not the head?"

How do the Chinese keep in touch with what others are really thinking and feeling, or with what is going on in their world? Some would answer that it is only necessary to know what one is required to do. In a Chinese organization, this often means that one merely waits to be "tapped on the shoulder" by one's superiors. This is the orientation of people happy to be followers, whose greatest pleasures lie in the security of their job, the patronage of their boss, and the certainty of support from social connections or intimate friends.

Main Points of Chapter 2

- Since Chinese recall the humiliation visited on them by foreign countries over the past 160 years or so, the initial attitude of many Chinese toward foreigners may be one of suspicion.

- If not respected, the Chinese believe they will lose face, which in China means they become a social nobody.

- The Chinese believe that their country is destined to be great again, and that it has a spiritual culture superior to that of other countries.

- Conflicting feelings of love and fear are held by Chinese toward Americans.

- According to Chinese mores, the better-off should share with the less fortunate.

- Chinese businesspeople are sometimes described as ambiguous, prone to lose focus on their subject, lacking in logic, and unable to express themselves clearly.

- Chinese culture advises younger individuals meeting people for the first time to say little, be well prepared, make no mistakes, and avoid making fools of themselves.

- Being unguarded and artless is not a desirable attribute in members of a foreign team meeting a reserved, quiet, alert, and observant Chinese team.

- Chinese assume that they do not need to give you a background briefing before making some request of you. They believe that you know most or all of the basics, so to give such a briefing, they commonly reason, would be offensive. In the same manner, they are often not fully briefed themselves, which will sometimes lead to an unraveling of initial agreements and require further negotiations.

- Discontent or annoyance regarding those with whom one is dealing should not be expressed directly to the Chinese if amicable relations are to be maintained.

CHAPTER
3

WELL-MANAGED
NEGOTIATIONS

The Individual Approach

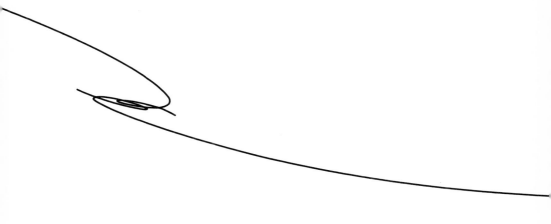

The ideal negotiation is well managed. Both sides employ styles and adhere to approaches that make them compatible, and moments of miscommunication or conflict are soon resolved without the development of animosity or suspicion.

The cases reported in this chapter are well managed. They illustrate how professional, individual negotiators were supported by excellent teams and achieved success. Only one of the negotiators, Wang Sheng Cu, might have been able to succeed without the support of his team. The non-Chinese, meanwhile, shared some traits that are critical to successful negotiations with Chinese and that can all be learned. These individuals were:

- Skillful negotiators and rapid learners, with excellent support teams.

- Exceptionally talented in bringing about good agreements.

- Flexible and mature.

- Comfortable with a team approach rather than a lone-wolf approach.

- Sensitive to the culture of China and possessed cross-cultural communication skills.

When we take up the story of each negotiation, both parties already know a great deal about each other and trust is mutual. Despite each being the first negotiation with the Chinese parties, the cases are well and truly past the stage of an arm's-length relationship. Moreover, the foreign negotiators depended on the support of people in China, and their achievements reflect the wisdom of their approach.

The cases show good negotiating behavior, as is brought out in the discussions following each case. Following the presentation and analysis of each study, general statements are offered regarding how best to prepare for most negotiations with the Chinese.

HOW GIVING FACE CAN BREW SUCCESS

OVERVIEW

Peter Benjamin, the owner of an Australian chemical engineering consultancy, has a warning for those wanting to do business in China: "Many Chinese see it as their patriotic duty to shoot down foreigners, so you can be like a clay pigeon at target practice." Despite this, Benjamin has been successful in China and is responsible for the design of many of the country's modern breweries.

He was invited to submit a proposal for a huge Guangdong brewery by Dr. Pasteur Lai, the son of a former Chinese minister of health and now an Australian citizen. Lai had many connections deep within the Chinese government, had done his homework on Benjamin, and was able to report to the Chinese that Benjamin was the premier brewery designer and builder in Australia.

THE SCENE

Benjamin was initially cynical. "We get a lot of 'tire kickers' in this business—people who aren't serious about a project but just want to test the waters," he explained.

Benjamin sent the Chinese a questionnaire, asking for information about specifications, resources, brewery capacity, products they planned to produce, budget, and business plans. The response he received convinced him to head to China to discuss a potential deal to build Guangdong province's largest brewery—a $20 million project. But, having heard from others about their China experiences, he decided to pitch only for the business in which his company had special technology to offer.

"One of the first things you need to understand about China is that you can't compete against cheap, local rivals," he advises. "The Chinese only want foreigners involved if we can offer special technology they can't get at home. We knew if the Chinese could have got locally what we offered, they would not have approached us."

PREPARING TO NEGOTIATE

In the lead up to the negotiations, Benjamin knew his business could provide strengths the Chinese business lacked. He had access to technology that could increase the capacity of the planned brewery while also reducing waste. He specialized in understanding and predicting market trends and had access to sophisticated, international market data the Chinese company lacked.

The Chinese party had no experience in designing breweries whereas, since 1983, Benjamin had built or redesigned all Australia's major breweries and most of its boutique breweries. Before starting negotiations, he did extensive research on the Chinese market, including its beer industry and the Guangzhou company. He found that, despite the company's listing on the Shanghai Stock Exchange, it had direct links to the Chinese government.

"If you're working with a brewery in China, you're working with the government, because the industry is so tightly regulated. I also found that the government department in charge of the alcohol industry is run by ex–Red Guards, so I knew I was dealing with people who had to report back to important government figures. I thought that, if I could find ways to make them look good in the eyes of their bosses, it would help in developing a beneficial business relationship," he said.

When Benjamin arrived in China, he discovered that the Chinese were also talking to German, French, and Belgian companies, and that the Chinese company's plans for the brewery were not as well defined as had initially appeared.

"I decided my job was to be the expert, and I knew I should tell them what they needed, rather than let them tell me. It was clear they knew nothing about designing breweries."

Benjamin also understood the sensitivities in pointing out the shortcomings of the Chinese plans. He had spoken with Chinese Australians (including two on his staff who had become the key members of his team in China) and read widely on Chinese culture, so he recognized the risk of causing the Chinese to lose face. To avoid doing so, he offered to work with the Chinese on developing the competitive brief using the latest technology.

This would allow him to begin building relationships with the Chinese before the tendering process had begun. It would also give the Chinese lead negotiator face with his bosses (and the Chinese government officials), as he would be able to develop a better business brief using foreign technology. It also gave Benjamin's business a head start in the tender competition.

UNCOMMON TACTICS

"Before tendering began, we were working with the client to develop the brief while the other companies were sitting around," he said.

The Chinese arranged the accommodation for the tendering companies. Each foreign team—the French, Germans, Belgians, and Australians—was lodged by the Guangdong government at the same hotel.

"We would go and have a meeting with the Chinese. When we got back to the hotel, the other businesses would always be waiting in the lobby to be picked up for their meetings. It was made pretty clear that we were competing against each other," Benjamin said.

Working in such a specialized field—brewery design—meant that the foreign negotiating teams knew each other, and they used this to their advantage.

"We knew the Chinese were trying to pit us against each other, so we turned their tactic around. We met every afternoon in the hotel bar and compared notes. We could then work out together whether this negotiation was about price, technology, reputation, or some other driver. Of course it was about price and technology—it always is," he said.

The negotiations took place over several weeks, during which each of the foreign companies met with the Chinese team almost daily. "We talked about the price and technology constantly. We were always discussing the scope of the project, to fit it in with a budget with which they were happy, but which still delivered excellent technology. There were perhaps thirty Chinese, and every time we met, there would be different people talking. You'd think you had an agreement, and then one of the Chinese would suddenly pull you aside and tell you the complete opposite. It was very confusing."

SHORING UP ADVANTAGE

To ensure he was not misunderstanding the negotiations, which were being conducted through an interpreter with the Chinese team, Benjamin had brought from Australia two of his China-born staff— a chemical engineer and an accountant.

"I decided I needed to use my two Chinese team members as my interpreters, because the Chinese language is often not explicit: The meaning of what they were saying was often only implied. It was the best decision I made, because I got the chance to log onto real feedback."

Benjamin also began to see the language barrier as an advantage. "Not knowing the language gave me carte blanche to completely change my mind on things I already had said, because I could use the excuse that I had not properly understood. They kept changing the negotiations on me, so it gave me the chance to do the same back and get away with it."

Benjamin had great respect for his competitors. They were professional managers, corporate people. But they also had superior attitudes toward the Chinese, and indeed also toward Benjamin and Australia. They refused to believe that a world-class brewery designer could be found in Australia.

After several weeks, the French and Belgian businesses pulled out, frustrated at the drawn-out negotiating process. They had offered their best price when first challenged and had left themselves no room to maneuver. Between them, the French and Belgian negotiators had two other problems. First, they were both professional managers involved in a number of projects, so it was easy for them to give up and go home to take up other projects waiting on their desks. Second, no one on the French team liked Chinese cuisine, so returning home looked very attractive to them.

Benjamin, however, was a specialist chemical engineer who owned his own business, had already invested $350,000[8] in preparation, and was not inclined to walk away.

PATIENCE PAYS

"I went in suspecting we were going to spend ninety percent of the time arguing price, particularly since the Chinese started negotiating by crying poor. They kept saying they had a limited budget, so I started high and kept shaving off the smallest amount, but never near my limit. I knew from my initial questionnaire and research they could afford to pay what the technology and I were worth. Even though this represented a great opportunity to enter the Chinese market, I also needed to get properly rewarded," he explained.

"When I first got to China I was told of a Chinese saying—'China has 5,000 years of history, so what's an extra hundred years?' This basically means that they are patient and will wait for the right deal. We had invested a lot of money to go to China, and we were not about to turn around and come home just because it was taking longer than we wanted."

The Chinese team tried to use Benjamin's planned return date as leverage, in a bid to pressure him into agreeing to their price terms on the basis that he was leaving the country. But he recognized the ploy. "I realized they were dragging negotiations out until my departure, so I told them my date was flexible and I'd just stay until we finished. I acted as though I no longer had a deadline, and politely pointed out they were the ones who had to build a brewery within a certain time frame."

Benjamin spent every evening with his Chinese negotiating team, analyzing each day and trying to figure out the Chinese strategy. They would probe and explain to him Chinese cultural perceptions, which Benjamin found invaluable for understanding the Chinese tactics.

BEING TESTED

"There was one meeting in which one of the Chinese team became very angry and distressed. That night one of my interpreters told me that the individual had probably been testing my reaction. He explained that Chinese don't do business with people they don't know, and that sometimes they will use different emotions to see how the other party reacts under pressure.

"Chinese culture is so different that you need that local Chinese input. You can never have intuitive understanding of everything that influences and drives them—that would take fifty lifetimes. The next best thing is to have local contacts to guide you."

Benjamin found other confusing elements about the negotiating process. "We would have in-principle agreement on issues, and then they would just change their mind. We have since learned this is standard. Even if you have something in writing, it is only ever a 'discussion document.' The Chinese expect you to 'be like bamboo and bend with the wind.'"

With the negotiations down to just two companies, Benjamin tried a new tactic. He pitched the environmental benefits of his brewery design, explaining how his technology could make the Chinese brewery a world leader in waste management. His technological solution would diminish environmental waste while ensuring maximum capacity and building up the Chinese company's reputation as a world leader.

Meanwhile, the Chinese team had also done its homework and was secretly favoring Benjamin's company based on its reputation for delivering on time and to specifications. In the end, the specialist technology Benjamin could offer ostensibly won him the contract.

But Benjamin believes it was more about relationships and face. "I put effort into helping them look good. I designed the brief with them using the latest technology. I helped solve other problems they had not considered, such as environment management that would save them money. I suggested my solutions would make their business a world leader. It was about giving them an opportunity to shine."

THE LAST ROUND OF NEGOTIATIONS

Before agreement was reached, and after the last of three proposals had been delivered and considered, nine separate negotiations were held to discuss:

- Payment terms and advance payments
- Currency decisions
- Inspections policy
- Warranties
- Delivery of overseas and local components
- Commissioning and training of the Guangzhou company's personnel
- Penalties
- Performance requirements
- Capacity to deliver

By this time, the Chinese team was reduced to twelve people. While Benjamin and his team were in China on the last occasion, the Chinese team split in half and each went abroad—to Europe and Australia—to evaluate Benjamin's suppliers (and through them, him) of pump valves, electronic equipment, stainless steel, and laser welding. His suppliers all appear to have given him a pass mark, but one subjective problem remained.

While Benjamin's team was well ahead of the other teams on all criteria, some members of the Chinese team remained opposed to the Australian team—because it was Australian—saying they wanted, on the basis of image and reputation, a brewery designer and builder from Europe. The vice governor of Guangdong province finally stepped in, we understand, and made the decision in favor of Benjamin's company. Within forty-five minutes of his decision, the negotiation leader was on the phone to Benjamin at his hotel.

"We want you to sign the contract," he said out of the blue and with no preamble. "Come to the office now. Also bring $2,000 to pay for the celebration banquet at lunchtime."

Benjamin and his team went directly to the provincial office. Before he signed the contract, he said to the team leader, "Thank you very much for your agreement to commission us to build your brewery. In consideration of that, we wish to present you with a five percent discount."

The step was artful. Bringing the project in five percent under budget gave face to everyone on the Chinese team, including the vice governor. They would not forget this.

Commentary

After winning the job to design the Guangdong brewery, Benjamin was exclusively commissioned to design a $5 million winery in Xinjiang province. This demonstrated how trusted he had become in China.

In his time working with Chinese, Benjamin believes he has learned a number of valuable lessons from the challenges he has faced. "First, do not be distracted by cultural differences. Understand them, learn to work within them, but do not be led astray by them. In my first negotiation, I probably spent too much time on the cultural aspects and not enough on the business elements.

"Second, know that nothing is ever fully resolved. The Chinese see a contractual agreement as only a starting point in business. You need to be flexible and work with this, rather than fight against it.

"Third, know that face is most important. I have seen the Chinese build bad breweries they knew were wrong, just because they did not know how to acknowledge they had made a mistake without losing face. Learn how to give face.

"Most importantly, be prepared to make the Chinese look good. China is all about reciprocal favors, and if you make them look good, you will do an enormous service to yourself."

OUTFOXING THE CHINESE

OVERVIEW

Some years ago, I worked as a salesman for an agent of the Japanese packaging printing press manufacturer, Kumi (name changed). It had just acquired a German manufacturer of printing machines—Chantdung (name changed).

Chantdung made a superior press specifically designed for cigarette packaging. It was relatively simple compared to the machines of its competitors, which made it all the more suitable for countries lacking technical sophistication and First-World infrastructure. The press was reliable, easy to operate and maintain. It was perfect for a China that was emerging just then from the Cultural Revolution and had a population of heavy smokers. The Chinese government was interested in the profits to be made from their need, as were companies such as the British American Tobacco Company (BAT) and Kumi-Chantdung.

THE SCENE

Kumi-Chantdung was keen to get its machines into the massive Chinese market ahead of the opposition. One of its problems was that, as Chantdung was a subsidiary of Kumi, the Japanese salesmen wanted to lead the charge and make the sale, which angered Chantdung's German salesmen who had the technical expertise and manufactured the special machinery. Eventually, the Japanese acquiesced and allowed the Germans to lead the negotiations.

The internal conflict was not lost on the Chinese, who exploited it to their advantage. On every point they asked whether the Japanese agreed, which infuriated and belittled the Germans. The Chinese also made no secret of having invited a rival British company to Beijing, at precisely the same time as the Kumi-Chantdung team, and even put them up in the same hotel.

The German sales director was an immensely proud and haughty man, with little experience in dealing with the Chinese. Being something of a gastronome, he often chose to comment negatively on the food. This, too, was not lost on the wily Chinese, who went out of their way to make sure the quality of the food eaten by the Germans was kept at a mediocre level, while delivering great food to the British team.

TESTING REACTIONS

While the packaging presses were to be installed throughout China, the trials were conducted in Beijing, where the electricity supply was stable and the infrastructure satisfactory. This highlighted the fact that the opposition's machinery outperformed the tough and capable Chantdung-built machines that lacked electronics and high-tech features but could cope much better in the Chinese countryside where electricity supply was not consistent. The Chinese also noted this apparent discrepancy in performance.

When the time came to sit down and negotiate at the end of the trials, the German negotiator was despondent. Since the Chinese had been so aggressive toward him, he was convinced that Kumi-Chantdung stood no chance of success in the negotiations.

One of the Chantdung sales team, Freddy Mitra—an Indian schooled in England but with a wealth of experience in dealing with the Chinese gained at a previous company—asked to take the lead in the negotiations. The request was granted and the German went home, leaving Mitra at the helm. He suspected that Kumi-Chantdung was the front-runner, but that, having played into the hands of the astute and experienced Chinese negotiators, it was now at a distinct negotiating disadvantage.

THE HUMBLE SUCCEED

Mitra, using his instincts, a suitable level of Indian humility, and a lot of patience and courage, played the game to perfection. He explained that, since the Chantdung press had performed so poorly compared to the opposition's equipment, and his superior's behavior had been uncomplimentary, he, as lead negotiator, had no choice but to withdraw his machines and team from the negotiations.

He then began going through the motions of dismantling the machinery and packing up. He also made a point of seeing the government official responsible for the project and relaying the same message to him, as well as thanking him and the government for their interest in the Chantdung machinery.

Within hours, the Chinese team made it known that, since it had made the Kumi-Chantdung team travel so far and spend so much time in China, it would be only polite to hear what their proposal would have been. Mitra presented the original proposal. With a few minor negotiations relating to installation and training, and an ongoing supply of some of the rotary dies and gravure cylinders, the proposal was accepted almost immediately—and at a fair market price.

These machines have become the backbone of the Chinese cigarette packaging industry, which is still thriving, in contrast to the situation in most other countries.

(with Gervaise Sutton)

Commentary

This case shows a successful (Mitra) and an unsuccessful (the German salesman) negotiator performing in the same negotiating session. It demonstrates a clear understanding of the tactics the Chinese are prepared to use to gain the best possible outcome.

Fortunately, Mitra's negotiating skill was equal to the task. He was well prepared, remained calm and flexible when all appeared lost, and, knowing the contortions through which the Chinese often put the opposition, came up with a clever counter plan that not only called their bluff but put the government representative in the hot seat. Mitra remained polite and humble to the end, never giving offense, and kept the government official in charge of the project in the loop when playing his trump card.

Mitra's negotiating skills and his reasoning were outstanding and, while it helped that he had previous experience with the Chinese and was a seasoned negotiator with cultural sensitivity, anyone could accomplish a similar feat with adequate preparation and foreknowledge.

The German leader made a major mistake when he failed to recognize the talent and experience in his own team. Mitra had not been able to reveal his ploy until the leader—self-centered and frustrated—had gone.

The lesson here is that every negotiating team leader should take advice from all his team members. This may sound obvious, but it is advice often not taken, and the number of failed negotiations should suffice to remind each of us to use our team's full resources and skills.

THE COST OF DEATH ON CHINESE ROADS

OVERVIEW

Mark Rogers is an English expatriate in Beijing, where he is the finance director of the branch of a U.S. multinational. He has been in China for seven years, during most of which he has held a Chinese driving license and driven on Chinese roads.

In 2004, he was driving to the famous Shaolin Temple, a few hours south of Beijing. An hour out of Beijing, it started to rain heavily, and on taking a sharp turn in the road in Hebei province, he accidentally drove into two pedestrians, Wu Hua and his sister Wu Jiao. From the nearby village of Suixi, they had been forced to walk on the road because of flooding. Rogers braked, but his car slid and he lost control, side-swiping the Wu siblings and hurling them onto a stone wall by a flooded storm-water drain.

THE SCENE

Shocked and shaking, Rogers pulled up and rushed to help them out of the drain. He pulled the woman up onto the road and ran after the man, who was floating away slowly, and pulled him onto the road. Cars kept passing, in both directions, but no one stopped to help. Unable to find any sign of life in either of the bodies, he was horrified.

Rogers used his cell phone to telephone his secretary, Betty Xiao, in Beijing, and told her what had happened. She told him to cover the bodies and wait in his car for help to come. Three hours later, a farm truck pulled up, and two farmers got out. They both came up to him carrying cell phones. Repeatedly they nodded to him and one offered him his cell phone, pointing to the mouthpiece and flapping his lips.

Rogers took the phone and heard the familiar and reassuring voice of his secretary: "Oh, Mark, what an awful experience! These two men have come from the nearby village. They will drive the two people to their village for help. You follow them. You can communicate with them through me, using our cell phones." "Thanks very much, Betty. It's a bad scene here. I've killed both these people," he said, grief stricken.

Thus, horrendously, did Rogers start his involvement in a civil suit brought against him by a diverse group of plaintiffs from Suixi village, including the deceased's workplace union, their family members, village officials, and others who were never precisely identified.

Although, technically, Rogers would not have been at fault three months earlier, the law had just changed. Drivers in such situations were liable for all damages, even if pedestrians or other parties were at fault (as was the case here).

A CIVIL APPROACH TO A CIVIL SUIT

Rogers' insurance company was the recently opened Beijing office of Carolina Greater Insurance Co. (CGI). They took over the compensation negotiations with the group of parties who were eventually to assemble in Suixi to seek compensation for the death of the Wu siblings.

CGI decided to employ a professional company that was well established in China, Security International (SI), to represent them in the negotiations with the Suixi village plaintiff group. SI appointed two people to handle negotiations: their Beijing manager Brian Monaghan (a former member of the Royal Canadian Mounted Police and a security specialist) and his Chinese manager Wang Sheng Cu (a former People's Liberation Army officer).

Six weeks after the deaths, they arranged to meet with the plaintiff group in Suixi. There were fifty people present representing the plaintiffs, but Monaghan and Wang persuaded them to appoint only two to negotiate with SI. The deputy mayor of the village and a lawyer were chosen.

NEGOTIATIONS BEGIN

Negotiations were held each morning for seven days until agreement was reached. The two Chinese reported on their progress every evening to a large village meeting, while the SI team reported to their CGI client every night.

Monaghan spoke Chinese quite well but stayed in the background, while Wang acted as spokesperson. Negotiations moved from one set-piece speech or proposal to the next, followed by long, private conversations on both sides. The Chinese presented detailed calculations of the compensation they sought, the largest item being a solatium (*jing shen pei san jin*).

This was also the item on which most time was spent, the Chinese view being that there was a potentially unlimited amount to be paid when a formal apology could not make up for the spiritual damage caused the plaintiffs.

The SI team, under instruction from CGI, conceded that this type of damage payment was appropriate—according to precedent, with poor rural families in particular. Opposition to this claim would have met resistance and seen the claim multiplied due to the perceived intransigence of the defendants.

SI was able to achieve a compensation payout satisfactory to CGI, totaling only seventy-five percent of the bottom-line target figure they had previously agreed with CGI. The Chinese were also happy, the figure being twenty-five percent higher than what they had privately decided to target.

In recognition of the win-win outcome, SI funded a banquet in Suixi for the entire village on the last night.

Commentary

In reflecting on this case, Monaghan said he was modestly proud of what they had achieved, the goodwill generated, and the fact that the payout was within budgetary limits. Most of all, he was thankful to his colleague Wang, who had managed the entire affair masterfully. "He was the real negotiator," Monaghan said. "I was just the figurehead."

Modesty aside, without someone of Monaghan's maturity and experience to allow another to step in, the suit easily could have escalated into a drawn-out conflict, ultimately costing twice as much or more than the figure for which they settled.

But more importantly, they had avoided taking their suit to a Chinese court. Had that happened, the suit might have taken years to resolve. The final lesson to be drawn from this case is that clever, experienced Chinese are a mandatory element in any negotiations with the Chinese.

REGIONAL AUTHORITY VERSUS CENTRAL GOVERNMENT

Since 1993, Larry Porter has been a senior partner at the Beijing office of a well-known multinational management consultancy, where he has been assisting foreign companies to establish joint ventures. He also spends time at the company's Shanghai office, which opened in 1995.

Porter's business forte is such that a number of client companies only go to him when they get themselves into unrealistic, unmanageable commitments with prospective Chinese partners.

These clients would often tell Porter that the Chinese government, in spite of its original promises, would not permit them to remit more than a token amount of future profit back to their head office in hard currency. This problem arose repeatedly because foreign companies naïvely assumed that they could even remit home their profits from domestic sales in China. They chose to ignore the fact that only export sales generated hard currency for China, especially in the 1990s. Domestic sales brought in the local currency—the yuan, which the Chinese would gleefully inform foreigners was only good for lighting one's pipe.

Inevitably, Porter had found, by the time companies had taken this information on board, they were already committed to investing in land and facilities, trapped by their own lack of prudence.

The first question Porter would ask a troubled foreign client was: "Who have you spoken with?" What he feared, and what usually proved to be the case, was that the foreign companies had approached regional authorities, rather than the central government in Beijing. Even today, regional authorities rarely receive permission from Beijing to authorize investments but, to preserve their own face, they will issue authorizations—*which is no permission at all*. After that, it is up to Porter to find the right department in Beijing to give permission, one of the most difficult and time-consuming tasks he can undertake on behalf of a client.

These days, an increasing amount of Porter's work involves identifying suitable manufacturing sites, organizing China visits for the CEOs of blue-chip companies, and conducting due diligence studies for joint-venture studies. This often involves studies of the Economic Development Zones (EDZs) that are now widespread, and conducting field visits to determine the suitability of given EDZs for a client's proposed plan or investment.

The strength of Porter's company derives from his range of contacts throughout China but, even so, he must tread carefully. Since some government officials are particular about not wishing to be connected with regional authorities that are known to be corrupt, Porter's Chinese managers carefully check out each contact in their network. His Chinese managers also advise him to avoid officials when they are losing their power base. His company needs to be as neutral as possible and not appear to take sides politically. Moreover, after negotiations with the Chinese, he always asks his Chinese staff for feedback—and listens to the answers.

"My staff have to be so comfortable with me that they can tell me what they really think, not what they think I want to hear. It takes a long time for them to develop that sense of security. Most Chinese are super cautious about telling you what they actually think. Chinese staff belong to FESCO [Foreign Enterprise Service Cooperation], and have to report back everything of consequence, so I am careful that nothing gets back that will damage our reputation."

Building on Experience

Porter has much personal experience in negotiating with the Chinese. They disguise their decision makers in true bureaucratic fashion, but he knows that he must identify them in order to achieve the best outcome. He must work out their bottom line, what they are really after. *It will never be clear at the beginning.* They always have their own hidden agenda and objectives. His goal is to work out what these are and to make them as hard as possible to achieve. He understands that many Chinese still live in a world characterized by criticism and self-criticism, left over from the Cultural Revolution, which has given them the self-control not to lose their cool in public.

Porter is observant and an astute listener, with seemingly little to say. He always takes two Chinese colleagues with him—one to take notes, one to observe. Both are thoroughly briefed beforehand. He always negotiates in English and one of his colleagues interprets. This slows the flow of the meetings, giving him time to think and observe. He feels greatly empowered doing this. It keeps him alert to little tactical ploys the Chinese commonly use, such as asking the same question in three different ways. He has learned to always give exactly the same answer—otherwise, they are quick to attack his perceived inconsistency.

"Sometimes," he says, "a simple question is loaded with dynamite. So you have to listen very carefully and then think about why they have asked the question."

Porter has learned to be patient with the Chinese. He is constantly asking himself what is behind their questions or statements. It is a puzzle, and he knows he needs time to mull over what happens at meetings. He thus has meetings for no more than half a day, to give himself time for problem solving and reflection.

The Chinese prepare very thoroughly, according to Porter. "They will test you out ... find out if you know what you are talking about and if you are to be trusted. You must not give them information you believe is not true, or about which you are not sure. It is best to say, 'I don't know' or 'I'll find out.' If you give them wrong information, nine times out of ten they will have asked somebody else and have been given a different answer, so they will wonder."

Porter says that Chinese officials take an extremely long view—fifteen or twenty years down the track—their primary consideration being what is best for China. He finds that foreign companies that understand this are rare.

❑ The ideal negotiation with the Chinese is well managed and well organized. A team approach is essential. Flexibility and cool heads, despite pressure, are mandatory. Team members should have negotiating skills and cross-cultural sensitivity (even if their experience is not China-related).

❑ Negotiating with the Chinese is not for the inexperienced or the lone wolf, yet the best China negotiators have all honed their skills by trial and error. The best China negotiator will:
  ■ not be distracted by cultural differences.
  ■ accept that nothing is ever fully resolved with the Chinese.
  ■ recognize that giving and saving face are the most important of all.
  ■ always be prepared to make the Chinese look good.

❑ Negotiations will be multidimensional and tricky, so one should listen to the ideas of all one's team members.

❑ While you may make the final decisions, be sure your team includes one or two astute Chinese members.

❑ Learn to recognize Chinese "red herrings."

**CHAPTER
4**

WELL-MANAGED
NEGOTIATIONS

The Team Approach

T he three cases in this chapter feature a team approach to negotiating, in which no particular individual shines.

 LONG-TERM THINKING PAYS OFF FOR VOLKSWAGEN

OVERVIEW

Volkswagen (VW), the first overseas carmaker in China, is the only foreign manufacturer to have been making a profit in China over the past ten years.

It all began in October 1984, when VW signed a joint venture agreement with China. One of the country's first major joint venture agreements, it involved several government authorities, including the Ministry of Foreign Trade and Cooperation (MOFTEC, now MoCom), the State Planning Commission, the State Economic Commission, the Ministry of Finance, the Bank of China (BOC), the Municipal Government of Shanghai, and the China National Automobile Industry Corporation (CNAIC).

A manufacturing facility was built in Shanghai, and VW's partners were Shanghai Tractor and Automobile Corporation (STAC), with a twenty-five percent share, as well as the BOC, Shanghai Trust and Consultant Company, and the CNAIC, which together had a twenty-five percent share.

IN THE BEGINNING

Being first into China has proved lucrative for VW. In 1986, its first plant had a capacity of 30,000 vehicles; in 2003, there were two plants turning out 400,000 vehicles. Again in 1986, national car sales were less than 30,000; in 2002 they were 720,000, of which VW had a fifty-three percent share.

The company has achieved market leadership through product quality, reputation, and pricing; indeed, every Chinese knows VW. In terms of the potential of China as a car market, it is still early days. Since its entry into the WTO, the prices of imported cars have decreased significantly, but no other carmaker has yet been able to whittle away VW's competitive edge. In addition, plans are afoot to import VW's lower-priced Skoda to China, to position the maker in the cheaper segments of the market.

VW was approached by the China National Technical Import Corporation in 1977, and in 1978 a Chinese delegation visited VW headquarters in Wolfsburg, Germany. The first VW delegation went to Beijing in 1979. So there were six years of negotiations, involving at least seven parties on the Chinese side, and major contracts were negotiated, including a joint venture contract, a technology transfer agreement, articles of association, supply agreements, and a planning agreement.

According to Heinz Bendlin, one of the original VW negotiators with China, even in the early days the Chinese behaved courteously. He has commented as follows:

"I learned in China that foreigners tend to have a typical mode of behavior. They want to achieve results quickly, get answers to all their queries, and immediately come up with solutions to problems. But in China one has to be patient and be prepared to spend considerable time solving problems step by step, or *ibu ibu*, as the Chinese say. Setting deadlines or showing impatience leads to disadvantages in negotiations.

"The Chinese like to negotiate in rather large groups. Fairly frequently, three or four VW people negotiated with ten to twenty Chinese. However, typically only one would speak while the others took notes. They were all very disciplined.

"There were times when they would cultivate a friendship, seemingly to manipulate situations. Our Chinese partners also frequently asked us to explain matters several times. This was not a sign of insufficient professional knowledge on their part, but just a tactic, as are the meticulously organized extras during negotiations, such as banquets, toasts, and sightseeing.

"We should listen carefully to the Chinese. Never try to convince them by saying that only your products or plans are outstanding. Instead, explain the facts and figures as often as they require; explain why you believe yours is the best offer; and explain why you are asking for certain payments.

"Do not show that opinions are divided on a given topic within your team, and avoid discussions in front of them. They cannot understand such behavior and will interpret this as a sign that you lack clarity about your concept.

"Try to take advantage of the Chinese way: Have a disciplined team, prepare carefully, speak as a team with one voice, and try to solve your problems during the breaks, or even ask for a break to avoid showing disharmony within your team on matters you are negotiating."

Commentary

Looking back on its successful negotiating style with the Chinese, VW suggests seven points as the keys to its success:

1. Have a small team and don't change the team members.
2. Show up as a team.
3. Remain patient and never negotiate under pressure of a deadline.
4. Explain facts and figures and your ideas as often as you are asked to do so.
5. Convince your partners through facts and figures that yours is the best offer.
6. Do not become nervous when the Chinese use the mass media to influence their position in negotiations.
7. Do not seek quick results, since they could be bad results—especially in China.

 A RARE SUCCESS IN CHINA—THE CELANESE JOINT VENTURE

OVERVIEW

One of the most closely studied Chinese joint ventures is that involving Celanese Corporation of the United States, a producer of value-added industrial chemicals, and China National Tobacco Corporation (CNTC). The venture produces tow, the fluffy synthetic fiber in cigarette filters.

In 1982, when CNTC decided to increase its production of filter cigarettes, it was on the lookout for international suppliers. Since all tow providers refused to sell their technology to China, CNTC approached Celanese, a highly regarded tow producer, with a view to setting up a joint venture. Celanese declined the offer after two years of arm's-length, long-distance discussions through its Chinese agent, London Export Company (LEC), which was well regarded in China. Celanese believed that the joint venture would destabilize the international market and adversely affect its cash flow.

In early 1984, LEC reviewed the negotiations and found there might be greater mutual benefit than had at first appeared. A senior LEC executive asked Celanese for permission to continue mediating the joint-venture proposal and, by mid-year, he had persuaded both parties of the potential joint-venture benefits. As a result, CNTC promptly made Celanese the preferred supplier of tow, even before the joint-venture plant was finished; classified the output of the new plant as import substitution, so that foreign exchange would be conserved and CNTC would not need to buy tow abroad; and would share top management decisions fifty-fifty.

FIRST STEPS

Next came face-to-face negotiations, discussions, and communications between the parties. Differences in formal communication almost stalled these discussions before they had got off the ground, with suspicion arising over the language used and the legal requirements put forward. Some of the main issues were:

- The Chinese insisted on a holistic approach, asking the U.S. team to agree to a macro-concept for the new venture, with details to be agreed to later. Meanwhile, the U.S. party insisted that they would only regard the overall venture as generally agreed to after agreement on each component of the new venture had been reached.

- The Chinese insisted on the prior development of friendship and harmony, while the U.S. negotiators were blunt in their demands for openness and frankness about differences.

- The Chinese opposed the U.S. company's proposal that lawyers be brought into the discussions.

LEC, which was respected by both parties and was an experienced China hand, helped resolve the problems and develop an atmosphere of trust, so that basic agreement was eventually reached.

STAGE TWO

The second stage, comprehensive planning, cost $1 million, took two years to complete, and involved the translation of the basic agreement into a new plant and business organization.

It had been agreed, in early talks, that Chinese regulations on technology transfers, feasibility studies, and joint ventures were not well suited to the new enterprise, so much time was spent anticipating problems related to the design and construction of the plant, its general management, human resources policies and practices, purchasing, finance, and accounting. As a result, specific plans were drawn up by U.S. and Chinese teams, with some fifty experts involved at any one time.

Cultural problems were not lacking, and included the difficulty the Chinese encountered when their Celanese colleagues argued with them or expressed differences of opinion. As one senior Chinese manager said: "I had to learn that someone could argue with me and still be my friend." Cross-culturally sophisticated LEC personnel mediated for both sides on a number of troublesome issues.

STAGE THREE

The third stage involved construction of the plant, in the city of Nantong, Jiangsu province. New cultural difficulties arose daily, as Chinese practices collided with Western performance imperatives. Celanese employees noted:

- Crews of Chinese subcontractors would disappear for days at a time, leaving work unfinished.

- In work units supervised by foreigners, the Chinese observed workloads; but in those supervised by Chinese, the workloads were usually reduced and additional employees hired.

- Many employees appeared indifferent to the satisfactory completion of the project.

- The Celanese habit of flagging errors or shortcomings was taken by many Chinese as a personal affront—compounded by the indignity of seemingly being "talked down to."

The Nantong factory was completed in 1989, when the joint venture went into operation, with a mixture of Chinese and U.S. managers and staff. Most of the Chinese managers appointed to the new enterprise saw themselves as loyal to CNTC, and their allegiance to the new venture was initially fragile. The Chinese managers discussed problems with their seniors at CNTC, rather than with their U.S. venture colleagues. Neither side could identify with the new entity at first, and managers held meetings in their native tongue, which upset those on the other side.

But overall, a long-term perspective was taken regarding the factory, where training was provided to enable employees to carry out prescribed operations.

At the same time, Celanese managers, believing that the performance of local suppliers had to be upgraded, spent much of their time helping suppliers improve deliveries. William Newman (1992, 72) points out: "Chinese plants...are accustomed to loose standards. Erratic delivery times are common with last-minute flurries of action to meet emergencies."

By 1992, the Nantong plant was meeting corporate goals and becoming profitable, and so it was expanded; and in 1994, the production of acetate flake (the raw material for tow) was added. Then two additional manufacturing sites for acetate tow, each a separate joint venture with CNTC, were built and started up in 1995—one in Zhuhai, Guangdong province, and one in Kunming, Yunnan province.

EFFORTS BEAR RESULTS

Looking back, Celanese says its joint-venture agreements reflect the learning and the changes that occurred in the wake of the original Nantong joint venture. In 2002, the flake facility in Nantong was expanded to provide flake to Zhuhai and Kunming. A senior Celanese manager said that the performance of the Celanese joint ventures in China had exceeded original investment expectations.

There are few joint ventures in China that have been as successful and learned so much from their own experiences. At the same time, the Chinese laws and regulations affecting joint ventures have seen tremendous changes since 1989, making it easier to do business in China.

In May 2001, after ten years of increasingly successful operations, the two partners announced they had "formed joint work teams to complete a feasibility study on an expansion of their joint venture to produce diacetate tow cigarette filters in China" (*Chemical Market Reporter*, May 21, 2001).

This coincided with the Celanese plan to phase out its Rock Hill, South Carolina, plant by the end of the first quarter of 2002. It is to be assumed that Celanese and CNTC will be more professional this time around in planning their joint venture, particularly since China is a growing contributor to the bottom line.

Celanese is now firmly established as a profitable corporate citizen in China, but cross-cultural learning and problems remain part of joint-venture life. A senior Celanese manager commented:

"My wife and I lived in Nantong from June 1997 until March 2000. We found the Chinese people, regardless of their personal circumstances or status, to be extremely friendly and supportive. One very unexpected aspect of life in China is the way we felt completely safe and secure, more so than in any place we have lived, including in the United States.

"Close friendships are developed between expatriates and people in every walk of life, including government officials. The only observation I would make here is that it probably takes longer and more effort to cultivate friendships at higher levels, and this usually requires a peer relationship.

"As I expected, I saw that there was a big variation in how well expatriates respected and adjusted to the culture. Those who tried to have things work the way they did back home became frustrated, and the Chinese quietly resented their attitudes. Likewise, some Chinese had no desire or ability to learn and adopt modern business and management ideas, and they became frustrated and were resented by the expatriates.

"In such cases, the performance of the venture was affected, so the Chinese and Celanese directors ended up looking for ways to resolve the issues, which usually meant moving someone out of the joint venture. Over time, this has made the directors much more careful in the management selection process."

Commentary

This case illustrates how vital it is that a very long-term view be taken when planning one's objectives, to ensure that every debatable issue—often resting on widely divergent cultural values and practices—is thrashed out among the parties concerned. We believe that the Celanese approach could not have been bettered. Both parties handled problems as they arose, choosing not to adopt stereotypical formats. Meanwhile, LEC's role as long-term mediator easily qualifies as the No. 1 point to note and mull over in this case.

 CASE STUDY ## SELLING WATER TO CHINA

OVERVIEW

Acqua International (AQ) is a Europe-based multinational company that has interests in water and other environment-related businesses.

In China, the company has joint ventures with medium-size and large municipalities to produce potable water. To increase its investments in China, the AQ Group arranged, through its local subsidiary Pacific Acqua International (PAQ), to enter into a strategic alliance with Tak Foy and Co., a Chinese conglomerate with strong roots in China and Hong Kong in the service industry (mainly leisure-related). The venture is called Haoyu China Limited (HCL).

THE SCENE

These negotiations concerned an urban water supply system providing potable water to around one million people. Through an agent in the province, the China subsidiary PAQ had secured a contract to construct a water treatment plant for the system.

Some time after the completion and commissioning of the plant, PAQ learned from the same agent that the municipality was short of funds for some urgent development projects. One of its options was to privatize the municipality's water supply facilities.

The sale value of the facilities was set by the municipality, and bidders were sought from within its jurisdiction; there would be no recourse to the central government for approval.

HCL, located in the municipality, submitted a purchasing proposal to buy the facilities, to set up a joint venture with the municipality's water company on a 3:1 ratio, and to operate the facilities on a twenty-five-year contract.

The unresolved issues when bids were called for were:

- Initial water charges. The only things that had been agreed on up to this date were how much would be invested in the facilities and spent on improvements.

- The demand for water. To make the business financially viable, a take-or-pay mechanism would have to be introduced, and local wells would have to be closed.

- The formula to calculate annual water tariff revisions. Devaluation of the yuan would affect foreign exchange–based investment.

- The new company's structure. Who would be the shareholders, board members, and those responsible for its day-to-day management?

NEGOTIATIONS BEGIN

At the request of the Chinese, a memorandum was signed by HCL and the municipality to record the issues still outstanding.

It was only then that PAQ—and through it HCL—was informed by the local PAQ agent (who was supposedly very close to high levels in the municipality) that other international competitors had also visited the municipality in connection with the same project.

After meeting high-ranking officials in the city, the PAQ team was advised to lower its starting price for water supply if it wished to remain the preferred partner.

In a bid not to lose the municipality's interest, PAQ organized visits to PAQ operations in other provinces for a group of municipal officials, whose reaction was positive. Then, believing it a good time to start negotiations, PAQ submitted a revised proposal, which it followed up by visits requesting discussion.

The mayor's office arranged a negotiating session to be attended by representatives of all the municipal departments concerned, at which PAQ and HCL were represented by four people: John King, Hans Christian, Cheng Peng Li, and Xu Jing.

For several weeks the unresolved issues and other matters were discussed, and every evening the municipality hosted a formal banquet, which lent ambiance to the talks. Cheng and Xu were the representatives on these social occasions, while King and Christian remained in the background.

STRATEGY APPLIED

PAQ did not begin negotiating using the water rates as the deciding factor in the belief that, were its ideas not well accepted, the entire project might be placed on hold. Instead, it picked secondary issues with non-critical impact to give both parties some wins to balance the losses.

Discussions started with water demand. Municipalities are generally optimistic about development and, therefore, ready to accept or propose relatively high demand levels where the take-or-pay mechanism is applied. Moreover, PAQ believed the municipality would not be in the joint venture if it were not ready to enforce the laws concerning wells. So an agreement was reached quite quickly on water demand.

Next to be negotiated was the tariff adjustment formula. Both parties agreed to an inflation-adjusted tariff, while the provincial government representative insisted that foreign exchange should represent less than five percent of investment and be used for no more than ten years.

Due to PAQ's favorable reputation, agreements on the shareholding structure and management were reached without too much difficulty.

Last came the water rate negotiations. PAQ impressed on the municipality that, as an old friend, it was right for the project, being technically and financially sound with a good track record in China. PAQ's sincerity was demonstrated by the number of Chinese staff on its team.

COUP DE FACE

Agreement was reached in two weeks, with the mayor himself voicing his support. Wishing to give face to their lead negotiator, and aware of Chinese sensitivity to pricing, PAQ then offered to reduce the starting water rate. In return, to give face to PAQ, the municipality offered preferential tax treatment over a five-year period.

IN RETROSPECT

Later, PAQ managers described some of the problems commonly faced by foreigners in negotiation situations, and how they might be resolved:

- Most foreigners new to China do not know how the Chinese perceive them, nor does it bother them.

- Many Chinese see foreigners as cheats, motivated only by the desire for profit.

- The Chinese point to history: relationships with foreigners are short term, the foreigners leaving after attaining their short-term goals.

- China has a high-context society. Who you and your associates are is more important to success than the mere excellence of your product or your competitive price.

- The Chinese may renegotiate a contract even after it is signed. They believe in people—not legal packages.

- China has a haggling culture; there are no ethics where price is concerned, and they will stop at nothing to get you to lower your price.

- Time is not money in China, although this is starting to change.

- The Chinese will not sign on the dotted line until they feel intuitively that the time is right, even if all points have been clarified.

- Chinese negotiators are not decision makers; the CEO or the government is the ultimate boss.

- Language is a big barrier in Chinese-foreign business negotiations.

SOLUTIONS

- Be patient. In China's family-centered society it takes time to build trust with non-family members.

- Local Chinese employees can help establish trusting relationships.

- Once the Chinese trust you, negotiations are less troublesome.

- Identify the negotiators. They may be top leaders at central and local levels.

- It is important to be honest and sincere with the Chinese.

Commentary

As a supplier of potable water facilities in many Chinese municipalities and cities, PAQ had a good performance record that brought with it and reinforced personal relationships, friendships, and trust.

The idea of leaving discussion of the water rates until after the easy-to-agree-on issues had been tackled proved a good move. The principal sign that negotiations were in PAQ's favor was the number and high level of officials invited to the meeting arranged by the mayor's office. That it still took some weeks to craft a final agreement is not, however, surprising, since there would have been numerous issues outstanding.

Most important of all, when the final agreement was reached, a gesture was made to give the Chinese face within their community.

Main Points of Chapter 4

❑ It can take years to reach agreement in negotiations involving many parties, Chinese policy, and cross-cultural issues.

❑ One should be patient and do things step by step, not set deadlines or be impatient, and listen very carefully to the Chinese.

❑ Teams should be disciplined, well prepared, speak with one voice, and try to solve their problems during breaks.

❑ If largely ignorant regarding how to negotiate with the Chinese, one should be advised by those experienced in negotiating with them.

❑ If one is patient, takes a long-term view, and thrashes out every debatable issue, final agreement can be reached.

❑ The international reputation of a company is critical to the Chinese willingness to begin negotiations.

LONG-TERM NEGOTIATIONS

Some complex business arrangements require long-term negotiations, since the issues are often convoluted, as in the trilateral toxic waste case presented below. Not only should operations be well managed throughout such negotiations, but the lead negotiators must know each other well and share mutual trust.

 TRUST BUILDING IN A TRILATERAL NEGOTIATION

OVERVIEW

This complex, ongoing negotiation involves three countries, each with players who have their own agenda and preferred outcome. Although the negotiation is yet to become hard-nosed regarding price, delivery, and technology, it shows how relationships develop over time and some of the dynamics at play in this relatively early phase.

THE SCENE

Our company (English owned, with regional headquarters in Hong Kong, a joint venture in Japan, and an office in Australia) has toxic waste technology that we are attempting to have accepted for a very large and politically sensitive project in China. Being negotiated is how to treat a large amount of toxic waste left in China by Japan at the end of World War II. For many years, China and Japan have been discussing who should bear the cost of treating the waste, and it was agreed only recently that Japan would clean up the waste and pay for so doing.

A project management company has been appointed in Japan to undertake the feasibility and technology selection aspects. The Japanese have long felt frustrated with what they perceive to have been a lack of cooperation by China, which has been attempting to get the Japanese government to tackle the entire problem, including many hundreds of tons of contaminated soil.

While Japan has admitted responsibility for the toxic waste—but not the polluted soil—it has long believed that China should fund all aspects of the project, including technology selection and the cleanup by Japanese companies.

The Chinese view, however, is that China should undertake the work, but that the Japanese should supply the technology and funding.

Our company has been working with both parties—assisting the Japanese to find a way through the approvals maze in China (so they could start some of the work) and guiding the Chinese so that they might use our technology, which would greatly enhance our opportunities in the project.

Although we have not been privy to the negotiations at government level, we have been working at the project level as facilitators with the Japanese project management team and the Chinese regulatory authorities.

Other parties involved include international experts (from government bodies) in the United Kingdom and the United States, who have been called on—because of the nature and substantial extent of the waste problem—to advise on issues such as technology selection and project requirements. The three main issues are:

■ Japan wants to limit the extent of the cleanup to an absolute minimum—which will cost, even so, hundreds of millions of dollars; China, meanwhile, wants to derive as much benefit as possible.

■ Japan believes that, as it will be funding the cleanup, it has the right to choose who is to do the work and how, and would prefer to use Japanese companies and technology; China wants Chinese companies to do the work, using technology chosen, provided, and funded by the Japanese. Although China has the final say—because work cannot proceed until it gives the nod—Beijing cannot but depend on Japan for the technology and funds.

■ We want our company's technology to be accepted for the major portion of the work. But for this to happen, we need acceptance by both the Chinese and Japanese players, so we plan to make maximum use of our joint-venture company in Japan.

NEGOTIATIONS TO DATE

In the role of middleman, we have been working with one of the newer breeds of Chinese companies, a partially privatized government department. Very large (20,000 employees) and still heavily responsible to the central government, it has unashamedly sought assistance and guidance from foreign companies, ostensibly to better understand the outside business world. The Chinese general manager with whom we worked is, at the age of 43, by Chinese standards a mere slip of a lad and considered exceedingly young to hold such a position.

We introduced the Chinese company to the Japanese (in Japan) and offered to assist the Japanese project managers to work through the authorizations labyrinth in China to facilitate and simplify their initial investigations and infrastructure development. To this end, we negotiated a memorandum of understanding (MOU) with the Chinese company to work together on the project and in order to promote our technology in China.

It was difficult to convince the Chinese of the value of our strategy, namely, that they should assist the Japanese company through the approvals phase in order to put themselves in a position of strength that would enable them to assist with the work. The Japanese, meanwhile, chose to believe that the Chinese would require the majority of the work to be undertaken by Chinese companies or personnel.

We recognized the need for us to build personal trust and a very strong relationship with the Chinese involved if the proposed arrangement was to be approved. The Chinese would have to trust our approach.

This took a long time, but we persevered, and they came to trust us and eventually accepted our proposal. But that was only after we convinced them that there was something in it for them in the long run.

Separately, our Japanese joint-venture company worked with the relevant Japanese government department on the technology issues. This move was designed to promote and allow acceptance of our technology as satisfactory for the treatment phase. We also brought some Chinese into those discussions to assist the Japanese project management company. The Chinese were pleased that we had given them face with both the Japanese government and the Japanese project management company.

Negotiations between the Japanese and the Chinese company we brought to the table have progressed, and the Chinese have started to undertake a number of pilot studies to help the Japanese gain approvals and to smooth the way for the project.

In order to further strengthen our position regarding the project, we continue to seek approval for our technology in China, realizing that the final say will undoubtedly rest with the Chinese. We have persuaded the Chinese company to arrange trials in China, using our technology for waste of a similar nature to that of the project, so that we might become an accepted technology in China, satisfying the requirements of the Japanese (through our Japanese joint venture) and the Chinese (by getting Chinese approval and having a Chinese partner to undertake the work).

The approval-related negotiations have been the most comprehensive to date, as is outlined in the next section.

THE DEVIL IS IN THE DETAILS

Negotiations started twelve months ago, with a presentation of our technology to a gathering in Beijing of fifty people, including government officials, university professors and department heads, as well as other experts. I presented the technology issues and outcomes to this group through a non-technical interpreter. This was a mistake.

The interpretation was quite often incorrect, the interpreter substituting the closest expression he knew for what I was saying. Fortunately, several technically astute people in the audience spoke very good English and were able to correct the official interpreter. It was a lesson I shall not forget!

Following the presentation, we answered the numerous questions that were posed, but otherwise the feedback was rather limited. It took a great deal of perseverance to keep the issue in the limelight and push for a pilot study to be conducted in China.

After almost twelve months to the day, we managed to arrange for a party of five Chinese, from different institutions, to travel to Australia to witness trials and further familiarize themselves with our company and its technology. Two members of the party were from a government department, two were from the host Chinese company, and one was from the province where the waste-related trials were to be undertaken.

Three members of our staff accompanied them: two from Beijing, one from Hong Kong, and me. The host Chinese company covered the airfares for the five Chinese, while we covered all other expenses. This allowed us to gain favor in the friendship stakes; we believe they will feel obliged to return the favor—we hope by arranging the trials and approval process for our technology.

The visit to Australia was really a relationship-building phase, designed to give the Chinese an overview of the technology, show them Australian hospitality, and build the all-important relationship of trust.

A lot of time was spent explaining the technology and answering questions, which were often asked in different ways by different people. To do so is typical of the Chinese when in information-gathering mode; they make sure that one is able to reply in the same way each time.

After we had already been working on the project for a year, we were asked what outcome we wanted from trials and why we wanted them carried out. The questions threw us. We had been under the impression that they all understood our hope to have our technology approved for future projects in both China and Japan.

But this was not so. Here we thus were, at this late stage having to explain the outcome that we were after. Fortunately, our Chinese marketing man from Hong Kong saved the day when he explained to the five Chinese that "We want to go to bed together and have many children!" They laughed heartily and the tension dissipated.

The whiteboard has become a very important tool in our discussions and negotiations with the Chinese. One picture is indeed worth a thousand words—and many more if you do not speak the language! It has enabled us to discuss many issues and clarify communications and misunderstandings. Moreover, having a Chinese manager from our company involved has also made a huge difference. Many times we would seem to have reached an impasse or a misunderstanding, only to have our Chinese colleague clarify the matter, allowing us to move forward.

Discussion and negotiations concerning the trials, as well as the transfer of information and understanding of the technology, have gone well. It was interesting to find that several Chinese who, unable to communicate with me during the first few days, were speaking with me in quite fluent English by the last few days of the ten-day visit. Initially, I had wondered if I had done something to offend them.

LESSONS SO FAR

- Avoid heavy lunches! A majority of participants fall asleep at the discussion table after lunch.

- In China, rank automatically makes people eligible for a trip overseas, regardless of whether the individual needs to be involved, has the relevant influence, or can contribute. Thus, to get the best value for money, time and effort should be invested in vetting the nominees for study tours. It is best to eliminate those who have little or no influence on major outcomes.

- A general nodding of heads does not mean one has been understood. One should repeat statements, draw pictures, and ask again, to ensure issues (especially if important) are well understood.

- The majority of the time that Chinese negotiators are with one should be devoted to them. It may be taxing to spend every night at dinner with them and accompany them all day every day, yet that is what they expect and it helps build trust and develop relationships. Moreover, relaxation after a few drinks can facilitate understanding all round.

- Avoid selecting expensive accommodations for your Chinese guests if they are to foot the bill. Since they may prefer more modest lodgings and the option of spending their allowances otherwise, one should ask before making bookings.

CASE SUMMARY

The prenegotiation phase, during which the teams were selected on both sides, is past. The next phase, involving meetings and opening moves in China, Japan, and Australia, has just begun. While different China-based players are at the Japan end of the negotiations, two of the China-based technical personnel have been on both Japanese and Australian visits.

The negotiating phase concerning the trials and technology approvals is advancing, and there are plans for further meetings in China involving the Japanese and Chinese parties, as well as our companies and UK experts.

This complex set of negotiations has required planning and strategy not only trilaterally, but also bilaterally between the Chinese and the Japanese. The dynamics of the situation are complex and this is still the early stage of what promises to be protracted negotiations.

We expect the trials and approvals process to become harder; the Japanese are still in the initial phase of shadowboxing to gain position, intelligence, and understanding vis-à-vis other interested parties, and continue to consider their options. Nothing is happening very quickly.

(with David Osborne)

Commentary

From the outset, Osborne's team understands the complex nature of the negotiations. It is spending a great deal of time laying a solid foundation based in trust, goodwill, and familiarity so that his company may achieve its goals and both outside parties attain their objectives. The team's patience is exemplary, as is its attention to detail, communication, and the concerns of all parties involved.

At this point, there is no place for a bottom-line approach—building friendly personal relations and sharing knowledge are crucial if the final outcome is to be favorable for Osborne. He recognizes that bringing both sides closer together and striving for a win-win situation for them will ultimately benefit the matchmaker.

CASE STUDY BEHAVING WITH PROPRIETY

OVERVIEW

This case outlines one Chinese individual's response to the thoughtless, inept negotiating manner of another, and contains valuable cross-cultural insights (adapted from Fang 2001, 51–63).

Chando, a Chinese shipbuilder, had agreed to change the main engine in a ship it was building for the Danish shipowner Danske. Although this would involve a lot of work and great expense for Chando, it was willing to substitute a low-speed engine for one of medium speed.

Prior to this, Jurgen Martens, Danske's vice-president and technical director, had made a very good impression on the senior Chando people, as had their sales and marketing director. Usually, a shipyard is entitled to refuse to change the type of main engine once a contract has been signed and, were a shipowner to insist, a charge could be levied.

But this is not how the Chinese in this case wished to do business. They believed they were obliged to reciprocate past kindness they had been shown by the Danes, according to the Chinese saying: "If you honor me a foot, I will honor you ten feet in return." In their eyes, Martens had previously honored Chando and it was now their turn to honor Martens. When asked how the Chinese had been honored, Qing Hua, the general manager in charge of the project, explained at length.

THE SCENE
"I always thought Martens was a very reasonable man. For instance, we had failed to realize that the specifications for the vessel's paintwork made the job of painting something we could not do, because the specifications prevented us from carrying out any welding once painting was finished. At that time, our shipyard lacked experience, and so the person responsible for painting had not recognized this problem when reading the specifications.

"I talked to Martens about the problem and he said, 'Okay, then do it by sectional painting. The price can stay as it is.' His answer helped us solve a big problem of our own making, and one we could not have solved otherwise. A shipowner has the right to refuse to accept a vessel that is not built exactly to the technical specifications. It will not pass inspection if the paintwork is not in accordance with the contract. So when Martens wanted us to change to a low-speed main engine, we were willing to cooperate.

"I then had to finalize the ship classification, and so went with five people from our shipyard to the Shanghai office of NOR [one of five classification companies in Shanghai], which had been recommended by Martens. Everything had been finalized except the price.

"'This is the first time we are doing business with NOR,' I said to both the company's Shanghai representative, a Hong Kong Chinese, and his assistant, a Shanghainese. 'You know our Chinese customs.

Today, I would be very grateful to get even the slightest discount from you. I would regard it as you giving me face.'"

COLD-SHOULDER TREATMENT

"There was no response. We sat in silence for thirty seconds, six Chando people on one side and two NOR people on the other. Finally, the Hong Kong Chinese broke the silence and said brusquely: '$240,000. Not a dollar less!'

"I slowly took out my pen and signed the contract. 'I agree with you, $240,000,' I said. After the signing, the NOR people invited us to stay and have dinner, but I declined, saying I had no time and had to go. I also said: 'I don't know if my colleagues would like to stay. I can ask them.' Bear in mind here that I was the team leader and that, if I wanted to go, no one would dare stay to eat. So we all left.

"As we were leaving, I left the NOR representatives in no doubt as to my true feelings. They certainly would have understood that I believed their price to be too high and that we would not work with them again because we had lost face badly in that encounter."

Chando stood firm, not accepting NOR as the vessels' classification standard, even though the company eventually reduced its price to a level lower than that of its competitor, LL.

Months passed and the time came for Chando to negotiate a new shipbuilding project with Danske. Agreement had to be reached regarding the classification standard to be adopted: that of NOR, LL, or another. Since a NOR representative had made them lose face once, they decided to use LL. But this needed a new provision in the shipbuilding contract that would allow the shipyard to choose from among the various classification societies.

Qing recalled: "NOR did not give me face, cornering me by using the fact that they were the only option in the specifications. This was not a personal matter: NOR looked down on my shipyard, a Chinese enterprise."

From the shipowner's point of view, there was little to distinguish NOR from LL. However, the shipbuilding contract that was subsequently drawn up between Chando and Danske—allowing Chando to choose from among NOR, LL, or an equivalent classification standard—provided Chando with an opportunity to take revenge on NOR.

PAYBACK TIME

When NOR managers approached Chando in connection with the Danske project, Qing was ready. He explained: "The NOR Shanghai office was managed by a Norwegian, who had once been NOR's regional manager in Dalian. One day, he came to the shipyard at around 11 A.M., accompanied by the Shanghainese I had met previously.

"I was in a meeting. When I was informed that the general manager of the NOR Shanghai office was looking for me, I realized immediately what it was about. I wanted to show him how displeased I was, but out of courtesy I told my colleague to ask them to wait fifteen minutes or so as I was in an important meeting.

"The two visitors were left alone to cool their heels in the waiting room. In fact, I could have left the meeting, which was not as important as I told them. About fifteen minutes later I came out to meet the gentlemen. The Shanghainese introduced his new boss to me and we exchanged a few words of courtesy. No doubt my behavior was cold.

"The visitors invited me to go out for lunch. I replied, 'Not necessary. If you wish to talk business, we can do it right here.'

"'Yes, we are here to talk business, but we can still eat and talk,' they said.

"'Let's do it this way,' I suggested, 'You have come to visit me; you are the guests and I am the host. Let me entertain you at our shipyard.'" Qing then telephoned to arrange three working lunches.

He explained to me: "Frankly, I have never entertained guests at a working lunch before. Whenever I receive guests, I always do so in decent restaurants, never in the shipyard canteen. This time, however, I intended to offend them, placing them and me on a par with the shipyard workers. We went to the works canteen for site supervisors and overseas service engineers, many of whom wore oily working clothes. I was in casual clothes that day, but the NOR visitors wore suits."

As they looked around the noisy canteen, the NOR visitors realized something was wrong.

Qing went on: "Then, I spoke to the Shanghainese in Chinese. 'You are Chinese, too,' I said. 'You know Chinese seldom hate or love a person too much. What the Chinese believe is *Li shang wang lai* [Courtesy demands reciprocity]. Please remember that.'"

Qing wanted both his guests to understand that the word "li" here meant not only a gift, but also something negative, such as an insulting action or a blow from the opponent.

"Then, they asked me about the price offered by LL. I said: 'Sorry, that's a commercial secret. You shouldn't ask such a question. I'm not in a position to reply. I can tell you that LL's price is on my desk right now. Just do your best.'" They whispered for a while before the Shanghainese said to me: '$300,000,' looking straight into my eyes.

"Smiling, I said: 'What I need is a written, not verbal promise. You may say $300,000 today, but forget and say something else tomorrow. To whom would I turn for help then? I must have your offer in writing.'

"After lunch, we went to the shipyard's guesthouse for visitors from abroad to drink tea. I answered their questions, one by one, except those concerning LL's price. They certainly found me annoying.

"Finally, before they left, the Shanghainese said: 'If $300,000 is still too high, would you give me a hint please? We can do $240,000.'

I smiled without saying a word, only asking him to send me a written offer. That evening, he sent a fax to my home. The price: $220,000 per vessel.

"NOR had reduced its price from the previous $380,000 to $220,000 per vessel. The offer was very close to LL's $210,000.

"We stood firm," Qing recalled. "At the next meeting with the NOR people, I felt the need to say a few words, in English, to the general manager, but I changed my mind because few of my colleagues understood English.

"Instead, I said to the Shanghainese: 'I will speak Chinese and you translate. Our cooperation for the first vessel was very unpleasant. I had never met anyone who treated me so poorly.'"

FORGET FACE AT YOUR PERIL

"I was looking at the matter not from the perspective of my personal face, but from that of the shipyard. I wondered why NOR had dealt us such an unmerciful blow when they had been in a negotiating position of strength.

"Further, I said to the Shanghainese: 'The Chinese attach great importance to the word 'li,' but I had no sense that you had understood the meaning of the term. So I definitely will use LL this time, even though your price is lower.'"

"The Shanghainese wondered how I could justify my decision, so I explained: 'I can say that your price is lower but your service is worse than that of LL. You may report this to the shipyard director, complaining about my having selected LL even though its price is higher than yours. But I believe that, were you to do so, you would lose our business forever. This time, what I want is to give you a lesson on how to deal with both Chinese shipyards and the Chinese. You are Chinese; you should help Western people deal with the Chinese, not just make money out of the Chinese.'"

Qing went on: "That evening, NOR invited us to dinner. We all attended, although we did not reach an agreement. I made no secret of my point: 'I did not sign the contract because you pushed me too hard the last time. I have taken revenge. This is *Yi ya huan ya* [A tooth for a tooth].'"

However, Qing reflected later: "Taking revenge should not go too far. Once you have let people know your strength, you should try to get along with them.

"My approach followed the maxim: *En wei bin shi* [Use the carrot and the stick]. The bottom line was that the vessel was being built in our shipyard, so whatever style was adopted, either *en* [the carrot] or *wei* [the stick], the purpose was to achieve *he wei gui* [peace and harmony].

Commentary

The case clearly demonstrates how the Chando manager acted naturally and spontaneously, adapting to the other party on the basis of the Chinese value of reciprocity in relationships. This Confucian value is well illustrated by two Chinese sayings: "If you honor me a foot, I will honor you ten feet in return" (or, "If you dishonor me a foot, I will dishonor you ten feet in return"), and "Courtesy demands reciprocity" (or, "Deal with a man as he deals with you" and "A gift needs to be reciprocated").

The Chinese values that stand out in the case are those of moderation and face. The NOR decision not to chase after the business it lost to its opponent reflects the traditional Chinese value of moderation. Moreover, face is a key issue in the Chinese business negotiating process and is critical in the first encounter between negotiating parties. Sincerity and the need to give face are expressed in Qing's appeal: "This is the first time we have done business with NOR.... I would be very grateful to get even the slightest discount from you. I would regard it as you giving me face."

The fact that NOR did not care about face or could not recognize the need to give it led to retaliation. It showed little appreciation of the nuances of Chinese business behavior. Qing took it upon himself to educate those involved, and they were fortunate in that he held no long-term ill will toward NOR.

Qing's approach provides a very focused set of lessons on face and Chinese sincerity. Even more important, his lesson on giving and returning honor is well worth our noting here.

Nothing in Western mercantile or economic negotiating theory can prepare those educated in Western ways for such a disjunction, for such generosity (honoring tenfold) when events go well, or such seeming venom when things go badly. Also noteworthy is Qing's total lack of resentment once his corrective measures had achieved their aim. It shows that a relationship can be repaired if cool heads prevail and bridges are not burned in anger or frustration.

In the following case, involving events surrounding a commodity transaction, few of the caveats about negotiations apply. However, one moral to be drawn from the case is that, even should you find negotiations to be a game with rules to which you are not privy, reciprocity is of the essence and will be rewarded.

 CASE STUDY

HOW NOT TO NEGOTIATE WITH THE CHINESE

OVERVIEW

In 1998 Simon Turner worked for Bassano, a large Australian womens-wear company with eighteen retail outlets across Australia. The following story recounts his experience in a negotiation in Beijing with Happy Clothing.

Bassano required a cheaper manufacturer of tailored womenswear and approached Happy Clothing, a tailored menswear manufacturer, to provide this service. Turner and his CEO Brian Thompson traveled to Beijing with a Chinese-Australian employee, Zhu Yi, who would act as interpreter.

While Turner went as the product specialist, management thought his previous experience working in India would be valuable. Turner, however, was not confident that this provided him with the necessary skills to negotiate in China. He had worked in high-context societies but was unfamiliar with Chinese culture. He thus decided to adopt a few of the basic approaches he had used in India, namely, being patient, extremely polite, and fastidious when it came to details.

THE SCENE

Thompson felt he had to finalize the negotiation in two days. Turner tried hard to convince him that more time might be required, but Thompson only added one day to their stay, assuring Turner: "I'm good at this, just watch and learn." Fully believing only two days would be needed, Thompson also scheduled other meetings for the three-day visit.

On day one, Thompson and Turner met Liu Baoping, Zhang Hua Ai, and Ping Ming. Liu spoke reasonable English, but the other two spoke no English. The morning was spent drinking tea, with discussion focused on Happy Clothing's capability. Thompson attempted to turn the conversation to Bassano's requirements, but the Chinese team did not seem interested. Soon after, the Australian team was ushered to lunch, followed by a ninety-minute drive to the company's factory. After an impressive and thorough tour of the facilities, they were driven back to central Beijing for a 5 P.M. banquet dinner. The timing seemed peculiar to Thompson and increased his frustration with the day's proceedings.

NEGOTIATIONS COMMENCE

Discussion began next morning. The Chinese knew a lot about Bassano and its competitors, which impressed Turner immensely, as he had not come across this approach in India. It also increased his confidence about Happy Clothing's ability to meet their needs.

The Chinese team confirmed they could meet Bassano's volume and price requirements. The deal meant that Bassano's landed cost for a fully tailored women's suit was $20. The retail price of $150 meant potentially high profits.

However, a problem arose when Happy Clothing identified its terms of trade. It was keen to maximize its foreign currency holdings, as this would lead to concessions from the government vis-à-vis control of their business. For this reason, the contract was conditional on Bassano managing distribution of Happy Clothing menswear in Australia. Thompson refused, but the Chinese remained firm that no deal could be negotiated otherwise.

A GIFT HORSE

Turner, meanwhile, believed their warehouse could easily accommodate more stock. He saw an opportunity to increase sales and profits by distributing this product or, as an alternative, the opportunity to subcontract the distribution to another company and make a profit as middleman. Thompson remained indignant and so did the Chinese.

Turner, however, encouraged Thompson to consider this option and to calculate the gains of both $20 women's suits and the subcontracting of distribution, together with the option of continuing to manufacture suits in Australia. Eventually Thompson consented—as long as the cost of the suits made the venture feasible.

Although Yi had said nothing on day one, at lunch on day two she told Turner that she thought the negotiation was going well: "I think they like you but I don't think they like Thompson." The afternoon session became more focused on the Happy Clothing rather than the Bassano contract, further infuriating Thompson, who made no attempt to disguise his feelings.

Knowing that the negotiation would take three days, Turner decided to provide Happy Clothing with information on required sizes and fabric considerations for an Australian market before moving on to what Bassano required. The Chinese were very pleased with this.

At the end of day two, Turner felt confident that a deal would be struck. But Thompson believed that only Happy Clothing would benefit, by gaining access to the Australian menswear market. As Thompson had another meeting on day three and possibly would not be able to attend the final stage of the negotiation, he provided Turner with the required agreement conditions that included the terms for a written contract.

The talks on the third day were slow. Turner was able to negotiate a price on Happy Clothing's menswear that would allow healthy profits for Bassano, even were it to subcontract the distribution to another company.

Bassano's contract was more difficult, however, not because of price or volume requirements, but because the contract was to include payment penalties applicable were certain terms not met. The Chinese told Turner that, not being usual practice, this would be difficult to accept. They gave Turner their word that they would meet his requirements, but he told them that he was not able to negotiate a contract minus those penalty stipulations.

SO CLOSE, YET SO FAR

Thompson was able to return to the negotiation, and he exploded when Turner told him that they were having a problem with the written contract. Standing up, Thompson pointed at Liu and said: "Now, listen, I've been waiting three days for a yes or no answer and we keep going around the block, giving more to you as we go. We leave tomorrow and want your commitment now. No more negotiation. If you can't do it then we'll find someone else; there are millions of people like you here, and if you don't deliver we'll piss you off and find someone else. It's as simple as that. Just let us know: yes or no."

Turner looked at the Chinese and knew the negotiation was over. Their expressions had become stern and cold; Liu left the room and the other two Chinese talked together quietly. Liu returned about twenty minutes later and said: "We will have to consider this. We cannot make a decision now." Meaning: NO DEAL! The Chinese then packed up their things, said goodbye, and left the room. Turner's comment to Thompson was: "You blew it, mate."

A week after returning to Australia, Thompson realized the offer of Happy Clothing distribution would be a good opportunity after all and decided to contact Liu. Turner asked Thompson not to do so, saying that he would contact Liu, as he had established a good relationship with him. Thompson refused his offer, determined to salvage the situation himself.

The Chinese response was: "We are not able to do business with you at this time." A further approach, two months later, met with the same reply. Three months after his visit to China, Turner left Bassano, which was then looking in South Korea for an alternative manufacturing base.

(with Anne Normoyle)

Commentary

The problems with this negotiation stemmed initially from Thompson's ethnocentric views. Assuming that the pace of the negotiation would be the same as at home, he failed to recognize that the Chinese needed to spend a day establishing a relationship. He was not prepared to deviate from the expected because of the Chinese company's desire for foreign currency. Further, he saw the Chinese reluctance to commit to a formal contract as an effort to weight it in their favor.

The Chinese behaved like Confucian gentleman, but Thompson showed them no respect. They offered a win-win contract, but Thompson dismissed it.

The case highlights the need for negotiators who can get along with the Chinese and for preparation before negotiating with the Chinese. Thompson was the wrong person to deal with the Chinese, and Turner was the right one.

In terms of preparation, Thompson lacked understanding of the economic structure and the close connection of companies to the government, knowledge of the potential negotiating styles, respect for the Chinese emphasis on trust and relationships, and their aversion to contracts. Bassano could have agreed verbally that the distributorship of Happy Clothing menswear was conditional on Happy Clothing meeting the standards required by Bassano for their womenswear. This would have provided the motivation needed for Happy Clothing to meet the Bassano production quality and schedules.

Although Thompson was afraid of being tricked by the Chinese and convinced that he could bully them into a deceit- and trick-free agreement, his cowboy tactics were anathema to the Chinese.

 CASE STUDY SCIENTISTS AND BUREAUCRATS—ORIENTATION ISSUES

OVERVIEW

This case study involves attempts to set up a bilateral scientific research arrangement involving Chinese scientists and Australian government representatives based in the nation's capital, Canberra. The discussions are ongoing.

Three face-to-face meetings between Chinese and Australians have already been held, the first in the United States in 1999 and the subsequent two in Europe in 2001 and 2003. The setting, each time an international scientific conference held every two years, has been used by the parties as an opportunity to meet and discuss the bilateral agreement.

BACKGROUND

With the initial contact in 1999 involving no more than discussion concerning areas of mutual interest, the Australians felt no need to take into account cross-cultural considerations. They found the Chinese quite Westernized in their approach to discussions, and nonscientific discussion focused on the then-forthcoming Olympic Games in Sydney.

The Australians regarded the rapport that developed between the two parties as being between scientific colleagues, rather than government representatives. At the conclusion of the conference, it appeared to the Australians that both parties would investigate the formalizing of an agreement on the exchange of scientific information and then share the discoveries of further research.

When they met again in 2001, the parties still seemed enthusiastic about cooperating and indicated that they had in-principle support from their superiors. Following that year's meeting, the Australians wrote several times to the Chinese in a bid to move things forward, but received only formal replies.

Two things should be noted here: first, that the Australians were trying to initiate business between their department (on behalf of the Australian government) and the Chinese government; and, second, that they attended the conferences for the purpose of work-related self-development and not at the behest of the government.

UNRESOLVED ISSUES

Essentially, all logistical and practical issues of the proposed effort remained unresolved at the start of the third meeting. Both sides had exchanged views and agreed, in principle, to cooperate by mutually making resources available in an effort to bring their hopes for joint research to fruition. However, no formal agreement had been reached.

Notwithstanding, the Australians remained eager to obtain a formal agreement. The Australian team organized the 2003 meeting. While both parties had signaled their intention to attend the 2003 conference, it was only some six weeks before the event that they agreed to have a formal meeting during the conference.

Max Wran, who took the initiative at the third meeting, is not a scientist and so has only limited ability to contribute and is essentially regarded as a support figure. But, with a background in industrial advocacy, he had developed a reputation as a no-nonsense person. Accompanying him was Kevin Porter, a scientist and the one who integrates any learning from the conferences into the department's operational framework.

AUSTRALIAN BLUNDER

The meeting took place over two afternoons. No agenda was prepared nor was an interpreter used, since the Australians believed the Chinese representatives had a sufficient grasp of English. The meeting, which the Australians expected to run for about two hours, was loosely chaired by Wran and conducted as a fireside chat.

Following the exchange of pleasantries and discussion on the progress of the conference, Wran steered the conversation in the direction of research cooperation. The Chinese, who agreed that the suggestions put forward were valuable, made many positive statements of support before digressing to discuss sightseeing. Wran, becoming noticeably agitated and increasingly directive in his comments, used the odd profanity to emphasize his point.

Porter noticed that the Chinese were taken back by the crude display, although they made no comment, and the first afternoon eventually ended amicably enough after two-and-a-half hours. The next morning, Porter apologized to the Chinese for Wran's outbursts and confirmed that a second afternoon meeting would be held. The Chinese appeared very understanding, but Porter sensed their enthusiasm had waned significantly.

During the second afternoon's meeting, scheduled to last two hours, discussion of the morning's conference proceedings was interrupted after forty minutes by the Chinese, who left for another appointment. Nothing had been agreed to or signed. The Chinese apologized, saying that the dialogue should be resumed as soon as possible. In a seemingly conciliatory manner, Wran agreed and said he would be in contact and get the ball rolling.

INTERPRETING EVENTS

The Australians, believing that an arrangement with the Chinese would be formalized in 2003, had expected a real negotiation during which they would convince the Chinese to commit to joint research. Wran's principal motivation (he later confided to Porter) was the number of trips to China he believed the project would give him.

The Australians adopted a laissez-faire approach to the apparently important meetings, on the assumption that, as both parties were attending an international conference, formality could be disregarded for the side meetings. With no formal or informal agenda prepared or discussed, meetings were held in the context of "let's talk when we get the chance."

Wran's belief that he could steer the meeting toward a positive outcome, using an informal approach and bullying tactics, was not borne out.

The apparent avoidance of specifics by the Chinese at each meeting and their failure to reply to follow-up letters indicate that they were no longer interested in cooperating with the Australians. Although discussions had been friendly on the surface, Wran's displays of temper and tactical maneuvering had been too unfriendly and unprofessional for the Chinese.

Interviews with the Australians outside the meetings indicated lack of focus on specific issues. There were no statements about the benefits that might accrue to the Chinese. The assumption was that the Chinese were only interested in the quality of scientific information, not its commercial aspects. Failure to include such elements in early discussions perhaps had left the Chinese cold on the idea of combined research.

As of this writing, nothing has been agreed to; there is only recognition that working together would be mutually beneficial. The Australians have yet to engage formally official government channels and have no idea of the extent, if any, of government support for their Chinese colleagues.

The Australians' approach to their discussions with the Chinese was not sensitive to the latter's views regarding age and social hierarchy. In 2003, Wran was sixty-one years old and second-in-charge of his organization, while Porter was forty-three. The Chinese scientists were in their early forties (but the Australians did not know their ranks). Given the age and senior position of the Australian lead negotiator, the Chinese may well have been concerned that he was not of sufficient status to engage in serious discussions.

SUGGESTED FIX

To end this impasse, the Australians might initiate formal representations to the Chinese Embassy in Canberra. Such an approach would help speed up negotiations, and the Chinese scientists might then agree to visit Australia, where local hospitality could enhance the chances of a positive outcome.

The Australians might also consider including neutral parties in negotiations. Outside support and recognition may help improve the credibility of the Australians in the eyes of the Chinese. As both sides are linked to an international scientific community that meets every two years, such a strategy easily could be managed.

Commentary

Without access to the Chinese version of events, it is difficult to draw definitive conclusions from this case. However, it is clear that the Australians were ill prepared to negotiate with their Chinese counterparts. They assumed no research or preparation was needed, simply because meetings took place on neutral territory. Adding to the difficulties was the assumption on the part of Wran that his personal and conflict-resolution styles would overcome all obstacles.

Additionally, by failing to demonstrate cross-cultural awareness, the Australians offended the Chinese, who simply walked away from the discussion. Wran's cowboy strategy was unsuitable for forging new relationships and negotiating a venture with the Chinese. Porter believes that the goodwill built up previously is in jeopardy and even may have been lost.

Porter has been in contact by e-mail with one of the Chinese scientists, on a personal level. However, there has been no formal correspondence with the Chinese since 2003. While the Australians believe themselves still to be serious about engaging the Chinese in this venture, with no understanding of how the Chinese are thinking it seems unlikely that they have any idea about how to proceed.

So, is it overstating the case to call the 2001 initial encounter a negotiation? The Australians believe not. They view those discussions as a successful prelude that had gone a long way toward establishing common ground between the parties.

Be that as it may, momentum has been lost for a number of reasons. Wran and Porter did not work together as a team. Wran, overconfident about his abilities as a professional negotiator, was not able to accept feedback on his style or undertake a postmortem on why things turned out the way they had.

It is intriguing to speculate what lesson Qing of Chando might have mandated for the Australians.

❑ The building of trust is critical, particularly in those negotiations in which a foreign team may have the task of mediating (as between the historical enemies China and Japan).

❑ In negotiations, everyone must be given face.

❑ It is important to choose the right interpreter.

❑ In long-running multicultural negotiations, sharing knowledge and confirming that everyone has the same understanding is crucial to success.

❑ Chinese values turn on the fact that the Chinese remember favors and disservice. Always remember the sayings: "If you honor me a foot, I will honor you ten feet," and "If you dishonor me a foot, I will dishonor you ten feet in return." Requests should be carefully considered before a reply is given, especially if they involve face.

❑ Choosing the wrong negotiator—overconfident, insufficiently prepared individuals—reflects an organization's lack of cross-cultural commonsense.

❑ Protracted negotiations require many subgoals, often feature political issues and other barriers, and call for negotiators with patience, long-term planning skills, and business diplomacy of a high order.

CHAPTER
6

BARGAINING OVER PRICE

As we have already seen, in China trust takes precedence over price, even though many foreign negotiators will expect to deal with price from the beginning. Moreover, foreign negotiators will give price concessions at the last moment to give face to their opposite number to boost personal prestige, which comes from being able to say that one was able to buy the best product or technology—while having beaten down the foreigner's price.

But there comes a time in successful long-term business relationships when foreigners give a thought to what is best for their Chinese partners, and when the Chinese conclude that the foreigners are genuinely trustworthy, true friends, rather than the greedy capitalists that many were accused of being by the Chinese Communist Party until the 1990s.

It is interesting to note an aspect of the business ethos pointed out by many foreign negotiators with experience in China, namely, that when emphasis is on price, there may simultaneously be indifference to quality.

A foreign retailer who buys leather goods in China has noted that when he takes delivery of goods, their quality is often not as high as that of the items he had initially agreed to purchase. The retailer, far from considering the Chinese dishonest, recognizes that many foreigners may not share the Chinese perception of the importance of quality relative to price.

Another aspect of the business ethos is the degree to which Chinese senior managers socialize in order to build and sustain business relationships. They invest more time and effort in this aspect of business than even the Japanese, who are renowned for their emphasis on relationship building.

As is illustrated by the following case study, price can be a major factor in negotiating final agreements. Essentially, the example is akin to, although more sophisticated than, the price bargaining at Shanghai's Xiang Yang market we saw in chapter 1.

CASE STUDY GAMING IN SHANGHAI

OVERVIEW

HyperHawk, one of the world's major providers of global supply management software and services, helps companies reduce costs through efficient product and services sourcing. It has handled more than $50 billion worth of products and services in the oil and gas, other natural resources, retail, transport, finance, and industrial sectors for customers including General Motors, Nestlé, Shell, Japan Energy, Mitsubishi, and Cadbury Schweppes.

Shanghai-based JJM, one of the biggest gaming and hospitality companies in Asia, is owned by Chinese businessman Tan Wu Bo. We take up the story when JJM has been a HyperHawk client for six months, and the companies have signed an agreement to conduct two projects. The first, completed in March 2005 and tremendously successful, saved JJM some $1 million, and the second one is set to start. Impressed with the results, JJM wishes to explore the possibility of other joint endeavors with HyperHawk.

To this end, a meeting is arranged between JJM's Senior Vice-President of Finance Iris Ma and HyperHawk's Regional Managing Director Drake Dubois, and attended by JJM's Vice-President for Procurement Henry Chow and HyperHawk Sales Group Director Layton Pang.

Ma is keen to explore more projects with HyperHawk and has tasked Chow to follow up with HyperHawk as soon as possible. The managing director of HyperHawk suggests that a session be arranged with key stakeholders from both companies to discuss and assess possible opportunities for other JJM projects.

THE SCENE

Ma and Chow agreed to the suggestion and asked that a proposal be submitted to JJM after the opportunity assessment meeting that was attended by Chow, his assistant Mary Xie, who is also the purchasing manager, and two members from HyperHawk. Both parties identified ten possible projects.

Xie asked for a proposal to be submitted to JJM through her, and

HyperHawk provided a competitive price package that included services over a twelve-month period. As is to be expected from a Chinese company like JJM, Xie asked for a reduction in the licensing fee, additional program management days (at no extra cost), and an extension of the software term from twelve months to twenty-four months.

In reply, HyperHawk put in writing its discussions to date with JJM:

1. JJM had agreed that HyperHawk could add value to the projects identified.

2. JJM would sign for a ten-project package to get a competitive price.

3. If HyperHawk could meet JJM's demands, the latter would sign the contract by May-end 2005.

Xie agreed to point one above, but was noncommittal on points two and three. After much discussion, HyperHawk agreed to lower its fee and provide JJM additional program management days at no additional cost. However, HyperHawk said it could not agree to extend the twelve-month term for use of the software without charging extra.

Then, to complicate matters further, Xie suggested that JJM could not commit to an agreement even if all the issues were resolved.

The most recent negotiations were conducted quite hastily, since HyperHawk knew that Xie was not the decision maker and approval had to come from her top management. Many Chinese companies put in place a structure whereby the foreign negotiator deals with multiple tiers of negotiators before working through the final deal with the senior key decision maker.

NEGOTIATIONS TO DATE

HyperHawk's primary concern was how likely JJM would be to enter into an agreement even if the issues were resolved, and within what time frame.

JJM argued that the proposed price was beyond what it could afford, although it recognized the need for help from HyperHawk to implement the projects, and that it needed twenty-four months to implement the ten projects due to its lack of manpower.

HyperHawk took the position that, while it was prepared to look into the fee structure and program management term as part of the total package, the request for twenty-four months was not reasonable. Although it reasoned that other organizations were able to implement ten projects in twelve months, to satisfy JJM, HyperHawk negotiated a mid-way solution: a maximum of eighteen months.

When one week passed and there was no response from JJM, Hyper-Hawk asked if it would be prepared to sign if HyperHawk acceded to its three requests. Xie replied that she would submit the proposal for approval to her superiors, Tan and Ma, but added that there was no guarantee the agreement would be signed by the end of May.

From HyperHawk's perspective, all the issues presented by JJM had been resolved—yet there was still no deal. When asked about the status of the project, JJM cited staff turnover, but then mentioned another possible IT project where there was a clear need for HyperHawk. The discussion ended with JJM requesting that HyperHawk prepare the preliminary work and submit yet another proposal.

Based on the updated information, it appeared that the IT project might get underway earlier than the previously proposed ten projects. Moreover, given that this project had an entirely different scope, there was a strong argument to negotiate a separate deal for it. Whichever proposal JJM wished to undertake first, HyperHawk was ready to negotiate and finalize an agreement, but it could not yet tell whether the latest development was a genuine project or a further stalling tactic.

EVALUATION OF NEGOTIATIONS

Both parties acted rationally in the way the negotiations were conducted, and it helped that the relationship between them was excellent from the start.

HyperHawk gave in to JJM's demands in the hope of concluding the agreement quickly and starting the projects. But JJM only introduced a new project, which took the parties away from the initial negotiations. It was clear to HyperHawk that JJM believed it had to win negotiations with vendors, perhaps a result of its corporate culture.

Meanwhile, JJM believed it was negotiating from a position of strength, having even gone so far as to assert that it had in-house a system similar to that of HyperHawk that could probably fulfill its needs, albeit without the sophistication of the HyperHawk product.

Going forward, it was critical that HyperHawk engage with Ma, the senior vice-president and decision maker, since the groundwork had been laid with her staff. But it was unclear if approaching Ma from the start would have expedited the negotiations.

HyperHawk reflected that maybe it should have asked for the agreement to be signed within a fixed time when it met JJM's initial demands, although JJM had previously delayed decision making on other projects. Perhaps HyperHawk initially should have found out how urgently JJM wanted to implement the projects and only then have proceeded with the negotiations.

Hyperhawk's experience certainly highlights the need to be patient when negotiating with the Chinese.

Commentary

This case is typical of what vendors face in a competitive, hi-tech environment, and illustrates the opportunity they have to reduce their price. Handled appropriately, a win-win outcome is not difficult to achieve. The buyer here assumed that the vendor could bargain from the standpoint of a large margin, while the vendor, who employs well-paid professionals, had to think of the high overheads to be maintained.

From this case study, at least two scenarios for short-term success can be derived. First, assuming that you, the vendor, are taking a tough stance, you can take a long-term perspective and conclude the first sale with a friendly, competitive attitude, countering the buyer's demands with suitable offers, while never losing sight of your determination to bag the order. But, besides showing friendliness, flexibility, and determination, you must show the potential buyer that you will be there for them over the long haul. For this you require people with leadership qualities in your team.

Should you lack high-quality leaders in your team, you have the option of a second scenario. In this case, you would show, right from the beginning, that your team comprises hard workers who will do whatever the buyer needs. By adopting Chinese-style service orientation and dedication—making your team indispensable to the potential buyer, being available daily, and making yourself virtually a part of your opposite number's staff—you could clinch a deal. HyperHawk failed to show the requisite service orientation and commitment.

From the perspective of longer-term success, an initial achievement provides the opportunity for friendship to be cultivated with the client company's key people, perhaps even with the CEO, the final decision maker. Should one eventually become accepted as "family," the client will telephone you for what they want and no longer require competitive quotations. But to reach that point, you will have had to develop a genuine friendship and service orientation with those at the top of the client company.

CASE STUDY SHANGHAI SOAP

Wang Dan is CEO of the Shanghai Soap Company, which produces high-quality, mold-pressed gift soap in animal and flower shapes for overseas clients, many of which are world famous.

Matsuoka Takehiko owns Tri-Pacific Commercial, a Tokyo-based export company that is the agent for a number of Japanese manufacturers doing business in Southeast Asia as well as in North and South America. Over the past few years, Matsuoka has been exporting machinery, especially labor-saving devices and automation machinery, to Asian countries.

Wang wrote letters to several automation machinery manufacturers, including YL Industrial Company, a Tri-Pacific Commercial client that, lacking interest in the matter, had passed on the letter to the agent Matsuoka. Wang indicated an interest in more advanced soap-pressing machinery, since his current equipment was unsafe, produced soap of increasingly uneven quality, and had to be shut down every few hours.

Matsuoka was the only one to respond to Wang, the other companies possibly having been deterred by the technological challenges of building the requisite machinery. Yet, Matsuoka said no more than that the machinery would probably be too expensive for Wang.

Two months later, Wang wrote to say he would be visiting Tokyo on business and wanted to meet Matsuoka—even though he realized the machinery might be too expensive.

Initially when they met, the main stumbling block was technical: how to design a machine that would pick up a blob of soap, set it down correctly on a mold, and then pick up the imprinted soap and position it for packaging.

After the meeting, Matsuoka was confident that YL had the talent to come up with an answer despite its earlier-stated lack of interest. Acknowledging that the price would be steep, he gave Wang an initial budget limit of ¥30 million (then about $150,000).

But when Matsuoka subsequently visited Wang in Shanghai, he discovered that each mold had a small ejector pin that pushed the soap out of the mold when the press was released. It was this information that attracted the interest of the YL engineers, who then came up with a design, rough drawing, and rough quote.

On Wang's return visit to Tokyo, Matsuoka quoted ¥40 million for the supply and installation of ten units of the necessary machinery, but Wang asked for the quote to include the dispatch of an engineer, spare parts, plus a variety of suction heads to withdraw the different soap shapes from the molds.

An upward-revised quote was sent, and Matsuoka traveled to Shanghai with a YL engineer. There Wang protested the increased price, saying he would reduce his order to eight units were he not to receive the extras at no added cost, but Matsuoka said that the reduced number would not affect the total price significantly.

It was only when Wang said that his father, the owner of the business, would never agree to the ¥40 million quote that Matsuoka reduced both his price and the number of units from ten to eight. He then negotiated a small discount from the YL plant and found the price further reduced when he learned from an engineer that the machines would need only one type of suction head.

When Wang again pressed for a price reduction, Matsuoka decided to show goodwill and give him face with a further ¥100,000 discount—despite already having indicated that the previous price was his bottom line. Wang agreed to this final price of ¥29 million for eight units.

Commentary

When asked what, if anything, he would change were he able to negotiate that deal again, Matsuoka said he would not have reduced the price as much. Yet, although he believed that Wang would have settled for ¥30 million, he did stress that Wang had the potential to become a good long-term customer.

Matsuoka also explained how, even after having taken delivery of the order, Wang had complained about the price of the spare suction cups. Then despite having been encouraged by Matsuoka to order a larger quantity of the cups in return for a one-percent discount, Wang had declined. His persistence and stubbornness had been noted by all. Wang had let it be known that, while he would never have bought the machines at the original price, he had found it a pleasure to do business with the congenial Japanese. After each round of negotiating, they had enjoyed dinner together, and once the machines had been installed and the details resolved, the two had been determined to remain friends. The degree of similarity in their values and needs was far greater than Matsuoka had experienced with another culture.

ROUND ROBIN PRICE BARGAINING

OVERVIEW

K. G. Marwin Inc. developed a particular technology in the 1980s, called the Trilliamp Process, that the Chinese government sought to integrate into an ethylene facility in Lanzhou, the capital of Gansu province. It signed a contract with Marwin, which in 1985 invited inquiries from U.S. and Japanese manufacturers for production of the machinery.

Marwin recommended the Japanese company Auger-Aiso as most capable of producing the turbines, while the Chinese invited two U.S. companies—Federal Electric and Pressure Inc., which manufactured through the large Japanese trading company Mitsubo—to compete for the multi-million-dollar contract.

THE SCENE

To undertake the negotiations with the three prospective suppliers, six Chinese officials and three representatives from the Bank of China were selected.

The Auger-Aiso chief negotiator was Todman Glazer, the company's Japan branch manager from the United States who resided in Tokyo and was assisted by his Japanese colleagues. Glazer remembered the tight deadlines he had faced on previous trips to China; now positions had been reversed, with the Chinese facing the pressures and deadlines. He realized the value of thinking like one's opponent—seeing things as they do. This was the first potential deal with China in the ethylene market, and Auger-Aiso faced stiff competition from Mitsubo, which had already cornered the Chinese oil-processing market.

At the first negotiation meeting in Beijing, the Chinese insisted that custom required the visitor—Glazer—to make the first presentation. This he did, even though he was accustomed to allowing his opponents to speak first.

Glazer began by addressing the excellence of Auger-Aiso technology, explaining that the manufacturing would all be done in Japan to ensure product excellence. When the Chinese offered no indication of their position or price, Glazer felt obliged to quote an upper-range price that would allow flexibility. The Chinese still made no comment.

In the afternoon, the Chinese heard offers from the combined Mitsubo-Pressure team, then Federal Electric. By the end of the day, Federal Electric had dropped out of the race, accepting that it could not compete.

REVOLVING DOORS, CHANGING MOODS

During the first week of negotiations, a pattern emerged. The Chinese would meet with Glazer and his colleagues in the morning and ask for a price, saying that their competitors had already bid such-and-such a price, which was invariably lower than the last Auger-Aiso bid. They would meet with Mitsubo-Pressure in the afternoon and use the same approach, causing the latter to drop its price. Moreover, each meeting would end with the Chinese saying, "We will call you tomorrow."

But, because they never called, both prospective vendors became panicky and visited the Chinese office without notice to present an even lower bid. As the Chinese kept the vendors guessing and in the dark, Glazer understood how the Chinese had earned a reputation as master negotiators.

At the second meeting, tactics changed and there were different people representing the Chinese side. An antagonist would suddenly burst out in loud Chinese and harangue the Auger-Aiso side for some fifteen minutes, complaining about the quality of the machines they were offering. A protagonist would then intervene and, apologizing for his colleague, would say he had been upset about the current situation.

Glazer regarded these outbursts as no more than arranged role playing, designed to make the protagonist (the good guy) appear more trustworthy to the foreigners. But, Glazer realized, all the participants were play-acting.

Then there was yet another change. The Chinese located the Auger-Aiso and Mitsubo-Pressure teams near the meeting room, in adjacent rooms. Mitsubo-Pressure would be called in and asked for its best price. After the team had returned to its room, Auger-Aiso would be called in, told the latest price, and asked if it could beat this. When the prospective vendors could drop their price no lower, they would add something to the package. Auger, for example, added oil gauges for its turbines, effectively a three-percent add-on. Even so, the Chinese still would not commit to placing an order.

WHEN THE PRICE IS RIGHT

Glazer could hardly believe that he had lowered his price twenty percent that week; to do so would have been out of the question in the United States. On the final day, Auger-Aiso made another offer—and, for the first time, the Chinese made a counter offer. Auger-Aiso accepted, and agreement was reached. A few hours later, Mitsubo-Pressure came back with an even lower price, but the deal had already been struck.

Glazer spoke later about how difficult it was to compete with Japanese trading companies, explaining that U.S. companies had so many factors to bear in mind, including insurance and a variety of liabilities. Meanwhile, Japanese trading companies, which had vastly different legal parameters to operate within, could more easily focus on getting contracts and closing deals. He believed that Auger-Aiso had been awarded the contract because it had been the preferred supplier right from the start.

Commentary

In most respects, the Chinese negotiating style for big-ticket items has changed little over the past twenty years or so. Vendors still go to China and submit to the pressures of intense bargaining, while the good guy/bad guy routine remains a tool of intimidation. Although Glazer saw through the tactic, it could be the undoing of less-experienced foreign negotiators.

Glazer's suspicion that Auger-Aiso was the preferred supplier from the beginning is plausible. Consider the case in chapter 3, involving the Japanese packaging printing press manufacturer Kumi-Chantdung, in which the successful vendor turned out to be the initially preferred supplier. The clever Mitra was able to intuit that his company was preferred, and so gained the upper hand. One can only wonder whether, had Glazer guessed that Auger-Aiso was the preferred vendor, he would have been less willing to drop his price toward the end.

No mention is made of socializing or banqueting because more than one team was competing, as in another chapter 3 study—which the present case most resembles—involving Benjamin, who was invited to submit a proposal for a huge Guangdong brewery.

It is also interesting to note that, compared with the Benjamin case, the one above places less emphasis on the technical package and specifications, including installation and engineering support. This may be because, over the years since 1985, the Chinese have become more sophisticated in terms of quality requirements, whereas in the past price was the dominant factor, and its reduction the best way of giving face. In the 1980s and 1990s, the Chinese bought a great deal of technology that could not be applied and machinery that was inoperable. From this the Chinese learned how to get the best package at the best price.

❏ While price is a key factor in Chinese business negotiations, some foreign negotiators have found it is in inverse proportion to quality. The price may be reduced, but the quality of the good delivered is often inferior to that of the product the foreign client had originally agreed to buy.

❏ The bargaining style is fundamentally the same across the board in China, whether you are dealing with a vendor at a tourist market in Shanghai or a major product manufacturer.

❏ Some companies see bargaining as a cardinal part of their corporate ethos, and so assume that the vendor has a broad margin within which to bargain.

❏ Negotiators face two possibilities in China: They can land their first order either by tough bargaining or by reducing their initial price and offering long-term service support.

❏ Bargaining involves a succession of maneuvers that allow the price to be trimmed gradually, until the limit is reached.

❏ While bargaining can be a protracted process, the friendship between the parties is key to finalizing the deal and laying the groundwork for a future relationship.

❏ A hard bargaining style can put the squeeze on all parties, in the presence of their respective competitors.

CHAPTER
7

THE CENTRAL ROLE OF GUANXI

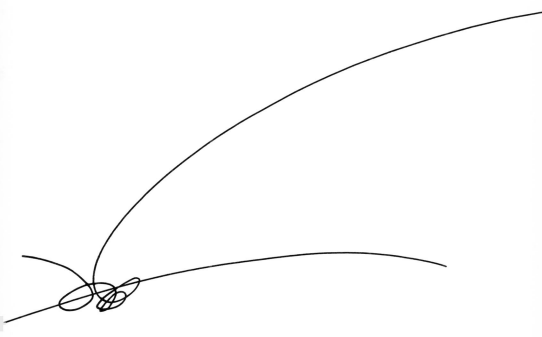

The commonest form of relationship is *guanxi* (phonetically pronounced gwan-sea). One of the best-known and frequently heard expressions in China is: "If you have guanxi, you have no problems. If you have no guanxi, you have problems" (*You guanxi, jo mei guanxi. Mei guanxi, jo you guanxi*). In other words, lacking guanxi connections brings dire consequences: No one will help you, there will be no support system for you, and you will be "alone in the world."

Guanxi refers to mutual relationships that are built on favors and permit the parties to make almost unconditional requests of one another. It requires that elements of mutual trust and obligation be in place. Meanwhile, apart from kin and friendship relationships, residents in big cities easily make friends with others who come from the same village, town, county, or province, or who speak the same dialect. These connections do not automatically evolve into guanxi relationships—being more disinterested, less calculating, and more caring than guanxi—but some guanxi relationships are offshoots of such connections.

These days, most Chinese businesspeople consciously develop comprehensive guanxi networks (*guanxiwang*) in the belief that without them it is not possible to do business. This conviction arose in times of food and goods shortages, when people could not get the basic necessities and resorted to their guanxi networks to acquire items they needed to feed, clothe, and shelter themselves.

The system still works because many Chinese are gatekeepers, providing access to goods and services. For instance, drivers in work units of government offices transport private goods for other workers and expect to be paid in cash for doing so. Transportation offices will hold back from sale some airline, railroad, and bus tickets for guanxi connections, while products in short supply can be obtained through guanxi networks. Large retail or wholesale organizations may give retail products three different price levels—factory price, wholesale price, and retail price. The price one would be offered would depend on one's guanxi membership, as well as the help one has given the corporation in the past to promote its sales. Guanxi networks of Chinese staff and consultants can extend into government, providing access to tax concessions, approvals for the domestic sale or export of goods, and assistance when problems arise.

CASE STUDY — GUANXI IN BUSINESS

A well-known, government-owned, five-star hotel in Beijing has an associated marketing company called High Jewel Marketing. With branches in six cities including the capital, it has both a retail division, which sells jewelry and handicrafts to foreign tourists at high prices, and a wholesale division selling export-quality clothing and high-quality home appliances.

One of the marketing company's senior managers was formerly a high Communist Party official who, over a career of thirty years, developed a broad network of contacts in commerce, government, and industry—in other words, his guanxi connections. These contacts were useful in providing High Jewel with information on supply sources nationwide, and the company benefited from having a special relationship with a prestigious Beijing hotel.

Out-of-town suppliers enjoyed the privilege of staying at the hotel—hotel bookings not being easy to obtain in Beijing—and many deals were completed in its dining room.

High Jewel sells its products at three different price levels, with factory price (*chu chang jia*) the lowest, followed by wholesale price (*pi fa jia*), and market price (*shi chang jia*). It is legally able to do this, with the only caveat being that the seller does not exceed the maximum price allowed by law. The company sets its price levels according to the buyer's guanxi connections and its potential to help High Jewel now and in the future.

The manager, son of a high Communist Party official, says that he tries to avoid doing business with friends, because it places excessive demand on human feelings (*renqing*). He thus gives friends a low price for the first transaction and after that treats them just like any other customer. Over the long term, only those customers who can do something for High Jewel consistently receive low prices.

Guanxi has an unconditional aspect that reinforces the common material-istic thread that runs through the relationships shared in the network. First put forward by Karl Marx, the Communist dictum, "From each according to his ability, to each according to his need," has become a contemporary moral doctrine among the Chinese. Requiring that the more affluent be generous and look after the less fortunate, the principle is extended to countries. Thus, someone from the United States or a European country would be feted on a visit to China but would be expected to reciprocate at a level reflecting the greater wealth of their country. It is amusing to hear the Chinese checking on the size of the bill a foreigner is paying for his return hospitality. "Ah, that is good," they might say, "More expensive than ours was. We can feel good about it, even though the food was terrible." This is an oft-heard comment following foreign hospitality at a Western restaurant in Beijing or Shanghai.

The word guanxi is used by all Chinese, but its tenets are most commonly put into practice and most frequently discussed in China, where the term *guanxi-xue* has gained currency. Translated as "guanxicology"—the art of using relationships—the expression has a certain ironic quality. To some it implies an under-the-table system of gifts and favors, and even a gloss for corruption and back-door dealing. To others, reinforced by the warmth of good personal feel-ings, it is seen as leading to and reinforcing trust between people.

Guanxi between Chinese and foreigners can develop from genuine warm feelings of friendship or as a result of the complementary needs of both sides—one side needing what the other has to offer—in the event that there is sufficient trust for a practical relationship to develop over time.

CASE STUDY · WITH TRUST, THE SKY'S THE LIMIT

It took Ron Gosbee, the general manager of AWA Aerospace, three years to win his first China contract. It was for air navigation equipment to be used at fifty-three airports. Next, he won another project for eighteen airports. The trend continued until the number of projects numbered well over one hundred.

Around this time, the Chinese civil aviation authority began to man-date AWA equipment, and individual provinces and cities with their own money to spend on airports were encouraged to approach AWA. This was the first major sign that the company had become "family" in China.

The second sign was that Chinese parties were now approaching Gosbee, saying: "We've got some business, if you are interested."

In one instance, AWA had an arranged soft loan from the Australian government, which was to provide Shandong province with a package of goods, including many things that AWA did not make—such as airport fire trucks, fuel tankers, and landing-system instruments. AWA obtained quotations for the goods from Australian suppliers. The Chinese saw the quotation and noted that the trucks in Australia were twice the price of those in the United States, for which reason they would buy them there. AWA, in turn, pointed out that the goods were coming as part of an Australian government soft loan package, and that the prices for Australian products—other than those made by AWA—were not negotiable.

The Chinese kept insisting that the price be lowered, and eventually gave the Australian team five minutes to lower its price. Unable to do so, they walked away in the belief that this was the end of the matter. Two weeks later, however, AWA's Beijing office advised Gosbee and his colleagues that the Shandong people were still indicating they wanted to do business with AWA, provided the price for the trucks was lowered to match the U.S. price. Of course, AWA could do nothing.

Three weeks later, AWA received a message in Australia from its Beijing office that Shandong would not go ahead with the soft loan, but still wanted to buy AWA equipment—for cash. AWA had achieved, without seeking it, that rarest of things—guanxi status based on established trust.

Commentary

The remarkable point here is that foreigners very rarely achieve membership in a guanxi network. Gosbee is a notable exception because he was trusted. He never had to ask for business from a customer's guanxi network, and his price was eventually met when the Chinese found a way around the "obstacle."

 BUSINESS EXPANSION WOVEN FROM TRUST

 Another example of someone who fitted in completely with the Chinese is the China trader Paul Winestock, who had been dealing with the Chinese since the 1960s. As a trader of textiles in China during the 1960s and 1970s, Winestock built up a large network of customers and friendly officials. One of the latter, who had known him since he was a young man living in drafty provincial hotels with no dining room, was Li Haoran, who had first appointed Winestock as a selling agent for the Textile Import-Export Corporation. When Li moved on to become managing director of the Animal By-Products Import-Export Corporation, Winestock approached him and asked to be appointed the exclusive distributor and wholesaler of Chinese leather shoes in Australia. Eventually, he was given control of twenty-five percent of China's shoe exports, with agreements for the regions where the best shoes were made, namely, Beijing and Shanghai.

In 1982, Winestock sold his business to the multinational corporation Pacific Dunlop and was asked to train George Preston, one of its senior managers. Preston had this to say about Winestock:

"Winestock's reasoning was this: When you made money in the good days, you had to remember that, if the Chinese needed to sell at a higher price, you had to be able to give it to them somehow.

"Winestock had an advantage: He ran his own private company. He didn't have to report to a board. He was able to take a long-term view. So he had the freedom to say, 'Well, I don't need to make so much profit this year. I can live without making $2 million this year. It's going to cost me half a million, but I know I'm going to get it back.'"

Winestock's style was blunt, but such was his acceptance by the Chinese that they are said not to be have been offended. He says, "I can tell them off and they take it from me. But before I do, I think" (Blackman 1993, 1997).

Chinese behavior involving guanxi can be far more businesslike and profit-oriented than was that of Gosbee, above. The following story about Mike Cardell, a senior international marketing manager, reveals a more salesman-like, drier personality, and shows what he achieved with guanxi relationships of a more market-driven variety.

"I had read that 'guanxi' means the use of personal contacts or connections in a relationship of reciprocal obligation. But until recently I wondered if it was fact or fiction in the modern business world.

"At a recent trade fair in China, I saw a range of seat covers that would provide my business with a better range than that of our competitors. The manufacturer, however, advised me that he was in the final stages of negotiating a global agreement with a Western auto parts distributor. If it went ahead, we would have had no chance to see the product in our region.

"We use an agent with whom we have conducted business for twenty-five years. I asked him to approach the manufacturer and explain that we could offer far better distribution in the Oceania region.

"Our agent told me that he actually had known the manufacturer since childhood. They had grown up in the same town and belonged to many of the same clubs. He told me confidently there would be no problem.

"The next morning, prior to the opening of the trade show, I received a phone call at my hotel inviting me to dinner that night with the president of the auto seat cover company. After a very pleasant dinner, I was offered what I was after—the regional distributorship for their complete range of products—with unbelievable promises of cooperation, which subsequently came true.

"Guanxi made it happen. Guanxi is real. It is not friendship as such, but sensible business reciprocity. Since then, through our agent, we have been able to direct a great deal of business from other parts of our group back, in return, to the seat covers president. These days, when I visit him, he often invites me to sit next to a potential customer near the head of the table, enabling me to talk business to that individual.

"This experience demonstrates to me the power of guanxi connections. We are always ready to do favors and help one another seize opportunities to make new business friends and new business."

An example of how guanxi can develop comes from a non-Chinese colleague who last year wrote us a letter saying, in part, the following:

> I have just returned from Beijing, where I am building up a close relationship with the construction department of the Ministry of Communications. We have formed a joint venture to bid on a major international bridge project and have spent many meetings getting acquainted and defining the various parties' specific scope of activities. Recently, however, I found the attitude prevailing at earlier meetings had completely changed.

Previously, the Chinese company had made it clear that, with their extensive ability and experience, what they required was not our services but, rather, to associate with us in light of our international reputation. We had been shown a Chinese-language PowerPoint presentation outlining their capabilities and, although I couldn't understand a word, I must say the illustrations were impressive. It was clear that they sought no more than our concepts and that our role would be limited.

The last two months have been a time of meetings and presentations. I have shown up, with one or two others from my company, and there have been some thirty Chinese participants. But, finally, there was a breakthrough after my last presentation to the company president in Beijing. I feel barriers have come down. We have been asked to participate on a much broader basis in this and other projects in which the Chinese company is involved.

I have the feeling that the company was initially embarrassed to admit it needed outside assistance. Yet, it was pleased when it saw our concepts and it seems that we now have the makings of a true partnership. In the Chinese scheme of things, trust and friendship carry far more weight than any written agreement. At last we have experienced guanxi and are happy because we believe we can do business with this company.

I can only wonder what would have happened had our Chinese partner been different. We have heard of many foreign companies that have lost their shirts as a result of teaming up with what turned out to be the wrong partner. Clearly, an understanding of the guanxi process can help one establish the credibility of one's Chinese partner.

Below, we see examples of how guanxi has been applied in a company setting.

THE POWER OF GUANXI

Frazier AC is a global organization headquartered in the United States. The company operates thirty-one manufacturing plants in nine countries and three core divisions—the product design and development (PDD), production (PRO), and sales and marketing (SM) departments—each in its Asia Pacific, Northern Hemisphere, and Southern Hemisphere regions.

In 1999, Hong Kong–based Frazier Asia was developing a new line of residential air-conditioning products that it planned to have manufactured by four Frazier factories in China, Thailand, France, and Egypt.

The Frazier Asia PCD team leader was Chen Li, who had seven years' experience working in China and before that had worked in Malaysia. Chen had three mechanical engineers, two control engineers, and a manufacturing engineer in his international team, which had three Hong Kong Chinese members, a Taiwanese member, and one member each from the United States and France.

Part of the PCD team's job was to search for and qualify component suppliers during the early stages of the design process, and most of the critical components were sourced in China in order to keep costs low.

At short notice, Chen was able to find component suppliers who solved design problems and shortened development time, both because he had worked with Chinese in Asia and because he could count on the many guanxi contacts of his four Chinese team members.

One of the PCD team's component suppliers, Hong Kong–based Tse Hao, enjoyed good relations with numerous manufacturers in China. Tse had built up his network by investing a little money in a number of companies, for which he then located customers. For this reason, Tse used many business cards, being variously president of precision metal company A in Shanghai; president of plastic and press mold company B in Guangzhou; director of industrial company C in Shenzhen, and so on. Most of Tse's customers were U.S. and Japanese companies.

Tse supplied the plastic parts for the Chinese, Thai, French, and Egyptian factories, for which he was also the plastic tooling maker (around sixty percent of the Frazier Asia air-conditioner parts were made of plastic).

One year after the new line of products went into production, a new manager, Ma Wannian, was appointed to the Frazier China factory. Transferred from one of the company's U.S. plants, where he had worked in the manufacturing division for twelve years, Ma was aggressive, hardworking, and keen to demonstrate his ability to Frazier's top management. It turned out that, despite having been born in Hong Kong, he did not understand the importance of guanxi in mainland China. Thus, some of his Chinese colleagues considered him to be more like a "capitalist exploiter."

When he learned that the parts provided by Tse were produced by other companies, Ma saw it as a chance to reduce materials cost. With this goal in mind, he planned to contact each supplier personally and request that Frazier be supplied directly, rather than through Tse.

The first supplier he contacted was the manufacturer Chow Fupei, a Singapore Chinese. Tse soon received word of Ma's approach to members of the Tse guanxi network and so, simultaneously, the Frazier factories in France, Thailand, Egypt, and China reported that Tse and his network companies had stopped supplying them with production parts and returned all purchasing orders to Frazier factories. This meant that all Frazier production lines would be out of parts within two weeks and production of air conditioners would cease.

When Ma telephoned Chow in Singapore, he learned that Tse had moved all the tooling from the Singapore factory. It was then that Chow admitted to having broken the network rules and predicted he would lose his China business. Ma started to feel uneasy.

On hearing this, top management from Frazier's Atlanta headquarters instructed Ma to fix the problem. Ma, who protested that he had only wanted to lower supply costs, tried to contact Tse by phone and by fax but was told he was out of town for two weeks.

Finally, the vice-president of manufacturing at the U.S. headquarters, Harry Boswell, contacted Frazier Asia's PCD team leader Chen for help. Chen knew they had no choice but to go to Tse with head bowed.

The following day, Chen contacted Tse by phone and, after apologizing on behalf of the company, requested a face-to-face meeting with him in Shanghai. Only Asia-Pacific Production Planning team leader Larry Markham was allowed to accompany Chen, and the meeting was held the next morning at Tse's Shanghai office.

At the meeting, Tse said this had been the first time he had had a customer such as Frazier, and pointed out that he had already made sure the renegade Chow in Singapore would never again do business in his network. Tse added that he could now only trust Chen at Frazier. Markham apologized for the incident, expressed gratitude for Tse's long-term support, and said Frazier wanted to continue its relationship with Tse.

Eventually, Tse accepted the apology, which Frazier headquarters was required to put in writing. Moreover, not only was direct contact between

Frazier staff and supplier manufacturers forbidden, except on technical issues, but Frazier had to promise that such an incident would not be repeated and that all price negotiations would go through Tse. The letter was to be signed by Vice-President of Manufacturing Boswell.

Within a few days, supplies returned to normal. Nine months later, Chow's company in Singapore went bankrupt.

Commentary

Tse was an experienced businessman, with a clear understanding of his ability to dictate whether Frazier had its orders filled. Production lines could not last long without parts, and Tse chose to negotiate only with Frazier top management. He won, and his prize was face.

Frazier, meanwhile, chose the right person, Chen, to conduct the initial negotiation. Both Chen and Markham knew their one objective was to restore the supply of parts to their factories.

This case study shows how guanxi works. Those who break the laws of a guanxi relationship are isolated from the network. It should be noted that most—but not all—native-born Chinese have the common sense to understand and play by the rules of guanxi.

 ## PROTECTING GUANXI FROM FOREIGN INTERFERENCE

"I want him out of this arrangement, Yong," Philippa Martin shouted into the phone from her office in London to Yong Bow Tian in Kuala Lumpur. "I can't see why it is necessary for us to keep paying him. We have a five-year contract with the Chinese." "But, Philippa...," Yong tried to get a word in. "No buts, I want him out!" Then the phone went dead.

Yong was a soft-spoken man who favored social harmony to conflict. Martin was trying to force him to cut the guanxi relationship with Alex Tang in Guangzhou, Guangdong province. In her view, they were paying him a commission that was totally unnecessary. Yong worked for the Kuala Lumpur branch of Educom International (ECI), an education consulting company based in London.

Martin was the branch manager, although for eleven months of the year she was in London. Aged thirty-seven, she was completing a Master's degree in IT management and, prior to running the Kuala Lumpur office, she had been a marketing officer for the north of England.

When Yong heard that she was soon to be married, he wondered if she would ever relocate to Kuala Lumpur. Yong is what most Malaysians consider typical of the Chinese residing in Malaysia: He speaks fluent Mandarin, Cantonese, and Hokkien. Before joining ECI, Yong was operations control officer at a timber company in Malaysia, where he dealt with many clients from China.

ECI was the official education agent for China's Guangdong province. The company placed Chinese students in universities or other tertiary institutions in Western countries, particularly the United States and United Kingdom. The contract had been negotiated by Yong through an old school friend, who had introduced Yong to Tang, an education agent from Guangzhou.

Using his guanxi connections in China, Tang had managed to wrap up a contract between ECI and the Guangdong provincial authorities. In return, Tang received a two-percent commission from ECI for every Chinese student who secured a place in a Western educational institution. The commission was not a part of the contract, but it had been agreed to verbally by Yong's predecessor, who had communicated this to ECI's London head office.

Ever since Martin had been appointed to her current position, she had been pressuring Yong to drop Tang and deal directly with the Chinese. Tang was then due in Kuala Lumpur in two weeks' time and Yong dreaded having to tell him that ECI would stop paying him a commission. Yong believed that a two-percent commission was nothing compared to Tang's valuable guanxi links that would help ECI well into the future.

Yong knew that Martin wanted to terminate the verbal agreement to show her manager that she could boost the branch's bottom line, and that he would have to tackle the situation delicately.

First, he decided to communicate directly with Norman Black, Martin's superior, whom he believed would accept his arguments. Second, he sent gifts and complimentary letters to all provincial officials in China whom he thought were important in the current arrangement. Third, he sent Black a report telling him how many Chinese students the Kuala Lumpur branch had placed in Western institutions and explaining that Tang's help and cooperation had made this possible.

When he met Tang in Kuala Lumpur, Yong told him that ECI wanted to terminate the current arrangement and explained that he was powerless to intervene since there was no mention of Tang's commission in the contract, which was between the Chinese authorities and ECI in London, not the Kuala Lumpur branch. Although Tang said little, his displeasure was evident. Yong said that, since Tang and he were good friends, he would try to convince the London headquarters to continue the relationship. He then asked Tang to give him pointers, so that he could negotiate either a reduced commission or another contract for him with London. Tang said he felt cheated and would persuade the Guangdong authorities to appoint another agent and reduce the number of students sent through ECI.

Yong was alarmed. "There is no need to do that," he said, trying to placate Tang while rifling through letters on his desk. "See, these are letters from Guangdong congratulating ECI and this office for maintaining a good and close working relationship with them."

Tang, looking over the letters, was taken aback and, requesting copies, said that he would think the matter over. That evening, Yong took Tang to dinner at a high-class restaurant and then to a karaoke parlor. Tang returned to China the following day.

For the next ten days there was no news from Tang, and Yong was worried. When he telephoned Tang, the latter seemed quite happy and said he had decided to lower his commission to one percent. He also informed Yong that he had managed to convince the authorities of another province to seriously consider making ECI their appointed agent. He had used the copies of the letters Yong had received as evidence to support the value of appointing ECI, and the authorities of that province had indicated they wanted to invite the top people at ECI to visit them soon.

Yong was elated, but he had only four days before Martin arrived in Kuala Lumpur for her one-month stint. He called Black to give him the good news and said he would make the necessary arrangements for Black to visit the prospective client, adding that this would not have been possible without Tang's help and his extensive connections in China. As a sign of gratitude, he suggested, ECI should leave Tang's commission at the current level, which was the standard rate for an agent in China. He also advised Black to quickly seal the arrangement with a formal agreement. Black asked him to draw one up for Tang and him to sign.

Yong called Tang to give him the good news. Tang was elated, and promised to convince the current client to send more students through ECI and make sure that the prospective client appointed ECI as its agent.

On Martin's arrival in Kuala Lumpur, she was quick to scold Tang for what he had done, but it was too late to do anything save accept the good news. A contract with the prospective client seemed likely after Black visited the province with Tang, and four months later the province officially appointed ECI to be its agent. Even Martin congratulated Yong, saying she had learned a lot from what had happened.

Yong confided that he believed in a saying of Sun Zi, the great military strategist: "If you know yourself and know your enemy, then one hundred wars means one hundred victories" (*Zhi ji zhi pi, bai zhang bai sheng*). In other words, if one is to win a battle, one must know oneself and the enemy. "I not only won, but I won gloriously. And it was a win-win situation for everyone," Yong said with unaccustomed elation.

CAN FOREIGNERS CREATE GUANXI NETWORKS?

In spite of misunderstandings, guanxi emerges as a critical factor in the success or failure that foreigners experience when doing business in China. In most of the examples we have seen so far, the appeals to guanxi contacts have involved Chinese colleagues and employees. The question therefore arises whether foreigners are able to build guanxi relationships of their own. The Chinese see the issue as follows.

A relationship without a certain amount of emotional feeling (*ganqing*) would be regarded as cold and businesslike. Some ganqing is essential for longstanding, close social connections but, the Chinese tend to believe, many foreigners find it difficult to develop ganqing because friendships in some cultures are more shallow than those in Chinese culture.

Most Chinese believe that friendship among foreign businesspeople is detached, cold, impersonal, mechanistic, and economic. Many even believe that when foreigners dine out, they each pay for their own meal. Rumor even has it in China that some foreigners have to pay for their own meals when they visit their adult children's homes. Chinese ganqing has a certain element of self-sacrifice blended in with the generosity, but to the Chinese, foreigners display no warmth, no self-sacrifice. This suspicion is a reason why it is so important for foreigners to display warmth and friendliness (by fitting into the value system) when building relationships with the Chinese.

There are two main lessons to be drawn from the Chinese perception of friendship as it pertains to foreigners. One is that, when appointing managers to do business in China, human resources departments should send individuals with the capacity to make friendships with genuine emotional feelings (ganqing)—warmth, affection, and good humor—that the Chinese will recognize and can praise. The second is that an individual's readiness to enter into business relationships based on warmth of friendship will dictate success or failure in creating their own guanxi network.

MAIN POINTS OF CHAPTER 7

❑ The most common form of relationship is guanxi, of which the Chinese say: "If you have guanxi, you have no problems. If you have no guanxi, you have problems." This means that, if you lack guanxi connections, you will suffer dire consequences, since you will not be helped, you will have no support system, and you will be alone in the world.

❑ Chinese businesspeople develop comprehensive guanxi networks of people who are, or might become, of value to them. Apart from businesspeople, not every Chinese approves of guanxi. Some think it immoral, an under-the-table system of gifts and favors, and a gloss for corruption and back-door dealing. Yet others see it as positive, stemming from friendship.

❑ Underestimating the importance of guanxi can have serious repercussions. Chinese who have been away from China for many years have been known to spark serious problems and cause people to lose their jobs.

❑ The misplaced desire to rationalize procedures and save money can threaten the integrity of a guanxi network. It takes a clever individual to resolve the resulting problems in a face-saving manner.

❑ When appointing managers to work in China, individuals should be chosen who have the capacity to build friendships with genuine feelings (ganqing) that the Chinese can recognize and praise.

❑ An individual's ability to form their own guanxi network and enter into business relationships with Chinese is greatly helped by their ability to form friendships based on feelings.

❑ Although few foreigners manage to form guanxi relationships with the Chinese, those who do achieve this by displaying the human side of their character and demonstrating what they have to offer as businesspeople.

CHAPTER
8

THE THIRTY-SIX STRATAGEMS

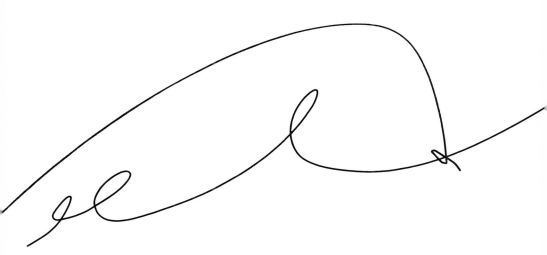

Gems that speak to the core of Chinese society, the three dozen stratagems are embedded in its culture. Some are used by astute businessmen around the globe, but they do tend to overwhelm the unprepared.

Tactical stratagems are not unique to China, being commonly found in low-trust societies and relationships. But their history is long in China, where low trust is longstanding because of the size of the country and its ancient political structure in which hundreds of independent states fought many wars against one another.

Stratagems have been an important part of Chinese culture and everyday life for more than 2,500 years. Even today, the stratagems are learned and practiced as a matter of course. One of our Chinese students put it this way: "In Chinese business and politics, friends and enemies come and go depending on what is offered. People strive for advantage over others by using tactics and strategies."[9] Some Chinese believe stratagems are used subconsciously, and that people would be embarrassed and feel uncomfortable were they made aware of the cunning aspects of their stratagems.

China negotiation specialist Tony Fang points to the prevalence of counterfeit products and economic crime in China today, and to the cupidity of merchants, concluding that "Chinese stratagems can be adopted even by decent people as a defensive weapon to keep evils at bay" (1999, 176).[10]

Mao Zedong (1893–1976) was a superb strategist and a terrific mahjong player, and greatly influenced the Chinese people's belief in strategic thinking. The fourth-century B.C. philosopher Mencius, the greatest Confucian thinker after Confucius (551–479 B.C.), justified the use of stratagems by declaring that people ought to revenge themselves on those who treated them like dogs or dirt. With the view widespread among the Chinese that "the marketplace is like a battlefield"—counterfeit products such as baby formula, instant coffee, and instant soup having become a serious problem—a defensive attitude may today be necessary for survival in China.

A familiar Chinese maxim states: "There can never be too much deception in war." Sun Zi, author of *The Art of War*, declared, "Engage the enemy with your normal force and defeat it using your extraordinary forces." Deception and stratagem-based behavior are central topics in all ancient Chinese classics about military strategy. The ancient Chinese formulated their extraordinary strategies so long ago because there were 480 wars during China's so-called Spring and Autumn period (722–481 B.C.). During this time, when demand for strategy and strategists was greatest, Sun Zi and most of the other great military strategists witnessed major wars between the lords of powerful independent states within China's borders. This is also the period when the great philosophies of Confucianism and Taoism sprang up and began to flourish, and when the *I Ching*[11] was studied most intensively.

The *Secret Art of War: Thirty-Six Strategies*, a remarkable book that deals almost exclusively with schemes of deception, is the work of an anonymous scholar who lived about three hundred years ago. It was first published in the 1940s, since when it has attracted the attention of military authorities, business strategists, and general readers. Today, the thirty-six stratagems are being used in the branch of Chinese military thought known as Information Warfare to devise entirely new kinds of war strategies that are barely understood by the U.S. armed forces—the world's most sophisticated military strategists (Thomas 2004).

Since 1990, a number of English translations of the original text of the *Secret Art of War: Thirty-Six Strategies* have been published, including those by Chu in 1991, Gao in 1991, Sun Haichen in 1991, von Senger in 1991, and Tony Fang in 1999. (Citations in the remaining pages of this chapter refer to these works.) The translations are similar, and each of the stratagems is explained by reference to historical or legendary events from ancient battles in the Spring and Autumn period.[12]

THE STRATAGEMS OUTLINED AND APPLIED

Among the cases given below to illustrate the stratagems are non-Chinese examples, included to point out that the stratagems are universal. Proper preparation should enable you to recognize their universality, rather than to believe they are exclusively Chinese and exotic. Were you to find them alien, you would play into the hands of the Chinese you face. Meanwhile, familiarizing yourself with how the stratagems are used, often artfully, by non-Chinese businesspeople should make them easier for you to adopt.

Stratagem 1: Cross the Sea without Heaven's Knowledge

Sun Haichen quotes classical author Guan's explanation of this stratagem: "One who is good at marshalling troops does so by putting the enemy in the unfathomable situation of fighting with shadows. He assumes no posture and reveals no shape so there is nothing he cannot achieve. He reveals no shape and shows no movement so there is no change he cannot make. This is the supreme art of war."

Fang sees this stratagem as variously involving deception of investors, the use of half-truths and white lies, and pretending something is true that is not.

APPLICATION

- The principals of a Chinese-owned property development company attempted to use this stratagem against a syndicate of private investors. The company used a separate set of management accounts and drew up several (unsigned) contracts supposedly submitted by major retail chains that expressed interest in engaging the development company to construct a number of shopping malls.

   These falsified contracts inflated the company's value. Initially, the unsuspecting syndicate showed interest when presented with the tailored accounts and false contracts. On reflection, however, the investors realized that the figures were unachievable given the company's size.

   Moreover, before discussion had ended, the syndicate had taken the precaution to contact the retail chains. It discovered that there had been no dealings between them and the property development company.

Stratagem 2: Besiege Wei to Rescue Zhao

The legend behind the second stratagem involves deception that led to the slaughter of the crack troops of the state of Wei and the restoration of freedom to the state of Zhao. The underlying advice is to concentrate one's strength on the enemy's weak point.

The stratagem is not a simply-applied directive but, rather, a ploy that requires thorough assessment of a situation and ruthless decision making.

Stratagem 3: Murder with a Borrowed Knife

On the basis of classic annotations to this stratagem, Sun explains it as follows. "When the enemy's intention is obvious and the ally's attitude hesitant, induce the ally to fight while preserving one's own strength."

Tony Fang, in his book *Chinese Business Negotiating Style*, sees such modern examples as a company playing its competitors off against each other (as we saw in the chapter 3 case study How Giving Face Can Brew Success); people taking detailed notes of what others say to possibly trick them later with their own words; and holding back of approval (by, for example, a government ministry) until foreign investors accept additional requirements. International businesspeople have found they encounter this stratagem most often. Here are some first-hand accounts of their experiences.

APPLICATION

- Ashley Burton was negotiating the acquisition of Prima Company as a management buyout. Prima at all times had Burton believing that his company had a reasonable chance of coming out as the lead investor. Prima did not offer definitive answers, but it recognized that it was an attractive buyout proposition, with sound financials and good management.

  During the course of the negotiations, the door to the key man at Prima was continuously revolving. Thus, when Burton would exit after having come in with a new interest rate or condition, his competitor would enter. Once the transaction was settled, Burton thought he had lost a tough fight. Only later did he learn that Prima had used him to reduce the cost of the funding to which it had already agreed with Burton's competitor.

- This Western-Chinese negotiation was going well; it was friendly and civilized. Then there was an outburst from one of the Chinese participants regarding an issue he could not accept, although the foreigners were adamant that it must be. After the meeting, the Western manager, Clyde Marchant, was asked by a particular friend among the Chinese negotiators: "As a friend, can you change your stance on this?" The pressure applied on Marchant was immense, but Marchant replied, "I personally could agree to this, but head office in the United States says it is an absolute requirement." Head office was the borrowed knife.

● In the final stages of a pre-bid agreement, the Chinese finally told the foreigners that they were also talking to other consultants about entering into the same kind of joint venture.

They said the ultimate conditions had to be in a form acceptable to the Chinese government and to their company president (who was never present). The foreigners felt under pressure and revisited all the items to see what they could concede. The stratagem, they said later, "worked well on us."

● In a technical meeting on pressure-vessel safety, the foreign party assumed a position different to that which it had adopted during the previous meeting. The Chinese brought out the first meeting minutes to remind them what they had said. The foreigners were suitably embarrassed and conceded the point.

● This is a non-Chinese case that reflects how universal stratagems can be. AMC, an aircraft maintenance contractor in Saudi Arabia, wanted quotes for inbound logistics programs and infrastructure. To the contractor's surprise, the Saudis invited all suppliers to the same meeting—FedEx, DHL, UPS, and TNT—for a brief review. A heated debate soon developed.

This suited DHL very well. They insisted that service solutions and quality were paramount, and often referred to competitors' failures in this regard. AMC wanted price to be the primary factor, but the DHL analysis of the shortcomings in its competitors weakened its emphasis on price alone.

In subsequent one-on-one meetings (AMC and DHL), DHL took the business by showing that (1) it was the only supplier that could meet all the requirements; (2) it would implement pricing in line with global U.S. military contractual benchmarks; and (3) future benefits would accrue from continuing to develop the AMC-DHL relationship.

● The following non-Chinese case involved telecommunications infrastructure planning at a major insurance company. The company designed a new architecture and specifications for a new installation. While ten solution providers were invited to submit tenders, screening reduced the companies to two, which had very similar solutions.

Realizing that the preferred solution was more expensive than had been expected, the insurance company negotiator told each company that it had made the short list and told the preferred company: "If you drop your price to $1 million, I will recommend your solution." The stratagem was effective because the insurance company got a superior solution at a good price.

● A foreign manager related: "I was getting many angry complaints about decisions I had to make, so I transferred perceived responsibility for decision making to an executive committee that included the CEO. This made me seem more powerful, and the decisions appear more irrevocable. Complaints dropped markedly. If anyone was still upset, I asked them to take it up with the executive committee."

● A Chinese manager gave this personal account. "I say to suppliers, 'This requirement comes from my boss. If you don't fulfill it, you will lose our business.' The supplier will usually accede. When I have arguments with other divisions in the company, I say, 'I'll report it to the boss.' He is my shield, and I borrow his knife."

Stratagem 4: Await Leisurely the Exhausted Enemy

We have found that this is the second most often chosen stratagem. Sun gives an apposite quotation in explanation of this stratagem: "When the enemy has come from afar in high spirits and seeks a quick battle, we should stay on the defensive behind deep trenches and high bulwarks and ignore their challenge, waiting for it to wane. If the enemy challenges us by creating incidents, we must not move. The principle is: when secure, remain immobile."

APPLICATION

● A Chinese provincial government contacted us seeking a supply of seed potatoes, with a view to making its province the supply hub for China. However, after our team arrived in China, the government body seemed to be playing games with us. There was no briefing or agenda for meetings; we had no timeframe. Since they needed us more than we needed them, we interpreted their tactics as counterproductive and waited them out.

● "We always try to hold international negotiations at our head office in Zhuhai," a non-Chinese manager told us. "There we have easy access to information, resources, and experts. The visiting groups always arrive tired, are working on short time frames, and have fewer members than originally planned. When we act as hosts, our teams perform better, are less frustrated by travel, and are more relaxed and in control."

Drawing on his Chinese experience, this manager also admitted that "The Chinese are masters of stratagem, and their foreign visitors get weary and on edge because the timing and agenda are controlled by the Chinese. Boredom, cigarette smoke, and Chinese patience seem to be the factors that most exhaust foreigners involved in extended negotiations with the Chinese."

Stratagem 5: Loot a Burning House

When the enemy suffers trouble or crisis, look for your advantage. Sun quotes the classic author Shi Zhan: "When the enemy is in disorder or hubbub, attack immediately."

Fang, meanwhile, says, "Use the Chinese 'fishing' tactic—that is, take advantage of foreigners' ignorance about local markets." Since Fang wrote that, the "fishing" metaphor has come to mean taking financial advantage of foreigners.

APPLICATION

- The global management consulting firm KPMG mounted a campaign to win several major clients away from Arthur Andersen after the Enron and WorldCom disasters. It succeeded in rapidly increasing its audit and consulting business, since the business environment was in crisis and clients wanted to waste no time in announcing new auditors. Arthur Andersen was unable to defend itself, while its clients were under pressure to abandon old ties to build market confidence.

- A foreign manager tells the following story: "I planned to ask for a raise after twelve months with the company. Just before the twelve months were up, one of our competitors started restructuring and hiring key staff.

  "One of my colleagues was approached by the competitor and submitted his resignation, but the company made a counter-offer and so he stayed on. A senior manager who was also approached did join the competitor. The timing seemed right for me, so I approached my boss and was fortunate to be retained with a raise even higher than I had expected."

Stratagem 6: Make Noise in the East But Attack in the West

Sun writes that noise in this stratagem refers to false moves in warfare. Make noise in the east and attack in the west means confusing the enemy about where to place his guards.

Quoting Blackman, Fang writes: "The Chinese deliberately discuss small matters or make unexpected or ridiculous demands, thereby drawing the other party off the main course."

Stratagem 7: Create Something out of Nothing

Sun explains this stratagem as follows: "Make a false move, not to pass it off as a genuine one but to transform it into a genuine one after the enemy is convinced of its falsity. Genuine strength grows under the cover of false appearance." Fang says: "Make the unreal seem real. Gain advantage by conjuring illusion."

APPLICATION

- Riall is a wheeler-dealer air compressor retailer in Malaysia. He tries to get extra for himself by subterfuge. He will, for example, allege he has received an order and payment from a customer for a premium compressor but finds he has none in stock, and so can only deliver a standard item.

  He then asks his salesman if he would be so kind as to let him have a premium compressor at a five percent discount while the salesman keeps the standard one in stock for himself. This way, Riall creates something out of nothing. Interestingly, when a salesman declines to supply him, he "miraculously" persuades the customer to accept the standard compressor.

- A Chinese interpreter relates the following: "I've experienced this many times. When I was interpreting for U.S. nationals in China, one of them told a joke that could have damaged the relationship. So I told a different joke, which the Chinese appreciated."

● An expat living in Shanghai once told how he would "watch in disbelief when foreigners pay high prices in China for goods that are overpriced to start with." He went on to explain that, "When they have no reference point for a fake Giorgio Armani jacket, they cannot make realistic comparisons. The unreal becomes real to them when it is offered at a high price. The point lost in translation is 'fake.'"

Stratagem 8: Advance Secretly via Chencang

Sun quotes Guan Zi as explaining this stratagem as follows: "Go where the enemy is ignorant; attack when the enemy is unprepared. Ignorant, the enemy cannot forestall our move; unprepared, the enemy cannot cope with our attack. Thus we achieve complete victory unharmed."

Meanwhile, Fang describes this as "play[ing] overt, predictable, and public maneuvers against covert, surprising, and secretive ones." He says the Chinese can make sudden demands and changes, or they can negotiate openly with one supplier while doing so secretly with another.

Stratagem 9: Watch the Fire Burning from across the River

Sun explains thus: "When the discord of the enemy becomes apparent, do nothing. Wait for the oncoming upheaval." Pye (quoted in Fang) comments, "The Chinese are masters of the art of stalling while keeping the other party's hopes alive; they freely use stalling tactics and delays."

APPLICATION

● The recommended candidate for promotion had approval withheld by a senior executive who did not want that candidate in his department. However, the executive knew that the company did not want to lose the candidate. Knowing that the candidate would retire in four months were he not promoted, the executive sat on the recommended candidate's file. Three months later, that candidate was promoted to another department. The strategy had worked.

● The stratagem was cleverly put to use in a Western setting, as a salesman relates: "I was selling IBM mainframes to a major insurance company that wanted to do a deal before the end of the year. I had already achieved my yearly quota.

"The client company needed a major mainframe capacity upgrade and had delayed its decision to year-end, expecting to do the deal then. For me, the benefit of making the deal before year-end meant a significant bonus, but the prospective client was unaware of this.

"My boss and I thus agreed on a do-nothing strategy, to include no end-of-year entertaining of the client; no discussion with the client of the order; leaking to the client the information that both my boss and I had achieved our quotas; and subtly suggesting there were supply problems with the equipment.

"In short, we led the insurance company to believe that we did not need the business and were experiencing a capacity shortage, which might result in higher listed prices for those placing orders the following year.

"This was highly effective, and the client ordered an upgrade at list price before Christmas."

Stratagem 10: Hide a Dagger in a Smile

Sun says this stratagem advocates working to put the enemy off guard, while working secretly to defeat it. One should prepare fully to prevent the enemy from changing its mind, and then take action, having hidden one's strong will. Fang says that the strategy includes "letting foreign friends speak first"; addressing the foreign clients as old friends; as well as showing the graciousness and bountifulness of Chinese hospitality to make it hard for foreigners to be too businesslike in early meetings.

APPLICATION

- A non-Chinese employed by a Chinese-foreign joint venture reported the following incident: "The chairman of our joint venture, Zhang Daifu, uses this stratagem at every meeting. He starts by saying things such as that the business is going well, the key indicators of production, costs, and safety have improved in the six months since I joined the company, and positive feedback is coming in. Then, just as I start to feel buoyed, Zhang bangs the table and shouts angrily, 'Why haven't we sold our concentrate to [a certain smelter]?' 'Why haven't you bought supplies from our approved supplier?' 'Why are lights left burning in the factory?' and so on.

"His tactic on the first and second occasions was successful. I came down to earth with a crash. But since he uses it at every meeting, the stratagem has lost its sting."

● The following example is drawn from an informal hearing about an incident of sexual harassment in a Western country. The chairperson, Sue, said, "I'm satisfied. There's nothing to this, just a waste of time as far as Mary [the plaintiff] is concerned. She just hates men." Thereafter there was a boy's club atmosphere as the men, feeling relief, joked with each other.

Eventually, Jack (the defendant) jokingly confessed. "Next time, I'll wait until she's had more to drink before I try that," he said, as though in confidence, and adding "But she really enjoyed it, you know."

There was silence as Jack realized he had been tricked. He had let his guard down, and concluded he could say anything. "He was never considered too bright," others said.

Stratagem 11: Sacrifice a Plum Tree to Save a Peach Tree

Make a small sacrifice to gain a major benefit, comments Fang. Meanwhile, Sun quotes a Tang Dynasty (618–907) general, Li Su: "One who looks into the distance overlooks what is nearby; one who considers great things, neglects the details. If we feel proud of a small victory and regret over a small defeat, we will encumber ourselves and lose the opportunity to achieve merits."

APPLICATION

● The application of this stratagem in a Western setting may be familiar to some.

The lease was to expire on one of the buildings we were renting, and we had the option of moving and taking with us the furniture. It was expensive but of little value to us, on top of which once it had been removed, we would be required to refurbish the offices, which would be quite costly.

We thus offered to leave the furniture and equipment for the owner, who accepted. In other words, we sacrificed a small amount—the near $7,000 depreciated value of the furniture—for the $40,000 to $50,000 we would have had to pay to refurbish the building.

● A union called our entire staff out on a protracted strike after we had sacked a casual worker. We took the union to court, won our case, and the staff were ordered back to work. But morale was low, and productivity almost zero.

So, we talked to the union and gave in on a number of small issues, hoping thereby to increase productivity and profit. Both sides were happy over the following years, in the belief that it had been a win-win situation. Management had given up something small to achieve a more productive and profitable yard.

Stratagem 12: Lead Away a Passing Goat

According to Fang, this means that one should "take advantage of opportunities when they appear." Sun is more precise in his perspective, suggesting that the reader should "Take advantage of the smallest flaw. Seize the smallest profit."

APPLICATION

● A Western shopper in Beijing once related the following gem: "On several occasions, when I thought the final price had been agreed to at a Chinese open air market, the vendor would ask for between five and ten yuan more as they put the product in a bag. At first I was caught off guard and conceded something extra.

"But after that I countered the tactic saying, 'I'll bring back some of my friends next time.' I also gave the vendors the impression that I was staying permanently in Beijing, which made them more inclined to concede on price. In other words, I turned their tactic back on them."

● A foreign manager in a southern Chinese province related how "once our joint venture was established and our plant up and running, the Chinese provincial government came up with ever-newer methods of extracting money from us, supposedly a rich Western company.

"The government's latest ruse was an annual land tax, equivalent to $10,000. Our counter-strategy was for our staff to build guanxi with provincial government staff, hoping that we can have some future leverage on other attempts to bleed us."

Stratagem 13: Beat the Grass to Frighten the Snake

Sun interprets this as meaning that one should find out about the enemy before taking action. The ancient Chinese referred to this as testing the enemy by conducting a brief foray against them to see how they respond and to learn everything possible from the response.

Fang quotes Western writers on Chinese negotiators as seeing this stratagem manifest in various forms, including: not preparing a Chinese draft of an agenda or proposal until the English one has been read; asking probing questions that encourage their counterparts to tip their hand; shaming people and then expecting them to do things the Chinese way; and initially applying pressure to see how their counterparts react.

APPLICATION

- The Chinese ask many probing questions of our technical personnel, who, not generally involved in commercial discussions, give away more information than we would like. This effective tactic proved short-lived, however, since we have learned to withstand attempts to obtain more of our intellectual property. Our guideline to staff is to be suitably vague.

- Another application that is often seen in China requires a great deal of patience but is cost-effective. Were one, for example, to want to ask a supplier for a discount, one would approach the company wishing to discuss the following year's forecast. The good news would come first, followed by the downside at the end of the meeting.

Stratagem 14: Be Reincarnated in a Borrowed Corpse

Sun suggests this can be interpreted as meaning that one should make use of the useless. Useful things do not ask to be used, but useless things do. He proposes that one should secure a good name for oneself and give the enemy a bad name because name and righteousness are everything in war.

Fang cites Chen as giving the example of dying Chinese companies that see teaming up with a foreign partner as a way of solving their financial, technological, and management problems.

Stratagem 15: Lure the Tiger out of the Mountain

One should not attack the enemy on contestable ground, according to Sun. The key here seems to be to gain a position of advantage, by maneuvering before attacking. A Chinese saying that expresses this vulnerability is, "Stranded on the sandy beach, the dragon is teased by shrimps. Descending to the plain, the tiger is bullied by dogs."

APPLICATION

● A local Chinese bank was seeking major services from multinational consulting companies, most of which were bringing in experts from their U.S. offices. One of the consultants, however, decided instead to fly a group of the bank's decision makers to the United States to tour some of the consultant's clients, with the trip hosted by the consultant's number two man. The visit lasted three weeks and provided the client with all the due diligence it required. Before returning home, the host was able to get a verbal agreement from the bank to proceed. The contract was scheduled for signing in China one week after the bankers had returned home.

● Ahead of a client's visit from overseas, it is common in China for the host to make sure that all the areas that are going to be visited are immaculate. No attention is paid to other areas, where visitors are not expected to go.

But sometimes the unexpected happens and visitors go where it was not expected they would venture. The problem with this stratagem is that, should visitors discover the untidy areas, the stratagem would lose its value, since the visitors would realize that the clean setting is artificial and would thus doubt the integrity of the supplier.

Stratagem 16: To Capture the Enemy, First Let It Go

Rather than close in on a defeated enemy (which might cause it to strike back), surround it loosely, and let it fritter away its strength and willpower. Rather than embarking on hot pursuit, give unhurried chase.

One experienced Japanese negotiator sees this stratagem played out in the Chinese practice of describing a foreign negotiator's initial concessions or flexibility as "a certain degree of progress"—before seeking further concessions.

Stratagem 17: Toss out a Brick to Attract Jade

This is the trading of something minor or counterfeit for something of major value, or as one classical writer put it: "Give profit to the enemy to lure him."

APPLICATION

- The Chinese only wanted to deal with the best company that had the most advanced technology—in that case us. They began the negotiations with their top guns: the CEO, professors, provincial governors, and city vice-mayors (the brick). They wanted to use our world-renowned name and technology (the jade) but wished to pay nothing for doing so.

- A foreigner in Asia related how he had traded the use of certain herbicides for permission to develop plantations in a small Southeast Asian city. Win-win situations such as this are an oft-repeated illustration of this stratagem.

Stratagem 18: To Catch the Bandits, First Catch Their Ringleader

The Chinese regard the leader of a group of bandits as the cohesive element and decision maker of the entire posse. Once the leader has been captured, the group will disintegrate and join its captors. This stratagem is often applied to business situations in China.

APPLICATION

- We wanted to attract the business of a major Australian bank, Westpac, for which we had not previously worked. I studied the thinking and priorities of its CEO and, together with my company chairman, obtained an interview with him. The CEO invited us to be tested on one of his personally sponsored projects within the bank. We were successful and were thereafter invited to offer solutions to other problems. We were increasingly successful. Thereafter, the bank's executives followed their CEO's commands without question.

Stratagem 19: Remove the Firewood from under the Caldron

The Chinese advise that one should avoid a contest of strength with the enemy, yet at the same time seek to weaken its position. This stratagem shows they believe that one of the biggest blunders is to confront a superior enemy head-on.

● When a large supplier of wine chose to move in on a small supplier, it did not attack the quality of its competitor's product, which was superior. Rather, it attacked the smaller company's poor distribution and inconsistencies in its product range.

Stratagem 20: Muddle the Water to Catch the Fish

This stratagem was designed to point out that, when the enemy is suffering internecine wars, one should take advantage of its weaknesses and poor judgment. One should create a disturbance or an ongoing annoyance until the opponent capitulates.

● A foreign mining manager in China recounted one of his experiences: "We spent months negotiating to lease part of the tenement adjacent to ours from the holders of the gold mining lease. Previously, there had been some debate about the exact location of the common tenement boundary, and claims by both parties that the other party had mined across the boundary, but nothing had been done. Then suddenly, just when discussion was focused on the area we wanted to lease, we were amazed to find that all the other party would do was to accuse us of illegally mining ore from their tenement. They even threatened to take legal action, called for meetings with our CEO (who was not in China), and refused to provide technical data on their tenement so that the boundary issue could be resolved and leasing arrangements made.

"The leaseholder's approach was effective. We were frustrated and delayed, and when we thought all the issues had been resolved, they were all put back into play. We were then willing to pay the leaseholder more than we had planned, just so that we could get on with our lives."

● A foreign negotiator has shared some advice based on his experience: "Continual verbal bashing has been used on me a number of times. It wears you out and makes you drop your price just to end the abuse. What I have learned to do is to start with a somewhat inflated price and slowly work down to a price that suits me. That allows them to believe they have won."

Stratagem 21: The Cicada Sloughs Its Shell

This is advice to maintain the appearance of inaction while secretly taking action. In classical Chinese military strategy, each side would count the other side's cooking pots and banners to determine the number of troops in the field. This invited deception, with opponents putting out far more pots and flags (the shell) than they had troops (the cicada).

Fang suggests that a parallel can be drawn in negotiations, with the side that does not want to continue placing excessive demands on the other side, thereby forcing a breach in the negotiations. The cicada's shell represents the excessive demands.

Stratagem 22: Lock the Door and Catch the Thief

This stratagem is about trapping an enemy in a situation from which it cannot escape. This is akin to luring a thief to an empty house or an empty campsite, and then surrounding it.

Business analogies could be a trap: for example, foreign parties in a situation requiring them to make decisions or concessions when they are to leave China in a day or so; organizing conferences or meetings at such inconvenient times as just before Christmas or other religious holidays; or generally manipulating schedules to put pressure on visiting foreigners. A number of the longer case studies in this book illustrate this stratagem only too well.

APPLICATION

● An Australian negotiator shared his experience of this stratagem with us as it applied to a cross-Pacific deal: "We had negotiated an agreement with a U.S. company, but a few issues remained unresolved. The time frames were set, but representatives of the U.S. company were refusing to come back to Australia to settle the outstanding matters. With only three days left to get an agreement in place, the U.S. party held all the cards.

"We were forced to make concessions we would not otherwise have made and moved on many issues to show flexibility, because we believed the ongoing relationship needed to be maintained."

Stratagem 23: Befriend Distant States While Attacking Nearby Ones

The message here is to keep peril at a distance and seek profit nearby. To this end, we should deal with our enemies one by one, beginning with the enemy that is closest. And, in order to make sure that the trusted followers of our enemy keep us informed of events, we should cause division in the enemy camp by befriending some of its followers.

In the spirit of this stratagem, the Chinese will occasionally befriend members of a foreign team to unsettle the chief negotiator.

Stratagem 24: Attack Hu by a Borrowed Path

Deal with enemies one by one, suggests Fang: Use a nearby state as a springboard to reach a distant one. Sun suggests that a small state sandwiched between two great powers might be threatened by one of them, in which case the other large power might take control on the pretext of assisting the small state.

APPLICATION

● The experience of a foreign manager working in China brings home the point quite well: "Our company was the only wholly foreign-owned company operating in China's agricultural sector. The Chinese authorities promised they would not inspect our premises, because we pointed out that this would expose our secret technology (not patentable) to scrutiny. Yet the competition has been trying to attack us via the Chinese authorities (the borrowed path), who have thus been putting increasing pressure on us to allow inspections.

"We, in turn, have been crafting clever responses to deny them access. However, even should they get in, we would still feel relatively secure because we believe it would be difficult to copy our production system without our technological smarts. We also have the option of threatening to withdraw our technology from China to protect our global position."

Stratagem 25: Steal the Beams and Change the Pillars

Consider that, over time, your negotiating team develops a structure of key proposals and demands, a well-thought-out game plan, excellent individual negotiators, and a sense of being close to success. Under such circumstances, how could the Chinese undermine your success?

Fang says it is not uncommon for the Chinese to switch negotiators and change the terms of a deal while discussions are underway. This is destabilizing and may cause your structure to collapse.

Stratagem 26: Point at the Mulberry Tree But Curse the Locust

If mulberry leaves fall, disappear, or wither, the cause could be that there is something wrong with the tree, or it could be that locusts are attacking the leaves. The key element in this stratagem is the cursing, which can be taken to mean a way of scaring or intimidating someone.

The Chinese also have another saying: "Kill a chicken to scare a monkey," which is essentially a stratagem. A monkey is hard to kill, but letting it see a chicken being butchered should scare it into submission.

There are a number of examples of this stratagem in our case studies. Note the Chinese negotiators who, putting on temper tantrums to intimidate their foreign counterparts, get their way. This is akin to the classical Western good guy/bad guy stratagem.

Stratagem 27: Feign Ignorance and Hide One's Intentions

On the battleground, surprise attacks can be achieved if the enemy believes you know nothing and are motionless. This stratagem applies equally well to negotiating teams; it requires secrecy, quietness, and self-discipline on the part of all your team's members.

Ignorance can be a powerful means of gaining information, but it does not necessarily mean that the information will be enough to allow an effective surprise attack to be planned. Pye (quoted in Fang) notes that the Chinese will "steel themselves against feelings of empathy and are quick to move aggressively if they sense that the other party has problems." Clearly, one has no need to reveal to the Chinese any problems one might have.

APPLICATION

- One businessman has revealed some interesting applications of this stratagem: "This is an incredibly deceptive tactic that I have used to purchase real estate, get the lawn mowed for free by the local council, and pay bills that are in arrears. It has saved me time and money, and more importantly, got me out of uncomfortable situations."

- A foreigner in Shanghai shared his different experience of how the stratagem might be applied: "A Chinese professor used this stratagem on me when I went to him, inquiring if he had received my application for a job in Shanghai. Thus he created an environment where he was the listener and possible benefactor, and I was the applicant starting from scratch."

● Another foreigner also gave a positive assessment: "This stratagem has stood out for me in Asia. Many people in different countries have used it against me as an opening gambit: I know nothing so please tell me. Or they have simply been silent and waited for me to talk or continue and give them more and more information. Westerners are bad at keeping their cards close to their chests, especially when they interpret silence as an expectation that they will keep talking. Silly questions often elicit the same response."

● An interesting story came from a foreigner who related how this stratagem had been put to good use by one foreign company when dealing with another: "Once my company became aware of the subtlety of this stratagem, we used it on a number of financial services providers we wanted to evaluate. We deliberately held back information, and at times purposely appeared inept to the providers. This led to extensive question-and-answer sessions, which lengthened the negotiation and wore them out. They thought we were bumbling, uncertain, and vague, and so gave us large amounts of information to 'compensate' us for our lack of knowledge.

"The service providers thought that by thus compensating, they would be in a commanding position, but what they really did was enable us to compare their systems with ours. We were thus able to reduce the services we required (and, hence, the price) in the agreement we finally signed with a provider. In sharp contrast to what had been seen as our bumbling behavior, our level of professionalism in the eyes of the service providers increased dramatically and magically once we had signed the financial service contract."

Stratagem 28: Lure Them to the Roof, Then Take the Ladder Away

The ladder in this stratagem is the means by which an enemy is lured into an ambush. This can be achieved in a number of ways, including by playing on the weaknesses of the enemy leader.

Much of what the Chinese write about this stratagem, however, deals more with giving the troops courage to fight their way out of an ambush—such as by destroying their provisions and equipment, and so making them willing to fight to the death.

Fang suggests that the Chinese practice of taking advantage of foreign visitors' schedules to squeeze out a last-minute favorable agreement and the practice of pushing foreigners to the brink of terminating negotiations are examples of this stratagem.

Stratagem 29: Flowers Bloom in the Tree

Attaching lifelike silk flowers to a flowerless tree makes it look more attractive. Similarly, feigning advantages you do not have, achievements that are not yours, and strength that you do not have can make you intimidating.

In the same vein, claiming government approval can enhance bargaining power, just as "borrowing" a foreign party's strengths can make Chinese stronger when dealing with their own government.

Stratagem 30: Host and Guest Switch Roles

Foreign negotiators recognize that, *if* a Chinese team visits foreign negotiators in their country, the Chinese will quite often find it difficult to utilize many of their stratagems. It is a matter of turning one's defensive, reactive role into an offensive, proactive one.

It is interesting to note that in joint-venture negotiations, the Chinese customarily use the size and potential of the Chinese marketplace to put themselves in a powerful position and foreigners on the back foot. Similarly, they use their perceived economic weakness as a basis for obtaining concessions from foreigners. Indeed, we believe this stratagem represents the Chinese rationale for the common final face-saving concession or discount before a deal is closed.

Stratagem 31: Beauty Trap

This is one of the most commonly used stratagems. Sun says two political maneuvers were popular in ancient China—the use of double agents and of beautiful women to infatuate enemy leaders.

Chinese history has many stories of beautiful women causing the downfall of a kingdom on the basis of an underlying principle—the strong can be subdued by the "weak." In modern-day parlance, the weak include women, wining and dining, gifts, and travel.

● A foreign executive explained how he applies this stratagem to benefit his company: "When we advertise employment openings, we always get a few applications from employees at my major competitor. We usually interview them to gather intelligence, because most applicants feel they need to make a good impression."

● Another foreigner shares his secret strategy with us: "I conducted an alternative investments seminar recently and took with me a beautiful and outgoing woman. When the seminar finished, I invited fifteen of the most likely business prospects to dinner. They enjoyed her company and did not seem to notice how much their glasses were being refilled. This stratagem enabled me to skip ahead in my investment-selling format."

● A foreigner who lives and works in Saudi Arabia relates how, when he takes prospective clients out, he takes them to Bahrain for an overnight stay. Unlike Saudi Arabia, Bahrain is a liberal Islamic state, with many good restaurants and bars. This application of the stratagem would not be discussed in Saudi Arabia.

Stratagem 32: The Empty City Stratagem

Appearing to be powerless (when you are not) creates doubts in the mind of the enemy. This stratagem, according to Sun, works wonders if it is used by the weak against the strong.

Thus it was that, in the 1980s, the Chinese often said to foreigners, "If you give us this product at a very low price, your future success in China is assured" (Knutsson, quoted in Fang). Fang says a deliberate display of weakness can conceal vulnerability and thus confuse the enemy, while Sun points out that this stratagem can be risky. Superficially, it is akin to Stratagem 27, which advocates feigning ignorance to hide one's intentions (perhaps a surprise attack).

Stratagem 33: Turn the Enemy's Agents against Him

This stratagem advocates exposing an internal agent of the enemy to false information, allowing this to be passed on to the leader, and bribing spies to become double agents, so that they pass on false information to their bosses. It is more commonly used than Stratagem 13, Beat the Grass to Startle the Snake, which recommends that one find out about the enemy before taking action.

APPLICATION

- This stratagem was used some years ago by a due-diligence working party with which I was involved. A representative from an investee company was assigned to assist us in information gathering and checking. When we discovered that he was secretly sneaking glances at our due-diligence lists and relaying the information to his boss, who then altered key points in the information, we decided to place a fake due-diligence checklist on the table for the representative to see.

  This kept his principals busy for a number of days and, by the time they had finished looking through the fake requests, we had determined the actual state of the investee company and decided against proceeding with the transaction.

  This stratagem allowed us to redirect and distract the investee company while we conducted our due diligence, without anyone losing face. Had we decided to invest regardless of what we had discovered about the company, trust would have been difficult to establish had any accusations been made.

Stratagem 34: Self-Torture

One's own real or imagined suffering or injuries can sometimes elicit sympathy and more from the enemy. From the 1970s through the 1990s, the Chinese used their own poverty and ignorance as a tactic to gain greater concessions from foreign investors. A typical rejoinder was: "This is not much money for you," or "A small decrease for you is a large gain for me."

APPLICATION

- Our Chinese clients often say: "We need the best possible service, but we cannot afford to pay your prices." Sometimes we cave in, because the danger in many of these cases is that the customer will not otherwise be able to settle our invoices. But at other times we say: "Try so-and-so. That company has tariffs that will suit you better."

- This stratagem can be beneficial when used against the Chinese, as one foreigner found out: "Three years ago, I used this stratagem on the Chinese. I had to work on a quality problem with a Shanghai supplier. I visited the supplier once a week for two months. One day I told the supplier, 'I am only a small potato in my company. You need to help me fix this problem, otherwise I'll lose my job. You see, I am in Shanghai often and it is almost as though I have moved here. My wife is complaining about me being away so much.' Their response was positive, and they promised to help me solve the problem."

Stratagem 35: Stratagem on Stratagems

Many battle plans are built on multiple strategies. Promptly carried out, Sun says, they can trigger a chain reaction that demoralizes, weakens, and finally defeats the other side. Typically, he writes, the first aim is to reduce the enemy's maneuverability, and the second to destroy its effective strength.

In modern negotiations, maneuverability may be defined as having a wide range of options with which to counter the opposing side's arguments. Strength, meanwhile, might be the extent of one's support coming from such sources as governments, institutions, or industry groups.

APPLICATION

- According to an experienced foreign manager, the Chinese often only want to deal with the best company with the most advanced technology. They open negotiations with their top guns, who seek to ingratiate themselves with their counterparts in the foreign company. They also make it clear that they want to use the foreign company's name and technology, in return for which they will provide access to their market. But they do not wish to pay for the foreign company's services.

  This approach may be played out in a combination of strategies. It often derails foreign companies at first, making them wonder if they have anything of value to offer the Chinese. The best way to counter such an onslaught or avoid it is to establish guanxi and mutual trust as quickly as possible.

Stratagem 36: If All Else Fails, Run Away

Living to fight another day is at the heart of this stratagem. What is the point, it implies, of fighting to the death, surrendering, or suing for peace? Retreat is by far the best choice. Sun advises that an army should fight only at the right time and with the right opponent. Should the enemy be too strong, one should wait either for it to weaken, or until one has become stronger.

APPLICATION

> ● A foreign manager in China told us the following story: "We once had to resort to this stratagem because of a chronic cash flow problem. We were unable to pay a foreign organization the franchise fees due and so said we would pay when that company's representative visited us in three months for a review meeting. When the rep arrived, we said that our CEO was overseas and asked whether we could have another three months' delay. The foreign organization again agreed, and by that time we were able to pay."

WHAT WE CAN LEARN FROM THE STRATAGEMS

Those involved in Chinese business will find the stratagems interesting but memorizing the facts daunting. Fortunately, we have found that just four stratagems account for sixty-five percent of the cases that international businesspeople encounter. We can thus assume that they are the most commonly used stratagems in all negotiations with the Chinese. The four are No. 3 (Murder with a Borrowed Knife), No. 4 (Await Leisurely the Exhausted Enemy), No. 18 (To Catch the Bandits, First Catch Their Ringleader), and No. 31 (Beauty Trap).

CONCLUSION

Stratagems are strategic core responses learned by the Chinese to take the initiative and put the other party—whoever they may be—on the defensive. They can also be used diplomatically to avoid causing the other party to lose face.

One of the issues that arises whenever experienced non-Chinese businesspeople discuss the stratagems is whether they are legitimate strategies that are deceptive but not unethical, or whether they are unethical and illegal to the extent that they should not be considered acceptable in negotiations.

Here is a list of dubious behaviors reported in the case examples above. We have classified these as unethical (**U**), quasi-unethical (**Q**), or ethically neutral (**N**).

Stalling, delaying, deferring for a better opportunity—**N**

Manipulating the itinerary to favor your team—**Q**

Silence, waiting out, not responding, not making eye contact—**N**

Half-truths—**Q**

White lies—**Q**

Straight-out lies/deceit—**U**

Fake relationships—**N**

Faking ignorance, naïvety, gullibility—**N**

Manipulating the gullibility of others—**N**

Talking down to others—**N**

Verbal aggression—calling names, criticizing—**Q**

Shaming others—**Q**

Psychological coercion—**U**

As a Western-born, Western-educated individual, I believe that each of the three behavior classifications calls for a different response.

Unethical behavior includes lying and psychological coercion. If one detects and can prove lying, one can show the other party that their lie has been detected, thereby giving oneself a moral and possibly strategic advantage.

If coercion is attempted (as is the case when someone shouts at a non-Chinese), what one does depends on whether one is a member of the same organization as the coercer. If you are, then there is a penalty to pay if you respond with anything but cool logic. If you are not (as when negotiating with Chinese who are not in your organization), the most psychologically comfortable response is to ignore what is being said. But it may also be an opportunity for counterattack, depending on the topic.

The weakness of many non-Chinese negotiators is that they do not take time to think over what they have just experienced, take counsel with their team members, or consider what opportunities the other side's behavior has given them.

Quasi-unethical responses include shaming others, shouting, calling people names, manipulating the itinerary, and telling white lies. All of these actions can be accepted with a cool head and without a heated reaction. Each provides an opportunity for you to give an unexpected response—being skeptical and asking numerous detailed but polite questions about statements that you suspect are untrue; showing pain and hurt; turning away from the speaker and talking to your team about something unconnected to the offender; or even walking out, showing regret and courtesy as you do.

Finally, neutral behaviors are mainly techniques to gain the upper hand, at least temporarily. They offer opportunities to use your own techniques—if the behavior is silence, you can remain silent longer, or you can leave the room politely to take a break with your team. If it is stalling, you may face the problem of the amount of money being wasted while you are being held up. Under such circumstances, many foreigners cut their losses and get on with other matters. That is a sensible response.

In general, your reaction to a stratagem has to be decided according to the prevailing circumstances, but it should *never* be automatic and irritated. Taking time off to mull it over with your team is the essential first step. You do *not* need a team leader who reacts to stratagems without thinking about the consequences.

❏ Stratagems are strategic core responses used by the Chinese to take the initiative and put the other party on the defensive. But they can also be used diplomatically to avoid causing the other party to lose face.

❏ It is vital that every negotiator be familiar with at least the four most commonly used of the thirty-six strategies introduced in this chapter.

❏ The four most often used stratagems account for sixty-five percent of those encountered by international businesspeople. They are: No. 3 (Murder with a Borrowed Knife), No. 4 (Await Leisurely the Exhausted Enemy), No. 18 (To Catch the Bandits, First Catch Their Ringleader), and No. 31 (Beauty Trap).

❏ One of the issues that arises when experienced non-Chinese businesspeople talk about the stratagems is whether they are legitimate strategies that are deceptive but not unethical, or whether they are unethical and illegal to the extent that they should not be considered acceptable in negotiations. When on the receiving end of what one considers an unacceptable stratagem, it is wise to remain calm, take a step back, and review one's options.

CHAPTER
9

BUILDING TRUST AND RELATIONSHIPS

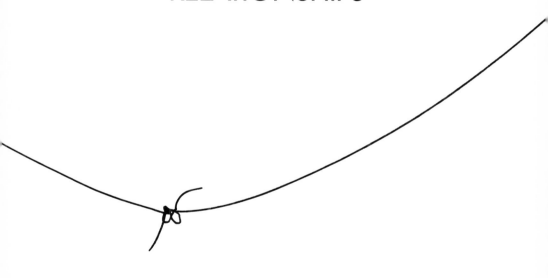

A major theme of this book is trust—what it involves, how it is built and sustained, how it can be lost. In China, nothing is possible without trust. Critical and earned, trust is shown to exist by shared experience and as a result of testing for sincerity, honesty, and dedication.

Foreigners are culturally and, often, physically different from the Chinese, and history gives no one an advantage. For four hundred years, outsiders have been the enemy, the invader, or remote alien figures variously seen as suspicious, exotic, and untrustworthy. The Chinese have had no sense of cultural affinity with them.

For this reason, some China specialists believe that the development of every close relationship with China is preceded by extensive negotiations, resembling psychological warfare, during which time is not an issue and winning is all the Chinese want. Trust, which does not flourish on such bedrock, can nevertheless be achieved.

 NEGOTIATIONS BUILD TRUST

OVERVIEW

This case involves negotiations between a private Chinese company and a private Australian company, the former requiring special technology that the latter possesses.

The negotiations were conducted during twenty-one formal and informal meetings held over three years in China and Australia. The meetings, lunches, dinners, and even karaoke and beer-drinking sessions were steps to build trust.

The case illustrates the importance of patience and preparation when dealing with the Chinese. One year of long-distance interaction preceded the first face-to-face meeting between the parties. The Australians spent this time familiarizing themselves with the project, the political environment, and the needs, resources, goals, and personalities of the Chinese company.

THE SCENE

Early on, the Australian company sought assistance from the Hong Kong trade commissioner, who brought both sides together and served as a trusted go-between. This use of an influential third party was one of the key elements in building the trust that led to the success of the project, since both parties had separately enjoyed a long relationship with the trade commissioner.

Then, when the fifty-year-old lead Chinese negotiator was on his first visit to Australia, the lead Australian negotiator broke the ice by inviting his Chinese counterpart home for a barbecue. The Chinese saw this invitation as a significant first step in developing the desired friendship.

Interestingly, while both sides had their own interpreters whom they used extensively during meetings, neither interpreter was present on some after-hours occasions. Yet the parties managed to bond and, after a few drinks at a karaoke bar, the Chinese became surprisingly eloquent and it became evident that he spoke an acceptable level of English.

THE AUSTRALIAN PERSPECTIVE

The Australians were initially skeptical about the Chinese company's ability to obtain the necessary approvals. While the Chinese had extensive experience and domestic contacts in the political sector and the business community, and their lead negotiator was a provincial council member, property developer, and hotel manager, this alone did not guarantee that the approval processes would be smooth.

TRIAL BY PATIENCE

When the requirements were not clear and the Chinese seemed to hold back information about whether they had received certain approvals and permits, the Australians were obliged to find out from others about obtaining authorizations. Chinese government departments and private companies earlier associated with the project had to be contacted and courted, all of which delayed negotiations and frustrated the Australians.

Despite the numerous unresolved contentious issues that could have damaged the negotiations if poorly handled, the Australians displayed patience in meetings, ensured their actions did not mean loss of face for the lead Chinese negotiator, and tried to increase the level of bilateral trust. This required restraint and no small measure of faith.

THE MORE THINGS CHANGE...

During the first few meetings in particular, the Australian team allowed some questions to pass and provisionally accepted puzzling details, knowing that the gaps would be filled in later. Although for months the Chinese kept changing their requirements and insisting on their ideas, it was clear that they wanted the Australians' involvement and technology for the project. On many occasions they adapted to and accepted the Australian way of doing things.

When there was disagreement on a particular timeline, the Chinese said it would have to be done in six weeks—although six months was more realistic. The Australians thus diplomatically pointed out the timelines for ASEAN projects they had successfully completed, enabling the Chinese to accept the Australians' timeline without losing face.

WE DO TOO

The contract-signing ceremony was conducted in Shanghai with pomp, ceremony, and government dignitaries present. But no sooner had the ink dried than the Chinese began to renegotiate the terms and conditions of the contract.

When one Australian mentioned this to the go-between, he was tartly reminded that Australians do exactly the same. As do others, on numerous pretexts.

Commentary

Both sides negotiated on an equal footing, and both made extra efforts to overcome culture- and policy-related difficulties. When the Chinese accepted many aspects of the original Australian proposal, the Australians were surprised, having been warned by others that most of their proposals would be unacceptable to the Chinese. From this the Australians learned not to prejudge the Chinese and the value of patient preparation. The importance of recognizing the following also became clear:

- Professionalism is vital; use a go-between. The Australians prepared for months before the two sides first met and involved a go-between throughout. They never assumed anything or accepted what they were told without double-checking the facts.

- Friendship and trust are crucial. The introduction of the Chinese negotiators into the Australian cultural milieu, via the barbecue, was significant. This glimpse of a more intimate side of Australian life was a glamorous, exotic, exciting, and memorable experience for the Chinese, which they would talk about for a long time to come. That the Australian lead negotiator's home overlooked the picturesque Sydney Harbour added to the ambiance.

- Face is pivotal. The Australians had a good understanding of face—how to give it and how to avoid anything that might cause its loss. The Chinese recognized the sensitive, thoughtful, and compassionate aspects of the Australians' face-giving and face-saving behavior. This made the Chinese feel more indebted and committed to their counterparts.

- Controversy should be skirted. The Australians maintained the principle of minimizing conflict and misunderstanding by deferring contentious issues and avoiding out-and-out no's.

- Flexibility is necessary. Both sides were flexible about their demands and positions, and responded positively and with good grace to the other side. Since the negotiation process is extended decision making, some contract items were negotiated after the contract had been signed. Some writers have criticized the Chinese practice of post-contract negotiation, but often it is closer to continuous improvement than to unethical behavior.

- There is value in restraint. The Australians were commendably restrained and calm throughout the negotiations, and both sides demonstrated their professionalism by the way they interacted.

This case shows that generalizations about what the Chinese will or will not permit are merely general propositions admitting of many exceptions. It shows professionalism at work, enabling both sides to build trust steadily and feel comfortable with each other.

The family-like business relationship is the cultural ideal. The longer business relationships with Chinese last, the more they will be expected to exude a family-like quality that over time allows generous-hearted trust to grow stronger than bottom-line obsession. Trusting others offers the best in life—a caring orientation that dictates freely given favors with no specific timetable for repayment—and, of course, no written contracts. This is how people treat close family members. If your brother wants a loan, you give it without quibbling or asking questions. Most would say that this is the Chinese way, ideally, of doing business.

When Chinese venture into talks with foreigners about some form of long-term business relationship, the cultural templates of close, trusting, family relationships in their culture unconsciously shape their expectations of you. They wish to know if you are someone whom they can trust and with whom they can feel comfortable. The last thing they want is a legalistic relationship, which to them seems cold and inhuman when measured against the close familial relationship. At best, they want generosity, compromise, and concession as needed, since these qualities ensure that no animosity or resentment lingers from misunderstandings or conflicts of interest.

BUSINESS RELATIONSHIPS MIRROR TRUST

As companies move from ignorance of one another to knowing each other well, and become (in a few cases) like family, they learn more about how to relate effectively with and sensitively to each other—just as do people in a successful marriage. Trust is at the heart of the process.

In a business environment, it is through their behavior, attitudes, and thoughts that negotiating teams evolve and learn to accommodate their counterparts. If one bears in mind that both sides learn from a cross-cultural, friendly relationship, it is easier to place the occasional problems in a wider perspective and see beyond the momentary irritations and puzzles. With both feet on the ground at the earliest stages of orientation and trust-building, it is good to consider what mutual benefits might arise from allowing interdependence to grow through its inevitable stages.

Stage 1. Orientation—Learning the Ropes

THE CHINESE	THE FOREIGNERS
Study the foreign company.	Consider market opportunities, technology, the Chinese company's performance, reputation, financial and growth potential, competitors, managers and their personalities, and the country.

Learning about Chinese culture and acquiring some understanding of the language are evidence of a beginning love affair with things Chinese. This allows one to become positive about the Chinese in a relatively short time.

Stage 2. Building Trust—Feeling Emotionally Secure

LEARNING TO TRUST FOREIGNERS	LEARNING TO TRUST THE CHINESE
■ Test their sincerity, honesty, suitability for long-term partnership. ■ Observe how they behave. ■ Assess how well they accept the country and its people.	■ Fit in with their ways. ■ Take a long-term perspective. ■ Make adequate introductions. ■ Explain one's technology, reputation. ■ Avoid argument and splitting hairs. ■ Create real friendships. ■ Be fair and honest. ■ Have no hidden agenda. ■ Socialize, get to know them.

At the individual level, trust can be built by being sympathetic, helpful, and thoughtful. By being patient and waiting for the Chinese to open up about issues, one shows that one has the skill to manage personal relationships across cultures. It can take the Chinese longer than people of some other cultures to develop a feeling of trust, and it depends on their seeing that one knows how to preserve people's face, expects no praise for what one does, and is sensitive to misunderstandings (things may not be what they seem).

Trust is built on a foundation of interdependence, which is the basis for joint ventures, strategic alliances, and successful transactions. As a relationship grows and builds on joint successes, a closer friendship and mutually respectful attitude develop. While trust may not be total, both sides will become increasingly comfortable with each other as mutual testing and evaluation continue, indicating that the basis for working together is widening and strengthening.

Stage 3. Growing Interdependence—Doing Things Together

THE FOREIGNERS—TOWARD INTERDEPENDENCE

- Manage, organize, and host exchange visits.
- Establish a policy about what the other side should or should not be told.
- Have home staff learn more about China and your (potential) China partner.
- Teach home staff to host visits, greet, and communicate with the Chinese.

The development of interdependence marks the beginning of doing business together; there is enough trust to trade, consider a joint venture, or create a strategic alliance to bring new technology to market.

The character of negotiations with the Chinese changes as a relationship grows. As we saw in this chapter's first case study, a seemingly unremarkable barbecue was an act of both genuine friendship and business professionalism at work. Business and private life, business and everyday culture overlap and are not in separate black boxes. The more one sees meetings with Chinese as deeply human and ordinary, the easier and more flowing relationships with them will become.

EFFECTIVE WORKPLACE COMMUNICATION

Understand how the other side communicates in terms of:

- Standard greetings.
- Courtesy.
- Avoidance of harsh words.
- Giving face.
- Anticipating what the other side thinks.
- Mutual unease.

While building trust with the Chinese, most foreign negotiators find themselves continually being reminded by their clients that price is the most important factor and competition is never far away. But once they start doing business together and become interdependent, many foreigners find that relationships start to feel secure and lead to introductions to other Chinese organizations and business opportunities—they are introduced to the Chinese client's network of business alliances. Becoming a friend of your partner's friend is a barometer of mutual trust and interdependence.

Foreigners have voiced their views regarding what is meant by interdependence in a number of ways. "In China, personal relationships cannot be separated from business relationships," one foreign manager told us. "When people become friends, companies become friends," said another. "The Chinese do not do business with people they don't know" and "The company and personal credibility are the same" are other sentiments we have heard. From these perspectives, through *guanxi* flow the networks of Chinese friendships that include the broad web of people, in business and government, whom one is always ready to ask for favors or to whose requests one readily responds.

At the operational level, experienced foreign managers conclude that the Chinese agenda is, generally, far simpler than that of either the Japanese or the South Koreans. With the Chinese, once the price has been settled, there is far less concern about quality or delivery and far less likelihood of renegotiation.

Stage 4. Familylike Relationships

By this stage, trust has been established, although this does not mean that there will be no more problems. Foreign managers enjoying familylike relationships with the Chinese identify the following characteristics:

RELATIONSHIP CHECKLIST	
▪ Effective meetings.	▪ The long-term sharing of profits and losses.
▪ Knowing correct techniques for gift giving.	▪ Total mutual trust.
▪ The sharing of corporate friends.	▪ Meetings like family gatherings.
▪ The good chemistry of all friendships.	▪ Aggression in some meetings.

Once interdependence starts to develop, a few foreign companies will work their way toward a familylike relationship with their Chinese partners. New attitudes and behaviors will be evident, including total trust, sharing of profits and losses (the most potent indicator of trust in business), deep friendship, meetings that have a familylike character, and the mutual incorporation of friends into the wider business networks (a major indicator of trust). The appearance of aggression may then be interpreted to mean that the Chinese side, now being family, feels able to express strong emotions that previously would have been suppressed.

The Face-Trust Stepping Stone

The Chinese seek to develop trust with companies that have a strong reputation and advanced technology, believing that this gives them face. Foreign managers working with the Chinese must learn to protect the face of Chinese managers. An example of how this might be done can be drawn from a Swedish joint venture in China.

At a staff meeting held after a new accounting system had been installed, the Chinese accountant commented that the new system was not sufficiently secure since an operator could easily change a customer's code. The Swedish financial appointee said nothing at the time, but a few days later discreetly pointed out to the accountant that the system was in fact secure. The Chinese then accepted this with no loss of face.

The point here is that the Swede recognized the importance of face and knew that under no circumstances should the Chinese accountant be challenged or corrected in front of others. This sensitivity and the resultant ability to operate effectively in the Chinese business world are necessary characteristics for those who would work with the Chinese.

Submitting Annual Tenders

A few foreign companies are involved in the annual submissions of tenders to supply commodities (such as coal) or products (such as plumbing supplies, can-sheet). Most foreign companies in this category have been dealing with China for many years and know their customers well.

All foreign companies taking part in the annual tendering for the supply of aluminum sheet for the can-making industries in China are involved in a series of meetings over a number of weeks. The participants include managing directors and purchasing directors on the Chinese side and divisional general managers on the other side.

The protocol for the annual series of meetings requires that the foreign companies submit their itinerary and proposed agenda in advance and wait for a response from the Chinese. That they have maintained relationships successfully for many years indicates that they have learned how to build and sustain trust and manage long-term relationships. To achieve that trust, they have been positive and committed, demonstrated sincerity and honesty with the Chinese over an extended period, and have never shown anger or frustration.

Ahead of each meeting, foreign companies (or their local China office, if they have one) sometimes have to undertake enormous preparations and detailed planning. To lend weight to their offers, foreign companies make sure one of their senior managers is in-country and always invite all senior Chinese decision makers and managers to meetings (if not invited, many would feel insulted). The foreigners attend all the banquets, New Year parties, other parties, and meetings to which they are invited, since these events offer otherwise rare opportunities to meet Chinese senior managers and senior government officials to whom access is not usually possible.

Those who have established joint ventures in China make it a point to invite representatives of every partner to visit the home country, at the foreign company's expense, to tour company facilities and production sites. The hosting of such visits is an important way to demonstrate trust and commitment to the Chinese.

Large Foreign Companies

Trust issues can be complex in business relationships involving extremely large companies. As a senior Canadian manager in Shanghai once put it: "The number one key to being successful in China is to have the Chinese like and trust you and believe you are offering the best deal for both them and their country." A study was conducted in 1994 and 1995 by Abramson and Ai (1996) of business relationship building by U.S. and Japanese companies in China. The researchers found that the Chinese respected the Japanese as masters of relationship building, since they know how to cooperate and gain cooperation. By contrast, the U.S. companies did not get high marks because the Chinese managers saw them as thinking of the bilateral relationship as dispensable and not permanent—or even long term.

For the Chinese, trust is severely damaged if a relationship is not cherished. Thus the U.S. companies that pulled out of deals at the time of the Tiananmen Square incident in 1989 have found it difficult to regain the trust of the Chinese, who had interpreted their withdrawal as the action of someone who is not a true friend. U.S. public criticism of China and Chinese leaders or policies also has deeply offended Chinese national pride.

One expatriate IT manager in China once spoke tellingly of what it takes for trust to be created. "It is a long process developing relationships. I was here six months before the Chinese even felt comfortable in my presence. It was nine months before there was a good relationship. Then I learned that there were issues related to managing the power structure here that the Chinese will not discuss with a foreigner. Western companies have to have local Chinese working for them who can network, build relationships, and get this information for you."

Losing Trust

Trust is brokered by many factors and is easily lost, as a foreign potash company in China discovered. It had been trading successfully in China for many years and believed that, since it had secured high market acceptance with a superior product, it could raise the price. The company began with an increase of only $5 a year, but sales began to slide. Its potash was red and so, in a country where red is considered a lucky color, the company had incorrectly thought it had a market advantage. Because Chinese customers believed that the company had increased the price just to boost profits, relationships and trust were seriously damaged.

When in Rome

Some foreigners consider the Chinese way of managing to be backward and inferior, particularly the Chinese insistence on keeping their superiors in the loop of ongoing discussions. These foreigners believe that advising and consulting superiors slows decision making enormously. But that is the way things are done in China.

It should not be forgotten that almost all Chinese partners are government organizations, working within a centrally controlled political and administrative system. The structure is bureaucratic, conservative, and generally more than foreigners can fathom. With each level asking the next one up for directions before making a decision, clearly even a whiff of condescension in a foreigner's behavior can drastically sour the atmosphere of a meeting.

Trust in the Marketplace

Out of the meeting rooms and away from the negotiation tables, trust is a major factor for Chinese merchandisers. The events described below speak for themselves about the speed with which Chinese may be offended, feel they are being treated badly, or believe their face is threatened.

 CASE STUDY FRIENDSHIP AND TRUST IN SHANGHAI

OVERVIEW

In September 2002, the Japan Broadcasting Corp. (NHK), a national broadcasting network, reported on the attempt by an NEC manager, Suzuki Haruo, to sell off one of the company's slightly older model mobile phones in the Chinese market. Suzuki was a typical late-thirties salaried employee moving on the fast track. It is likely that his boss in Tokyo had given him this job to see if Suzuki had what it takes to progress up the company ladder.

FIRST STEPS

In the NHK footage, Suzuki finds himself first of all in a huge electronics superstore in downtown Shanghai. Competitors such as Nokia and Motorola have meters of shelf space and seem to have garnered a high level of acceptance with Chinese consumers. Suzuki notices that, at the NEC counter, the sales staff look sick. Stock is not moving and the local staff are unmoved and poker-faced as Suzuki and his underlings from Tokyo try to ham it up for the NHK cameras.

RIPTIDE

Not to appear downhearted, Suzuki then speaks with the mobile phone division of China's largest telephone company about the benefits of NEC's slightly older and chunkier mobile phones. His presentation is in English and he is flogging this dead horse for all he's worth. He puts his hand into his bag and brings out the phone just long enough for the locals to catch just a glimpse. But that is enough for Xu Yan, a young Chinese female manager. She goes ballistic.

"You sell smaller, newer ones in Japan. Bring us your new models. We don't want this old-fashioned one. Do you think Chinese consumers are stupid or inferior to Japanese consumers? Why don't you bring the new phones? You should remember that we have a very big market here ... [and so on]."

Suzuki says nothing, but he clearly seems to be regretting having invited an NHK camera crew to follow him around Shanghai. From a cultural perspective, he is also pretty shaken, because in Japan the other party in a business discussion would never be so openly hostile.

CALM AFTER THE STORM

Three days later, it's a lovefest. Suzuki is back meeting the same people in the same place. Only the atmosphere is different. At last someone seems to have done their homework at NEC, which has decided to market its latest model G3 phone in China. Now Xu is smiling broadly, and calling Suzuki "my old friend." Now Suzuki is a hero.

DON'T BETRAY TRUST

This story is typical of what happens in China. It could apply to any foreign businessperson in Shanghai. Had Suzuki done his homework, it could have been a lovefest from the beginning. Suzuki, the clever man that he is, probably will not make the same mistake again—and certainly not on public television. Life is interesting in China!

A World Away from Trust

Most of the foreign businesspeople with whom I have spoken and who deal with the Chinese say that the Chinese are honest and there is little corruption. One person, however, told of a plumbing-products supplier that negotiates multimillion-dollar contracts annually and expects red envelopes (*hong bao*, which children receive each New Year from their father and other relatives), which in the adult world means under-the-table payments. Even so, the payments only guarantee that the giver will be considered for the contract, not be awarded it.

Some prospective Chinese buyers demand proprietary information—on technology, production techniques, manufacturing costs, wages, and conditions. One company currently works through an agent who knows China well, but it plans to build a manufacturing facility in China, believing that this will offer greater business security.

Another difficulty when working with the Chinese is the belief, held by many middle managers, that they can only wield power in an organization if they control information. Thus, a story is told about particular middle managers who, before going on holiday, lock their desks and so prevent people from accessing important, needed information.

Yet another story in the same vein concerns an up-country joint venture. When the company's one and only computer broke down, it was taken for repair to Beijing, an eight-hour drive away, to protect the information on the hard disc from local prying eyes. Since the computer repairman was on holidays for a week, however, the computer was taken back to the countryside and returned to Beijing a week later.

ANOTHER KIND OF TRUST—KARMA

Most Chinese believe that sharing karma (we translate the Chinese word *yuan* 缘 as karma) with anyone (including foreigners) favors a long-term relationship.

The word is of Buddhist origin, and it suggests that any event has occurred as a result of one's deeds, accumulated over many lifetimes. The belief that one has a shared destiny can arise when meeting someone for the first time. If the Chinese talk about a shared fate, it means that they feel comfortable with you and sense that the meeting was not accidental but was meant to have occurred.

Some educated Chinese consider the idea of karma mere superstition, but it is important to recognize that most of those you will encounter and with whom you will discuss business will have a sense of whether you and they have a relationship that was "meant to be." Should business or interpersonal troubles arise between you, the sense of this karma will weaken. But if they do feel that the relationship is karmic, you can be sure that they will take a responsible attitude, and the stronger the feeling, the deeper their sense of responsibility.

Relationships Minus Communication

This brings up a point of major difference compared to the West, where relationships are seen as shaped by and developed through interpersonal communication. As we share information, relationships become closer. However, communication does not strike the Chinese—especially those who feel there is a karmic dimension to a relationship—as being a major tool for solving relationship issues.

Since they do not regard communication strategies as essential for working on relationships, they are more willing to tolerate dysfunctional relationships, in the belief that no one can force a relationship to improve. Relationships, they believe, have to develop in their own, natural way. In business, they distinguish between interpersonal and business dimensions and decide on which aspects of the differences they will work and which they will leave for Nature to process.

A common Chinese saying is: "If you have karma with one another, though you are thousands of miles apart, you will still meet. If you don't have karma, you will never know each other even if you come face to face." Hence, the Chinese don't look for the reason a relationship fails to blossom; they believe that a relationship will not deepen unless there is karma. Should a close relationship fail, those involved are likely to say, "We probably didn't have karma."

That said, while karma may suffice for there to be warm personal relationships, it is not enough for intercompany business relationships. In that case, the Chinese require your company to have an international reputation, and you to be an astute businessperson who catches on quickly to how business is done in their country and who has far-reaching contacts, an excellent reputation, and the ability to advance their business.

HOW TO BUILD TRUST WITH CHINESE MANAGERS ABROAD

If you live in a large, international city outside of China, there will probably be an expatriate mainland Chinese community. You may meet some of its members or even have the opportunity to develop relationships or do business with some of them. They will have been posted to serve overseas for some years as a manager in their local branch office, subsidiary, consulate, or other organization.

Many Chinese expatriates play their cards close to the chest, do not trust many people, and are particularly careful not to put a foot wrong while abroad. The reason is that any mistake might lead to adverse comments being recorded in their personal files back at their work unit in China.

Can you help them when they are abroad, living in your country? It will depend partly on what seeds of friendship flourish between you. The fact that many have a strong fear of getting a bad report card while abroad can make them very guarded and prevent genuine friendship from developing. Problems are also exacerbated by the limitations of their English. Answering the following questions will help foreign managers to be more insightful, and—who knows?—become better, more understanding friends with Chinese expatriates.

THE EXPAT CHINESE	THE FOREIGNERS
First time abroad?	If it is, they may struggle for some time to adjust to the strange new world of your country.
Family not adjusting well?	The Chinese wife might be the one suffering from adjustment problems.
Poor English?	This may be a bigger problem than you can imagine.
Never wanted to come in the first place?	You shouldn't ask a direct question about this, but it shouldn't be difficult to work out the answer.
Square peg in a round hole?	He or she may simply not be suited to their post.
No friends here?	This does happen. It might be due to the paucity of Chinese expatriates in your city, the lack of shared interests or similar background, or some other issue.
Left unresolved issues at home?	If so, the issues may be family related.
Beijing head office makes all decisions?	Sometimes head office reserves the right to make all the decision, even if it manifestly misunderstands local conditions.
Can't get on with local people?	Some expatriates with no international experience misread the local people, soon developing fears and prejudices.
Personality problems?	As with every nationality, some Chinese are unsuited to working abroad.

When we lived in Sydney, Australia, there were one hundred or more mainland Chinese expatriates living there. Like everyone else who lives abroad, these people experienced issues of cultural adjustment and culture shock, and as a result it was usually difficult for them to trust the locals. Early on, they might ask local people for help, but as they settled in and met other expatriates, they would gradually come to rely on them for support and advice rather than on the local people.

Of course, you should never ask people if they have problems. To do so would threaten them with loss of face. But astute observation, indirect questioning, or asking those with whom they are working should provide ample pointers. It is important to assume a supportive, friendly attitude and not to pry. You should be kind, sympathetic, helpful, and friendly, treating them as individuals both at work and in private life. If you are a supplier, think of yourself as a service person.

WHAT TO DO	HOW TO DO IT
Wait for them to open up.	Don't push, probe, or prod. They may be shy and need to be given time and space. Be ready to accept that they may never fully open up to you. (See chapter 13 on composure, and the discussion on dealing with shy Chinese.)
Build trust on a long-term basis.	Think of them as friends for the next thirty years, not as temporary appointees. But don't be hypocritical or overdo it. Build your own long-term network. Your good Chinese friends may one day become your guardian angels who, when they are senior managers, may give you advice and support when you need it. While in your home country, they may well see you as their guardian angel.
Preserve everyone's face.	Don't criticize or accuse people, either to their face or behind their back. Always preserve a good, friendly atmosphere.
Don't expect praise or enthusiasm.	Your successes, efforts, or proposals will not be praised. It's not their way. Expect misunderstandings. They certainly will.

China has a highly centralized society, with power and decision making in the hands of the leaders—of governments, organizations, companies, and families. Moreover, it has a low-trust culture, meaning that those outside your group are not trusted.

In order to get along in Chinese society, one must preserve the face of others, display good manners, and know how to negotiate. Building trust is regarded as a highly important skill that is exercised prudently over time. People who talk a great deal are regarded suspiciously and not trusted.

At the interpersonal level, the process of building trust is much the same in China as in other cultures. Consider how trust is built in private life in your country. You meet someone with similar or complementary interests. A sense of compatibility soon emerges. You meet periodically and this sense is reinforced. Eventually, trust and compatibility build to the point where you both agree to do something together, such as see a movie, go to the races, or watch a football game. This first shared activity represents a significant increase in trust. If there are further joint activities, you may reach the point at which something more intimate, trusting, or long-term is considered. If it is a boy-girl relationship, the next step may be meeting the other party's family. If it is in business, the next move may be a joint activity, such as a transaction, discussion of a joint venture, or a joint investment.

If you think back to how you have developed a trusting relationship on the personal level, you will recognize what it takes to build trust in business dealings with the Chinese. You do not start off saying anything analogous to "sex now, trust later," "meet my mother right away," or "buy this incredible bargain now." That is what salespeople or con men are expected to do. Some salesman-type foreigners seem to believe that they can talk this way to the Chinese. Not true.

BUILDING TRUST IN CHINA

Based on what we know of ordinary trust building, we can say that the first steps in building a genuine relationship with the Chinese ought to be the following:

- Learn as much as you can about the organization and the members you are to face. Do so, for example, by talking with commercial attachés, informed people who may be long-term residents in China, specialists on China, or foreign companies that already do business with the Chinese company.

■ Do some preliminary study and read about China and the organization with which you are dealing.

■ During the first meeting, try to put each other at ease.

■ Judge whether you are comfortable with each other.

■ Assess what needs you have that the other party might satisfy.

■ Decide if you want to become more involved with the Chinese company and individually with your counterpart.

It might take several meetings for these first steps to be completed. In the meantime, your team ought to be concerned about the key questions of whether you can trust your Chinese counterparts and they can trust you—in both instances for the long haul.

If you have an analytical bent, you might consider assessing each of the other party's members on such aspects as: trustworthiness, integrity, traditional honorableness (never breaks a promise, is genuinely modest and polite), stability of background (the number of jobs held, extent of occupational mobility), personal versus corporate motivation (out to feather his own nest versus keeping the corporate good utmost in mind), and involvement in internal factional politics.

Ratings for these factors should yield enough material to permit an initial overall assessment of each individual's trustworthiness and, finally, the trustworthiness of the team and, perhaps, even the entire corporation.

This exercise will often lead to differences of judgment among the members of your team. You will find a lot of value in testing your judgment at an outside meeting with a China business specialist. He or she will introduce additional considerations—hypotheses about what else might be on the Chinese hidden agenda—that might help speed up your team's learning process. If you find a China specialist you can trust, use them often.

CAN THE CHINESE TRUST YOU?

The main thrust of this chapter has been to suggest how you can establish trust in the Chinese mind—where it is always the uppermost consideration.

You are assessed, scrutinized, and summed up as an individual by the Chinese far more often than you might expect. In the process, they will ask themselves the following three key questions:

1. Is the foreigner a warm human being or a cold, distant business-person?

One Chinese friend, who deals with people of many different nationalities in the Asia-Pacific region, once said: "Our relationships with Canadians and Australians are warm and friendly, but Americans, especially New Yorkers, are too cold and businesslike for us."

2. Can this foreigner manage to deal with us over the long term?

"We ask so many questions, and make things so difficult, that most foreigners find dealing with us very trying. Can we trust them to be here long term? Ours is still a developing country, and we lack the everyday small luxuries of advanced economies. Will they eventually give up and go back home where things are predictable and secure?"

3. Can he figure out how our social system works, and then accept it?

One of the prerequisites of being honorable in China is to keep promises. That said, sometimes in China senior managers give junior managers briefs without specifying the limits regarding what can be offered.

Let's suppose a junior is advised merely to welcome an important visitor and make him feel at home, without being given any specific guidelines or limits. Whatever the visitor asks for, according to Chinese etiquette, the junior is expected to provide.

Thus, were the visitor to say: "I want to stay in the imperial suite at the guesthouse over the weekend. Is that okay?" the junior in China would be unable to say anything except "yes." He might later tell a senior official about this, to which the senior might reply angrily, "Impossible. We have the Party secretary coming on the weekend." The junior would then have the unpleasant task of telling the visitor that he cannot keep his promise.

To foreigners, whether Chinese promises can be kept or not is a mystery, but the best advice we can give is to question any promise. Promises made by the Chinese are most likely to be kept when made by the CEO.

MAIN POINTS OF CHAPTER 9

- ❑ Nothing is possible without trust. Critical and earned, it is shown to exist by shared experience and as a result of testing for sincerity, honesty, and dedication.

- ❑ Negotiations can be strung out over a great many meetings, so one must learn patience and how to give the Chinese face, use a third party trusted by both sides whenever possible, and use interpreters to ensure mutual understanding.

- ❑ Foreigners should not be too direct or confrontational. Instead of saying "no," they might say "Let's look at this issue later." Conflict and misunderstanding can be minimized by deferring contentious issues and ensuring that one's actions do not cause the Chinese to lose face.

- ❑ There should be flexibility, restraint, and calm throughout negotiations. Post-contract negotiations are often closer to continuous improvement than unethical behavior.

- ❑ Trust building begins early in the development of a relationship with a Chinese organization. One should be kind, sympathetic, and patient, and allow the Chinese to take their time to open up, thereby preserving everyone's face.

- ❑ Once a trusting business relationship has been established, either or both sides may introduce the other party to their business friends, as a result of which further business may result.

- ❑ Over the long term, trust between Chinese and foreign parties can flower into a familylike relationship, as part of which they may share profits and losses, recommend and share corporate friends, and trust one another completely.

- ❑ Once the trust of the Chinese is lost, it is hard to retrieve. U.S. companies that pulled out of China after the Tiananmen Square incident in 1989 found it difficult to regain trust.

- ❑ Many Chinese believe that relationships depend on shared destiny (karma). If one feels a shared fate with someone, the Chinese believe, one can easily weather communication difficulties.

- ❑ When the Chinese you are dealing with is an expatriate living in your country, be particularly careful to understand his situation. It is probably far more complex than you imagine.

CHAPTER
10

COACHING NEGOTIATORS
IN STRATEGIC SKILLS

There are many options when preparing to negotiate with Chinese in China: read a book or two about China; attend a session given by a professional trainer knowledgeable about China and learn how they negotiate there; or take advice from people such as China-born Chinese who also understand your culture well.

Some people go to China without any special training, on a wing and a prayer, or with a book to read on the plane. The options chosen depend on past experience, the potential difficulties, and how much one trusts one's Chinese counterpart. Unfortunately, incorporating a China negotiation coach in one's team or preparations seems to be the least-used option. Not a good idea.

TRAINING SPELLED "COACHING"

The value of training or coaching depends on the past experience and self-confidence of the negotiator or team. Peter Benjamin, the successful brewery designer in the first case in chapter 3, had had a wealth of previous successes as an international negotiator. Essentially self-trained, he employed ethnic Chinese professionals in his business and used their counsel wisely. He was in the first place an exceptional person, who at age twenty-five had designed and built a chemical factory in Ireland for a blue-chip U.S. company. By the time the Chinese approached him to submit a proposal for a brewery in China (in competition with European brewery designers), he had developed a chemical engineering consultancy in Australia that had a worldwide reputation.

Only a few people can be stars like Benjamin. Most of us benefit in the beginning from participating in a focused training course. Although by the time Benjamin was invited to negotiate with the Chinese he was already an experienced, successful international negotiator, he lacked experience in China. So he needed—and received—both ad hoc training and coaching from his Chinese staff.

In our view, both coaching and training are needed for major negotiations with the Chinese. Most of us are familiar with the concept and practice of training, but what does coaching involve? A report from one of our China coaching sessions makes clear what coaching is and how it differs from training.

An established negotiator or negotiating team that is uncertain how effectively it can negotiate with the Chinese should consider working with a professional China negotiation coach. While every case is different, the following report relates work we did to coach Russell Finn, an experienced metals marketing manager who was new to China.

Coaching BRASS TACKS

Finn asked us to provide him with one-on-one coaching to prepare him for his first meeting with the Chinese Smelter Group (CSG). He had earlier attended one of our two-day training courses, titled "Negotiating with the Chinese," but still felt vulnerable facing CSG for the first time. He invited us to work with him because his predecessor was unavailable to brief him.

The coaching session started with us seated about three meters apart at each end of a long conference table in a large meeting room. That was a deliberate choice to see how he would handle the wide psychological distance. Finn began speaking in a small, hesitant voice, and his body was slightly slumped, as though saying, "This is a bit much for me."

He spoke of his concern about dealing with the Chinese. Early in the session, he used the passive rather than active voice, making such comments as, "Could this sort of thing be said?" We suggested that he use instead the active voice and be positive—saying, for example, "I want to say...." Using the passive voice sounds bureaucratic, and many Chinese could be confused about the point being made. Besides, we said, he would feel more in charge of both himself and the situation were he to use only the active voice.

We asked him how he was going to prepare, and initially he had no clear idea, no point of departure. We had him focus his mind on the first meeting, on who would be there, the personalities of the participants, and how the meeting was likely to unfold.

A senior Chinese manager had told him by e-mail that it would be an informal meeting with no agenda, presumably to put him at his ease. But he felt exactly the opposite. We could see that he seemed terrified of entering an unstructured meeting with people he had never met and who, he believed, would have no particular interest in him.

The first hour was spent focusing Finn on the idea of having an agenda that suited his need for security and predictability. If he could get the Chinese to agree to an agenda for the first meeting, it would be a small victory in the process of the Chinese taking him seriously. His reaction was predictable: "But what if they are offended by me asking for an agenda, when they've never used one before?"

We suggested an idea he found novel. "Use your inexperience to advantage. Be apologetic and insist on an agenda, say that you will feel incapable of contributing to the meeting if you are not forewarned." He intuitively grasped the approach. They would appreciate him showing his "true feelings" and being honest about his inexperience.

We then worked on the items for the agenda, beginning with the Chinese briefing him on the way they did business as a smelter group and then the precedents and practices that had been developed in similar meetings in the past. Together we created an agenda.

ROLE PLAYING

Finn was now feeling a little more confident, but he wondered what he would do if the Chinese refused to use an agenda. So, from this point on, we set up some hypothetical Chinese demands and rejections and explained how he could respond to them.

CHINESE: We do not need an agenda.
FINN: An agenda will help me understand the business relationship you have had with us for many years. I can then understand the matters of importance.

CHINESE: No, no, just a friendly chat. An agenda is not necessary between friends.
FINN: I am just the new boy on the block, and know nothing. Please advise me how to have more effective meetings

with you and reach better agreements. Please be my teachers.

We advised him to use such responses in the belief that the Chinese would feel obliged to help someone so inexperienced. They did, eventually, agree to an agenda.

On the question of metal price, Finn knew that the Chinese market price was set by the industry's No. 1 company, and that the rest of the market, including his own company, followed. Finn didn't know how he would handle price demands, so we supplied some alternative responses to hypothetical questions to give him a greater feeling of control.

> CHINESE: Let's cut to the chase. What figures do you have in mind?
>
> FINN: I have been looking forward to this meeting to exchange ideas and information with you, but it is premature for a small player like us to suggest a figure ahead of the big miners. But it seems very appropriate that we exchange estimates of supply and demand over the next two years so we can reach a better understanding.

Alternatively, we suggested that Finn could reply: Our company will look closely at the marketplace, particularly at what the big miners do. We will be guided partly by what they do. Or: It is too early for us—perhaps in a few weeks we can reply.

We suggested that, when market intelligence was discussed, a dialogue might go as follows:

> CHINESE: The market will be in oversupply soon (and hence prices will fall).
>
> FINN: I am tempted to draw the same conclusion. However, twelve months ago people were saying the same thing and, as we know, it didn't happen. So we feel we must be more skeptical about price fluctuation over the next year or so. We have learned many things from the Chinese. One is that when market intelligence is unclear, it is better to assume that everything will remain the same.

Many Chinese make a virtue of assuming that things will remain the same, we told Finn, so foreigners should take advantage of this. He knew that the Chinese had clear-cut goals: to buy the best quality copper concentrate agreed on and to negotiate for favorable delivery terms at the lowest possible price. But he did not know what tactics they would use at this meeting. We suggested he speak in general terms and not make any immediate offers (see the comprehensive opening statement explained in chapter 11).

We also suggested that, were he intimidated by any Chinese questions, he should repeat the question back to them using different words and asking if that was correct. Or, he could say he didn't quite understand and ask them to rephrase the question. This is an important tactic when dealing with non-native speakers of a language, because a question or statement that might sound aggressive often turns out to have a quite different intent or meaning.

GENERAL ADVICE

1. "The Chinese will probably praise and flatter you, your company, and your country, and that might induce you to do them more favors than under ordinary circumstances," we said. We praised and flattered him in ways that Chinese might. We praised the national character of his countrymen, his company's successes, then the sweetness of his temperament, his good looks, intelligence, impeccable manners, straightforwardness and honesty, and so on. He got the message quickly that he should not be affected by praise or flattery, but let them roll off him like water off a duck's back.

2. The Chinese would be very well prepared for the meeting with him, we stressed. Therefore, at the first meeting at least, he should repeat what was, in any case, true—his ignorance of past events meant he could only be humble, ask questions, and refer significant questions back to his boss. At the same time, the Chinese questions and statements would alert him to what their main concerns were.

3. He would be taking an interpreter from his company's Shanghai office and should have a prior session with her about this preparation and what he wanted her to observe and evaluate during the meeting.

He would later want to know, for instance, were his opposite number to make a promsie or give an opinion, what merit it had: whether it was an off-the-cuff comment of no substance or whether it had some significance and, if so, what that was.

4. We emphasized the importance of his self-introduction at the beginning. He should, we advised, write out and practice a short self-introduction, about his background and his family. For instance, he could start with his family name. His ancestors came from Ireland and, from the tenth century, were aristocrats and warriors in Donegal. His given name, Russell, is also Irish and means someone with red hair (Finn does have red hair). The Chinese would be intrigued and pleased with this romantic detail. We advised him to include in his self-introduction where he had grown up, his education, his family today (he should take some family photos to show them), his present job, and what interests him about China. "Don't make a speech—be crisp and confident," we added. "Two or three minutes will be fine. But be sure to rehearse it."

5. We told him to learn the names of everyone in the CSG team and to get help in pronouncing their names correctly. Be ready to ask each of them about their own lives and backgrounds.

6. While making friends with the Chinese, he should not believe everything they told him, we said. A part of being Chinese is to preserve one's face, even between man and wife. So saying something that would offend them or make them look bad is a no-no among the Chinese. If you want a long-term relationship with the Chinese, you need to learn this rule quickly. It is the hardest of all lessons for non-Chinese to learn.

7. Finally, we advised Finn to be on the lookout for misunderstandings, both on his part and on that of the Chinese. In the early stages, we suggested, he should make notes of their questions or statements and take his time to reply. If any word or phrase was unclear to him, then he should ask them to say that word (or statement) another way.

COACHING IN SUMMARY

The above case shows two reasons coaching and training cannot be combined. First, coaching requires focus and concentration on one individual, while one could train ten people simultaneously in the same group. Second, coaching is very personal, and the feedback will only be acceptable if it is private, just "between the two of us." Had others been present when we met with Finn, we believe he would have both been on his best behavior and clammed up about many things, while we probably would not have pursued some of the more sensitive questions.

With adequate coaching, negotiators acquire the strategic skills that enable them to overcome the characteristic (and possibly endemic) problems that arise at each stage of negotiations.

Yet the effectiveness of coaching depends on the basic temperament and the interpersonal skills of an individual, as well as on the extent of the individual's past negotiating experience and what has been learned.

Peter Benjamin (chapter 3) was the leader of his team and had a wealth of successful negotiating experience. Still, he had to call on his team of Chinese colleagues for culture-based coaching.

The bottom line in coaching, we suggest, is that an individual to be coached must want the coaching. Many people reject coaching, finding it threatening. Participants can be highly sensitive to and cautious about feedback, even when it is constructive.

Coaching is also feasible for negotiation teams once they are established, the members are comfortable with one another, and they have a leader who is respected by his team. Effective team coaching, however, frequently comes down to coaching the team leader, and so is similar in principle to individual coaching. The situation is most comfortable when the leader asks for coaching. We have faced situations where we went beyond coaching to act as stage directors—that is, we stepped in and advised the leader to do this or not do that. This has invariably occurred when a team is in actual negotiation with the Chinese over a period of time, and we have seen some problem emerging that urgently needed to be corrected. The relationship between the company, the team leader, and the coach needs a high level of trust for this to be effective and acceptable.

Main Points of Chapter 10

- Coaching helps negotiators handle the wide psychological distance between Chinese and foreign teams, develop confidence, take charge of negotiations, and overcome the characteristic problems that occur at each stage of negotiations.

- If one feels intimidated by any Chinese questions, one should repeat them back to the Chinese using different words and ask if that is correct.

- Advance preparation is necessary before all meetings. One should not succumb to praise and flattery, which might induce one to make too many concessions to the other party.

- A well-prepared, well-rehearsed self-introduction is important to start off a first-time meeting.

- Learn the names of everyone in the Chinese team and get help in pronouncing the names correctly.

- Be on the lookout for misunderstandings on both sides. In the early stages, it is a good idea to make notes of the other side's questions and statements and to take one's time when replying.

- Coaching is also feasible for negotiation teams. Team coaching, however, frequently comes down to coaching the team leader, and so is similar in principle to individual coaching.

CHAPTER
11

THE TWELVE-STEP PROCESS
FOR PLANNING NEGOTIATIONS

Negotiating involves a series of events over which you may have little or no control. Yet, as you meet the same Chinese team members repeatedly, your expertise will build and a hybrid culture may eventually develop—not entirely Chinese, not entirely your own—involving you and your counterparts that will lessen your feelings of uncertainty.

FOUR SIMPLE RULES

The first two of the most basic rules that any negotiator must bear in mind are:

1. *Always be thoroughly prepared,* and
2. *Always remain composed.*

Without composure (the subject of chapter 13), you are prey to tactics of the other side designed to put you off balance and shred your self-control.

Having the magical resource of time on your side of course helps enormously. It is essential for problem solving, review, and insight development. Related to the use of time are two more rules by which a negotiator should abide:

3. *Never put yourself under pressure,* and
4. *Take whatever time you need to process, understand, and respond to the events occurring around you.*

The following chapters are a platform for first steps that will be personalized as you become increasingly professional.

UNPREPARED AMATEURS

How do people who have no prior international experience or training and who lack a systematic approach generally negotiate with the Chinese (or any other foreign teams)?

Any group that lacks an agenda and a knowledgeable leader will roam all over the place, while talking about what strategy and tactics they ought to adopt. Without an experienced leader, such discussions lead to annoyance, irritation, and barely veiled competition among team members to dominate and lead the group. In fact, even *with* an experienced leader, there occasionally will be competition among individuals for recognition by the leader or others. Certainly a group lacking effective leadership goes off the rails very easily.

Weaknesses at Each Step

We have identified six main negotiating stages—prenegotiation, opening moves, bargaining, complications, revitalization, and agreement—in order to more easily highlight common problems, mistakes, and misunderstandings that we have been observing since 1985.

PRENEGOTIATION PROBLEMS

- Totally inadequate preparation.

- Inappropriate spokesperson chosen.

- Insufficient informal contact with the other side.

- Agenda not well handled, or nonexistent.

- Key words misunderstood.

- Negotiation background misunderstood.

- Decision makers not identified.

- Cultural differences not recognized or discussed.

Mistakes made in the prenegotiation stage become the seeds of most subsequent mistakes during the actual negotiations. They often lead to ineffective, confused leadership and eventual failure to reach agreement.

OPENING MOVES PROBLEMS

- Mutual understanding of terms, background not checked.

- Each side's needs, interests, problems, style not defined before bargaining starts.

- Eventualities unexpected.

- Chinese kept at arm's length as they try to socialize.

- Composure lacking; suspicion and some fear shown.

Unlike pleasurable meetings between strangers, on these unantici-pated or unarranged occasions, neither side shows pleasure at meeting the other side nor any indication of interest. A good atmosphere does not unfold, and the uneasy foreigner sees only poker-faced Chinese chain-smoking and sipping tea from lidded mugs. Although it is likely that they are looking their visitors over with real interest, few foreigners would guess that from the expressions on their faces.

Thus, many foreign visitors new to China (who have not yet had a chance to see the shining face behind the poker face at a boozy ban-quet) might well be thinking that they would rather be somewhere else. Or, had these visitors attended a banquet on the previous evening, they may well think that the people they had met there—who were warm and friendly then—are now like gnomes.

BARGAINING STAGE PROBLEMS

- Hard-sell approach.

- Too many people speaking at once.

- Much jockeying for position.

- Don't understand real interests of the other side.

- Impulsive changes in offers and proposals.

To go directly to bargaining and skimp on introductions and small talk, as many inexperienced Westerners are prone to do, is to rob the scene of a sense of human drama. This shocks the Chinese. It flouts their cultural expectations and etiquette.

Foreigners probably do this in the belief that the Chinese just love to bargain—and that's the end of it. They may imagine going to China to eat some good Chinese food, bargain, strike a deal, pick up some souve-nirs, and happily return home to tell their friends how smart they were.

Quite apart from not taking into account cultural differences or the need to foster friendship, such behavior fails to put the issue or product in its proper setting, where buyer and seller can pass the early mile-stones of getting to know one another and begin to trust one another.

Yet the Chinese are not entirely blameless in these matters. Many Chinese teams fail either to take a larger view of negotiations or to understand the cultural nuances of the way foreigners negotiate.

WHEN COMPLICATIONS SET IN

- Lose composure, balance.
- Stop listening.
- Lecture the other side.
- Aggression or avoidance based on perceived offense.
- Ignorance of the other party's changed behavior and attitudes.

The ill-prepared easily run into complications because one or both sides inadvertently have been rubbing each other the wrong way from the moment they met. Some negotiators handle problems and conflicts masterfully. But awkwardness, unease, and misunderstandings that occur right from the start result in complications—people misunderstanding each other, losing their composure, or becoming irritable or aggressive.

Many negotiators fail to develop beyond this stage, because the composure or personal balance of team members has been well and truly shredded by the lack of effective team leadership and management, and because the members hold negative views of the other party when what matters becomes interpersonally complicated. Thus, sooner or later, one or both parties may realize that the only solution is to have a cooling-off period during which the parties refrain from contacting each other for a day or a month—or indefinitely.

REVITALIZATION—STARTING OVER AGAIN

- Reassessment of stalled progress.
- Private discussions held with other party.
- Review of team structure, strategies, and leadership.
- Apologies and reconciliation.
- Conflicts and misunderstandings are resolved.
- Empathy is displayed.

People on either side with good conflict-resolution skills can pull negotiations into peaceful waters and help effect a win-win agreement. But not all negotiations proceed to agreement. Many fail to move beyond the complications stage, while revitalization, when attempted, might take months or years. Changes of leadership and personnel sometimes help achieve revitalization.

COUNTERING FLAWS AND FAULTS

The twelve-step negotiation process is the counterfoil to inept negotiations. It is a strategic tool like a cockpit checklist, itemizing the essential ideas, procedures, and protocol. It allows mistakes to be identified and remedied; it obviates misunderstandings, misperceptions, and other common missteps. It is the antithesis of chaotic brainstorming that results from a lack of leadership and team structure.

If you have no prior experience and are accustomed to spending your time devising sharp negotiation strategies, the following steps may seem counterintuitive. Be warned: *our* view is different. We know that *in*experienced and *non*professional international negotiators lack a systematic approach when they begin negotiating. They do need the help of a systematic tool like the twelve-step process.

Using a pocket-sized checklist (see table on next page) of the process keeps everyone focused on the same goals and procedures and reassures the team, enabling it to organize preparation and build confidence, thereby bonding the members. Some senior managers who are always engaged in meetings and negotiations with Asians even carry the checklist in their wallets.

OUTLINE OF TWELVE-STEP PLANNING PROCESS	
Organize the Team	1. Select the team leader. 2. Select the team members. 3. Assign roles to each member.
Analyze Thoroughly	4. Decide on the issues that are to be negotiated; table all relevant documents. 5. Study all factors affecting the scope of the negotiations, including history of the marketplace, the relationship, and other external influences. 6. Ensure common understanding of every item in step 5. 7. Assess mutual strengths, weaknesses; set goals, strategies, initial position. (i) Why do you choose that position? Is it tenable, defensible? (ii) You appreciate that you will not hint of your position until the comprehensive opening statement has been presented—right?
Make Final Preparations	8. Prepare, rehearse comprehensive opening statement. 9. Write out questions to be asked and who will ask them.
Develop an Agenda	10. Draw up own agenda; negotiate final version with other party.
Decide Protocol, Procedures	11. Draw up protocol, list procedures, appoint a secretary to help and support participants. Preparations should include: (i) Host checklist (meeting room, meeter, greeter, introductions); (ii) Opening welcome (remarks, introductions, seating, refreshments, small talk); (iii) Preamble to business of the day (meeting arrangements, breaks, messages, services and facilities).
Open the Meeting for Business	12. Negotiations so far, general items, other party's comments. (i) Discuss agenda items. (ii) Each side presents comprehensive opening statement. (iii) End meeting, review progress. (iv) Post-meeting initiatives. (v) Decide how minutes, reports are to be prepared.

ORGANIZE THE TEAM

Step 1. Select the Team Leader

The twelve-step negotiation process cannot be put into practice until a leader has been chosen and the team formed. From our experience with hundreds of negotiators in more than ten countries, we can say confidently that the best-led teams are the most professional. The best-led are also those that have been led from the beginning.

The best leaders take the view that each team member should understand all the nuances and information about the topic of the negotiation. With experience, leaders soon understand that the team must be multi-skilled, not mono-skilled—that is, not comprise solely engineers or marketers or accountants.

In flat organizations, the leader may be decided by age, as is often the case in China. Elsewhere, it is usually the most senior manager. Should that manager not have—and not recognize that they lack—the skills base to manage effectively a negotiating team in China, polite jockeying may be needed to get the best person into the role.

It is also better for the roles and focus of each member to be decided at the beginning. The leader should lead this discussion and ensure that all members understand their roles at the outset.

Step 2. Select the Team Members

We use two methods to choose and develop teams, depending on the number of candidates. The first approach—the pool approach—assumes that we are putting together a team for the first time from a large pool of candidates (say, twelve or more from a number of countries) to select a final team of, say, five people. The second approach—the selected-team approach—assumes a team of at least five people exists or already has been selected.

THE POOL APPROACH

The first step is to identify candidates with the right attitudes and interest to negotiate with Chinese. These attitudes can include being diplomatic; not being a lone wolf; being able to cooperate well with others in the team; controlling one's competitive drive so that it barely outweighs one's spirit of cooperation; not being a bigot; having reasonable social skills; having some role flexibility (can be a genuine presenter, listener, or socializer, as the situation calls for); and being a good team player who follows instructions.

Teams that have been formed already, and the members of which have experience working together, can be evaluated by being required to undertake role-play negotiations against teams playing the role of a Chinese team. This is done in the presence of a coach and experienced monitors who provide detailed feedback to the team and each individual. The teams can then be introduced to the twelve-step process, on the basis of which they can reorganize their negotiating techniques and operating methods.

Step 3. Assign Roles to Each Member

Skill diversity is essential. Ideally, a team will represent a spectrum of interpersonal and intellectual skills. Some members will have good presentation skills and most should have good interpersonal, cross-cultural communication, and questioning skills. A few will have analytical and research ability; strategy formulation, negotiating, and bargaining skills; and good intuition and cultural insight. Some may be adept at intercultural socializing and impression management.

Depending on the project, the business areas of team members can cover the whole gamut: technology, finance, law, marketing, production, human resources, and so on. Some members can double as observers who keep a record of what happens and what people say, also noting the nonverbal communication and interactions of the other team. All of your team members should have tasks to accomplish, motivation, and useful skills to contribute.

Teams are wise to choose an assistant leader or meeting manager to be the conscience of the team. This individual is responsible for requesting a break should some members feel something serious needs to be discussed. Calling for a time out is an acceptable way of creating a breathing space, enhancing teamwork, and giving members a chance to provide warnings or suggest new initiatives or counterstrategies. The assistant leader should sit next to the leader and channel all messages, in writing, from members to the leader when practicable.

The business roles of team members, based on their professional strengths and specializations as they apply to the specific negotiation, should be defined in some detail. An interpreter born in China is desirable when doing business in China and, when meetings are important, the interpreter should be included as a member of the team from the beginning.

ANALYZE THOROUGHLY

In this section, we look at a briefing and data-handling situation that ensures everyone is knowledgeable about everything believed relevant to the negotiation. The team leader must ascertain that all team members understand the matters raised for discussion in steps 4 to 7, and then explain the chosen focus.

Step 4. Decide on the Issues to Be Negotiated

Previous correspondence, reports from earlier meetings, related memos, and so on should be presented. These can be supplemented by prepared position papers, distributed to team members in advance.

Step 5. Study All Factors Affecting the Scope of the Negotiations

Define the negotiation domain and its history, politics, and dynamics for your side and the Chinese side, including:

- The background of the industry and market.
- The history of the product or service to be offered.
- An overview of the customer in respect to the product or service.
- An outline of the product, service, cost advantages, and benefits.

Obtain a complete picture of the personnel of the Chinese company, the expected members of their negotiation teams, and details of their associated or subsidiary companies that may have some connection to the forthcoming negotiations.

Step 6. Ensure Common Understanding of Step 5

Ideally, this requires a sentence-by-sentence discussion to ensure complete understanding. In our experience, the best-prepared international teams do this. It allows them to identify weaknesses and specific needs that may have been missed earlier. This is where the analytically skilled members of a team contribute most.

Doing one's homework and so achieving the appropriate level of under-standing takes much more time than many foreign teams are willing to spend. However, our experience is that the extra time pays off in producing better-bonded teams, and the resultant comprehensive knowledge allows them to keep on top of non sequiturs from the other side throughout the negotiation process.

Step 7. Assess Mutual Strengths, Weaknesses; Set Goals, Strategies, Initial Position

- Have position papers prepared in advance.

- Establish overall objectives.

- Determine your strategies to achieve your objectives.

- Decide your initial position.

You should appreciate that the logic and strategy of the comprehensive opening statement require that you give no hint of your position until after you have presented the statement in the negotiation.

MAKE FINAL PREPARATIONS

Step 8. Prepare, Rehearse Comprehensive Opening Statement

The comprehensive opening statement is the most strategically important statement you will make. It provides the best and perhaps only opportunity to present the full scope of your views and approach (thereafter, the discussion will shift to details, and new concepts or conditions subsequently presented will not get the attention they would have received had they been included in the comprehensive opening statement).

This means that time and thought must go into the preparation of the statement. It should be well planned, well researched, and well structured. An important underlying aim of the statement is to persuade the other party that your reasons for taking any position are sound and well supported. Should the other side present new information that requires changes or additions to the statement, you should make them immediately, before proceeding.

The benefits of working through a comprehensive opening statement are:

- It is a practical countermeasure to prevent conflict arising due to prema-ture bargaining.

- It emphasizes substantive issues rather than positions.

- Many Asians feel culturally comfortable with an approach that first reaches agreement on principles. Those of your team members who do not feel comfortable with this approach should be reappraised. Are they people with whom you can really feel comfortable over the long term?

- A systematic comprehensive opening statement will open the eyes of many Chinese teams to a level of professionalism in negotiating that they have not previously encountered. This will generate a higher level of respect, and they will feel you have much to teach them. All the previous points work in your favor to generate greater respect and friendliness and to enhance face on both sides.

You have a good chance of making your comprehensive opening statement the platform of the negotiation if you request to speak first. If the Chinese accede, it can be taken to mean they believe this will give them the upper hand. Interestingly, most Chinese are able to manipulate foreign teams into speaking first even if they do not really want to, and having a prepared opening statement makes the difference.

Even if the Chinese negotiators refuse to make a comprehensive opening statement, or offer only a feeble attempt, the one presented by the foreign party is the template and is on the table, publicly establishing key questions that you can hammer away at until you receive acceptable answers.

The comprehensive opening statement is critical to a serious discussion of the issues and should cover: the background to the present meeting, including the history of discussions so far, your views on the industry, its past and probable future, trends in direct and indirect competition, supply and demand expectations, the parameters and goals of investment and cooperation that you seek, and plausible sales projections or expectations.

It should not include your concrete offers or positions on price, delivery, or equity. Such offers should not be made until all issues have been presented and you know what they are thinking. The opening statement should only mention those issues on which you want their in-principle agreement.

Should you agree to speak first, you can invite the Chinese team to reply with their own comprehensive opening statement and provide them with the pro forma of yours. Even if the Chinese statement is not as comprehensive as yours, you will nevertheless have the initiative for some time, as you question them about what they have said and topics that you have covered in your statement.

Step 9. Write Out Questions to Be Asked and Who Will Ask Them

There should be a teamwide discussion of the questions to be asked. They may be strategic or information seeking but should not be offensive or aggressive in content or presentation. Those most familiar with the topic and with the most agreeable manner should ask the questions.

DEVELOP AN AGENDA

Step 10. Draw Up Own Agenda; Negotiate Final Form with Other Party

Remember that at this stage you are still preparing and have yet to meet the Chinese team. If an agenda has been agreed to in advance, the persons with most knowledge concerning the agenda decision process should share with the team what they have learned about the other side's thinking.

If the other side prepares an agenda prior to visiting you, ask for a detailed copy, stating it is "company policy" for agendas to be sighted and approved in advance.

You should study their agenda to prepare your comments on particular issues and to decide whether you wish to discuss any or all of these. You may also wish to include your own items.

You should also consider whether the agenda items are in suitable order for you; you may believe some items would be better discussed earlier or later. In short, the agenda is negotiable, so you should determine what form suits you best.

DECIDE PROTOCOL, PROCEDURES

Step 11. Draw Up Protocol, List Procedures and Preparations

Requests for a meeting format or special conditions (such as a private room for breaks) should be lodged in advance and are likely to meet with agreement.

Should you host the meeting or have the opportunity to organize a meeting the other party is hosting, every member of your team should understand exactly what to do. A meeting-room format, where your team can sit together and work as a team, should be requested when abroad and created when at home.

It is important that a secretary be appointed to help and support the participants on both sides.

The preparations in this step should include:

I   HOST CHECKLIST

- Prepare meeting room—seating, lighting, writing materials, refreshments.
- Designate someone to meet visitors and conduct them to the meeting room.
- Designate your official greeter, whose job is to welcome and make the visitors feel at home.
- Decide how and where one-on-one introductions are to be made.

II   OPENING WELCOME

- Welcoming remarks.
- Introductions.
- Seating.
- Refreshments.
- Small talk—how was the trip; how is the hotel, food, weather; how are mutual friends; what are plans while in the country?

III   PREAMBLE TO BUSINESS OF THE DAY (BY HOST REPRESENTATIVE)

- Meeting arrangements.
- Taking breaks.
- Sending and receiving messages.
- Services available.
- Facilities available (arranged in advance according to visitors' requests).

OPEN THE MEETING FOR BUSINESS

Step 12. Negotiations So Far, General Items, Other Party's Comments

I   DISCUSS AGENDA ITEMS

If an agenda has not been agreed to, in the first meeting the host team can delegate one of its members to list all issues on a flipchart or whiteboard, and then discuss phrasing and the order of discussion. Learning what topics and what order of discussion are desired by the other team may provide useful insight into their thinking.

II EACH SIDE PRESENTS COMPREHENSIVE OPENING STATEMENT

If you have thoroughly prepared your opening statement, it does not matter which side presents first. Since in China the Chinese usually ask visitors to present first, you should take this opportunity, which gives you a powerful strategic position.

The unfolding of the negotiation subsequent to the presentation of both opening statements generally, but not always, follows the stages of international negotiation.

Thus bargaining is assumed to follow the opening statements and discussions arising from them, after which some degree of complication (such as misunderstandings, personal conflicts, etc.) may occur and communication difficulties arise. As happens in long, complex, and very competitive negotiations (see the case study in chapter 3, How Giving Face Can Brew Success), when the Chinese draw nearer to decision making, they often apply an endgame of final pressure, involving new and unexpected demands about which you will have had no prior warning.

III END MEETING, REVIEW PROGRESS

Before closing the meeting, the leader should direct discussion with the Chinese team on what has been agreed to in the session, what is to be discussed at the next meeting, and what is still to be agreed. These points can be written on the board or flipchart, or they can be projected from a laptop computer.

Discussion should include what minutes of the meeting are to be prepared, bearing in mind that each side often prepares its own minutes to ensure full mutual understanding. Agreement should also be reached on the details of the next meeting.

IV POST-MEETING INITIATIVES

Meet as a team to analyze your performance at the last meeting and note what you can learn from it corporately and individually. Discuss the mistakes that were made and what might be done better next time, and set objectives for the next meeting.

The guidelines for managing team performance should be revised at this time. Tasks could be assigned to each member (someone else could be the leader) and procedures could be adopted should talks go awry.

V   DECIDE HOW MINUTES, REPORTS ARE TO BE PREPARED

Minutes should be prepared not only to the record progress of negotiations and track discussions, but also to facilitate the discussion process as it gains momentum. They should be short enough to allow a quick review of the last session but detailed enough to bring a new member of the team up to date efficiently.

FINAL COMMENTS

Developing a team to negotiate with the Chinese takes considerable effort. There is much to learn, and the team leader or team manager must take responsibility for organizing and directing that learning.

The team must be prepared systematically, following the twelve-step negotiation process; adequate time must be budgeted; consultants, advisors, a support team, interpreters, and Chinese liaison people should be consulted; everyone should be made to realize that collecting intelligence is high on the list of priorities; creative thinking should be encouraged; problem solving (especially responses to stratagems) should be carefully managed; team members should be alert to mistakes, misunderstandings, and miscommunications; and throughout the whole process, everyone should be aware that the task of maintaining trust with the Chinese is everyone's responsibility (dismiss anyone who does not promote trust).

Team leaders should accept that there may be times when someone other than the designated leader should be the spokesperson or leader. At times, the leader might even have good reason to embed himself anonymously in the team, not participating as a leader or spokesperson until such time as a critical, anticipated event occurs.

❏ Every team needs effective leadership, otherwise its members will quickly achieve mutual annoyance, irritation, and barely veiled competition to dominate and lead the group. Do not begin by talking strategy and tactics, and do not leave until the last-minute discussion of who will be leader and who will play other roles.

❏ The twelve-step negotiation process is a strategic tool like a cockpit checklist, listing the essential protocol, procedures, and ideas to be followed and the order in which they are to be presented. This helps identify errors, misunderstandings, and misperceptions.

❏ The twelve steps of the recommended process fall into six categories: organize the team; analyze thoroughly; make final preparations; develop an agenda; decide the protocol and procedures; and finally, open the meeting for business.

❏ There are two recommended ways of choosing team members and developing teams, depending on the number of candidates. The pool approach assumes one is putting together a team for the first time and has a large pool of candidates (twelve or more) from which to select a final team of, say, five people; the selected-team approach assumes a team of at least five people exists or already has been selected.

❏ The comprehensive opening statement is the most strategically important statement you can make. It provides the best and perhaps the only opportunity to present the full scope of your views and approach. Thereafter, discussion will shift to details.

CHAPTER
12

THE STRATEGIC
NEGOTIATION PROCESS

W hile developing the twelve-step process for planning negotiations, we were aware that there are critical strategic guidelines that
teams need to follow during negotiations. Our solution became the
Strategic Negotiation Process (SNP).[13]

Used in tandem with the twelve-step planning process, the SNP is formidable. Its most important elements are *opening negotiations with a comprehensive statement, delayed bargaining, quick resolution of conflicts*, and *using
key team skills*.

FOUR KEY ELEMENTS

Opening Negotiations with a Comprehensive Statement. In the last chapter,
we looked at what a successful comprehensive opening statement requires.
The opening statement features in the SNP because it is a preeminent tool.
Particularly if you present first, your opening statement provides you with the
opportunity to preempt the frame of reference for the negotiations (at least for
a time). Once you present your ideas, they can be (and ought to be) an agenda
of matters to which the Chinese should be asked to respond.

The Chinese may be intimidated initially, but it is also in their interest to
develop their own ideas. The opening statement is not ultimately a means of
maintaining strategic advantage over the Chinese but a way of encouraging
them to think through their own position thoroughly, *before* they start to bargain about price, quantity, delivery, and so on. Additionally, of course, your
opening statement should be thought of as a good-spirited way of driving
a wedge into any closed-mindedness on their part.

There are still negotiators, and not least among the Chinese, who believe
that they can win a negotiation through the use of their wits alone. It is frustrating when some Chinese negotiators say and do "what it takes" to win,
since this can mean puffery, faking the figures, and exaggeration. Be alert
to this possibility and cautious when they fail to support their claims with

figures or documents, or when you receive documents the provenance of which is uncertain.

Another benefit of the comprehensive opening statement is that it provides the best and perhaps the only opportunity to present the full scope of your views and approach. Go into any negotiation without such a statement, and you are certain to field questions that you might rue not having answered at the beginning.

Delayed Bargaining. Generally speaking, foreign negotiators not using a comprehensive opening statement are more likely to begin bargaining prematurely. One aim of the statement is to delay the onset of bargaining. Excessive demands—such as an unreasonably low or high price—can originate from a fear commonly held by Chinese that foreigners are out to make large profits at the expense of the Chinese, so they hedge against being caught out.

Such fears can be reduced by reasoned arguments in the opening statement. A response to their first demands is not necessarily required and can usually be deflected by asking them how they arrived at the price/quantity they have put forward. Such moves must be carried out politely and without hostility. If asked why one cannot respond with one's own demands, the answer ought to be that all the data needed to make a decision are not yet available. Still unknown may be what quantity of spares are needed, how much after-sales service they require, and so on.

Even if this is only a ploy on your part to obtain further market and other information from them, it is useful. After all, you are in their country, on their turf, and you may still not know all the questions you ought to ask. Naturally, a foreign team taking this approach needs to be indifferent to time constraints. It should be in China to spend whatever time is necessary to reach agreement.

Quick Resolution of Conflicts. Irritation, confusion, bewilderment, resentment, and much more of a negative character often emerge and then accumulate during sensitive negotiations with the Chinese. It may not be easy for foreigners to process and resolve such feelings when they are in China. Apologies and statements of regret should be made as soon as possible after any blunder.

If the problem has emerged from the Chinese side, taking a quick break is probably the best tactic, during which time you can thrash out the issues with your fellow team members. If the issues are complex, one should ask for advice from people outside the negotiations—an experienced consultant or a senior Chinese bureaucrat or manager with whom one is on good terms.

If the middleman who introduced you to the Chinese is someone with good sense, talk to him as well. Calming the waters of communication is an essential part of the psychological preparation one must undertake, and one must work at this at all times.

Finally, a more junior member of your team who has developed a friendship with a younger member of the Chinese party might take up the problem informally with him, seeking understanding and resolution in a way that preserves the faces of the senior people on both sides.

Using Key Team Skills. The best strategy by far in China is to have a strong team that includes:

- People with the appropriate functional and business skills for the particular negotiations—legal, marketing, production, etc.

- Individuals with good social skills—the Chinese are not impervious to charm and charisma.

- Team members who provide an array of intellectual and cultural competencies appropriate to negotiating with the Chinese. These should include the ability to read Chinese nonverbal behavior[14]; being intuitive and insightful about the behavior of individual Chinese; understanding the internal dynamics and leadership of the Chinese; and having strategic formulation skills as well as data analysis skills. Mainland-born Chinese who know your culture well are ordinarily the best candidates.

In general, regard your own team as your brains trust and encourage every member to comment on the problems you face.

The SNP assumes that, by the time you have stated your positions and demands (well after the presentation of your comprehensive opening statement), the heavy work of negotiating has been done, there is goodwill on both sides, a high level of mutual understanding has developed, and there is a minimum of bickering about offers and positions.

It can help at that point to list on a whiteboard the benefits and drawbacks of the various options proposed. The use of criteria for objective assessments, which can help settle on a fair price, is often essential in international negotiations. The most recent acceptable data on world prices, for example, should take most of the conflict or dispute out of price arguments.

At this late stage, when agreement is clearly in the offing, the question of concessions by each side is likely to arise. In our view, concessions should only be given when agreement has been reached and when they will serve as symbols of goodwill rather than as bargaining chips.

This is also a view commonly held by the Chinese, for whom final discounts are face giving—that is, they demonstrate to other people in their organization that their negotiations with the foreigners have been successful.

Extremely important in most international negotiations are informal communications, outside formal meetings, between the two sides. Such contacts regularly prove to help resolve problems or misunderstandings that seem unsolvable in formal meetings. This informal channel should not be thought of as involving only one person, such as the spokesperson or leader. Each team member is potentially able to home in on some members of the other side, with whom they feel comfortable and are on a par in terms of status, in order to gain intelligence or resolve problems. Younger members who have the least responsibilities can often speak most openly to one another or be used as subtle agents of influence.

How the SNP Works

The SNP was originally designed to reduce the characteristic (and possibly endemic) problems arising at each stage of negotiations with Chinese and other foreign nationals. It helps negotiators acquire the strategic skills that enable them to do the following:

Build good relationships from the beginning. Friendly conversation and good atmosphere from the outset and a helpful comprehensive opening statement build a good and trusting relationship quickly; without them, it's likely to be a rocky road.

Ensure all team members are motivated and involved. In all discussions and decision making, insights and intelligence about the Chinese should be shared with the whole team. Every effort should be made to understand the Chinese and their business and corporate cultures.

Minimize overt competition. This caution applies equally to members of one's team and to one's relations with the Chinese.

Delay the start of bargaining. This allows good relationships and mutual understanding to develop.

Recognize and resolve conflict quickly. This helps strengthen process management, which includes knowing:

- What comes next in a negotiation.

- What to do when the unexpected occurs.

- When to talk, when to be quiet.

- When to be firm or to yield.

- How to maintain contact and communication.

- How to keep team members composed and focused.

A CODE FOR SUCCESS

Some problems in China-foreign relationships stem from the use of teams and personnel who are steeped in the old ways of viewing the other side. These old ways include being cold and logical, cold and tactical, cold and crypto-aggressive, looking down on the other side, and mistrusting on principle. It is usually some variant of being cold/tactical/aggressive that causes unnecessary problems.

Such old-school ways surface among foreigners and Chinese alike. We know from our consulting experience that some non-Chinese with these attitudes come from non-management backgrounds, including engineers and scientists, for whom people skills have not been important in the past. Others come from commodity trading backgrounds, where it is thought that to be rational is to be right. Where demand curves and projections dominate debate about prices and long-term contracts, people are accustomed to arguing with exceptional rationality and coldness of manner.

Whatever the particulars of the interactions between the two sides, super-rationality tends to foster resentment, and a reactive style may emerge. In doing business with the Chinese, what is called for are good communication skills and a nonconfrontational approach.

I know one clever CEO whose style of communication is perfect for all occasions. Tact and politeness figure heavily in his style. His approach is based on the recognition that everyone wants to be treated with respect and consideration, given face, and consulted—rather than treated with condescension. Chinese grow up in a culture in which these values (except the last) are strongly inculcated and which ordains severe penalties (from scolding to ostracism) for those who violate the communication code.

As obvious as this CEO's approach should be, we are continually surprised at how often one or more of these basic tenets are ignored by otherwise intelligent people when they sit down at the negotiator's table. To assure success, this CEO is considering the adoption of a code covering all forms of communication with the Chinese, based on a recognition of the needs of the Chinese. As he sees it, the benefits in creating a company-wide code would include:

- Better understanding and developing greater respect for national and cultural differences.

- Improving the ability to observe, listen, and communicate, especially in relation to partners.

- Finding ways to build better bridges across cultural differences.

- Learning to avoid becoming critical, judgmental, or negative too quickly.

- Not allowing cultural differences to become an excuse for the lack of harmony in working relationships.

- Becoming more international.

To change team culture and attitudes to the Chinese, the CEO intends to initiate study groups led by China specialist consultants who would explain how and why problems arise at the interpersonal level between Chinese and foreigners, notably when they have little knowledge of one another.

❏ The most important elements of the SNP are opening the negotiation with a comprehensive statement, delayed bargaining, the quick resolution of conflicts, and using key team skills.

❏ If you do not use a comprehensive opening statement, you are likely to begin bargaining earlier than the Chinese. Excessive demands—such as an unreasonably low or high price—can originate from fears, commonly held by the Chinese, that foreigners are out to make large profits at their expense. This causes them to hedge against being caught out. Such fears can be reduced by reasoned arguments in the comprehensive opening statement.

❏ Irritation, confusion, bewilderment, resentment, and other negative reactions often emerge and accumulate during sensitive negotiations with the Chinese. It is not easy for foreigners to process and resolve such feelings. Apologies and statements of regret should be made as soon as possible after a blunder. If the problem has emerged from the Chinese side, taking a quick break is probably the best tactic, during which time one can thrash out the issues with one's fellow team members.

❏ The best strategy when negotiating in China is to have a strong team that includes (1) people with the appropriate functional and business skills for the particular negotiations—legal, marketing, production; (2) individuals with social skills—the Chinese are not impervious to charm and charisma; and (3) team members with an array of intellectual and cultural competencies appropriate to negotiating with the Chinese.

CHAPTER
13

THE CALM DESPITE THE STORM

Foreigners (particularly Westerners) are generally more ill at ease, uncomfortable, and awkward during business meetings with Chinese than are the Chinese with the foreigners. This flies in the face of received knowledge that the Chinese are shrinking violets, while foreigners are generally sociable and extroverted. That said, while the Chinese may be more introverted, they are also more composed than most non-Asian foreigners.

It is important that those who plan to be involved in business with the Chinese learn to be composed when encountering and communicating with poker-faced, unsmiling, seemingly humorless counterparts in formal settings. To this end, we developed a communication and consulting skills inventory to pinpoint the strengths and weaknesses of Chinese and foreign managers working in China.

Foreign managers are often responsible for supervising all aspects of a business relationship with a customer, including negotiating, developing, and managing joint projects; fielding difficult questions; handling complaints; and ensuring that work proceeds according to plan.

The broad array of tasks in negotiations with the Chinese offers foreign negotiators countless opportunities to lose composure and reveal their stand on different issues. Despite their often shy manner with strangers and foreigners and their frugal use of words, the Chinese rarely lose their composure, alertness, or powers of observation.

In order to enhance your composure in meetings with Chinese, it is necessary to understand the emotions involved. Becoming fearful, annoyed, or stressed can result in a loss of composure, and this can happen in a twinkling. The prime indicator of composure is breathing smoothly and deeply through the nose and from the diaphragm. Under stress, breathing becomes very shallow.

To ensure that all the members of the team maintain composure, they should all go through an advance two-step warm-up, as do sports people as well as stage and screen performers. The first of the two steps involves preparing for the negotiations. This process includes *stillness*, or being in the moment; *relaxation*, to free the body of tension and make it responsive to what you require of it; *proper breathing*, with exhalation representing the release of tension; and *concentration*, during which you feel no anxiety and focus on your role.

The second step requires role-playing, so that the team members understand what they will be required to do. By assigning work and self-defined tasks, the skills and concentration of all are rapidly enhanced.

TECHNICAL SKILLS TO DEVELOP IN COMPETITIVE ROLE-PLAYING

During negotiation role-playing, we require each team member to focus on developing for themselves four basic negotiating skills:

Showing team coherence and solidarity. These aspects are communicated to the opposing team in the role play by nonverbal cues and an obvious nonverbal display of your team's cohesion as a team.

Role focus. Each team member is to note down, and not share with others, points that:

- Reveal his/her own initial position on the negotiations.
- Define their individual role in the team in terms of a limited number of characteristics (e.g., observer; prudent participant; strong planner with strategic orientation).
- Indicate their political stance on the subject to be negotiated. For example, do you personally feel that few or no concessions should be given to the Chinese? Do you want to emphasize some particular aspect of the total deal—such as financing, long-term return on investment, retaining management control over some functional areas of the business, etc.?

Questioning. The team is required to prepare questions in advance, allocate them to different members, and ensure they are asked well. The team leader should determine who asks questions and when. Each member should contribute at least four questions.

Observation. At least one team member is to be assigned to observe the other team, noting down the proceedings, conclusions, and tasks to be handled later. In the final post-negotiation debriefing, each member should try to guess the other party's hidden agenda.

An example of tasks that can be set for team members appears in the box on the left. An exercise like this is perfectly appropriate for teams in real life to ask of themselves when facing the Chinese. These are powerful ways to strengthen the team.

COMPOSURE AND INTROVERSION

Being composed means feeling integrated as a person and not being under threat. One can be simultaneously composed and introverted, the latter characteristic including being timid and, often, diffident. Extremely introverted people have chronic and longstanding fears of being criticized, embarrassed, and shamed by others. They avoid stressful encounters by engaging in interpersonal contact only when guaranteed acceptance and support.

There appears to be a greater proportion of introverts among the Chinese than in some other cultures. Introverts are typically preoccupied with their own thoughts, feelings, and physical reactions, making it difficult for them to both relate and talk to others. One-on-one interactions with people of the opposite sex, strangers, or foreigners are typically the occasions when shyness arises. Introverts become less verbally and nonverbally expressive, and their self-consciousness can be painful to see. They have negative images of themselves as inhibited, awkward, unfriendly, and incompetent.

There is a caveat to bear in mind about shy Chinese, however. They generally worry far less about social skills than do many foreigners. They receive support and friendship from their group and friends, which means they have no need to work at developing new social skills or becoming extroverted.

It is important to understand that most Chinese are there to observe and listen. Their team offers acceptance and security, and so they can feel simultaneously composed *and* introverted.

SOCIALIZING WITH INTROVERTS

The subject of how extroverts might best deal with introverts, and introverts with extroverts, has long been recognized as important in the context of relationship building. When an extrovert encounters an introvert, the extrovert tends to get too close to the introvert (technically speaking, reducing the *social* distance), talking too much, putting them literally on the back foot, and metaphorically overpowering the other. A factor adding to these problems is that, in our experience, extroverts are often bigger and/or taller than introverts, which adds to the sense of intimidation felt by introverts in "close encounters" with extroverts.

Extroverts can manage relationships better with introverts if they speak more slowly, allow more time for introverts to answer, and take time to listen. Introverts, in turn, will do far better if they speak up more, are manifestly more friendly, and work at feeling less intimidated. If both parties follow these guidelines, they will be better equipped to maintain their composure and enhance the development of friendly relations.

STRATAGEMS AND COMPOSURE

It is difficult to maintain one's composure when being subjected to stratagems that one has never before faced.

Our analysis of the thirty-six stratagems in chapter 8 is a reminder that in China, negotiations will not be as they are in your home country. Chinese stratagems are tactical (in ways with which we are not familiar), intimidating (as few people at home are), and designed to gain control of the situation at your expense and to manipulate or ignore the agenda. Some Chinese may appear to be deceptive, employ diversionary tactics, and make feints, trying to put us off balance; or they may attempt to be manipulative and appeal to our pride, causing us to make errors of judgment. If you are prone to be suspicious of others, you can be sure that your composure will suffer with the Chinese.

One approach is to take a page from the Chinese copybook: Learn from them how to maintain composure. Speaking less, reigning in impulsiveness, taking counsel with fellow team members before responding, passing to another the spokesperson's duties, and taking time out—are all important countermeasures to adopt.

We need to be ready for the unexpected. Something might happen at any time that could instantly disrupt the situation and shred your composure. So it is best to go into negotiations with countermeasures that have been prepared with and understood by the whole team. Thus everyone will understand what to do when someone's composure is threatened. It is also best to accept that, if you do lose your composure, you will have little chance of hiding that fact from the observant Chinese, so think about any possible strategic advantages they could obtain from your loss of composure.

Those who suspect that negotiations might be rough going should pre-pare for undesirable options by preparing the following strategies that will enhance their composure, confidence, and negotiating strategies:

- Be prepared to cut your losses and terminate the negotiations if necessary.

- Know the bottom line beyond which you will not go.

- Be prepared to state your absolute bottom line and walk away (no faking) if necessary.

- At the start, inform the Chinese how your team does business: your pref-erence for collegial decision making, win-win outcomes, all-round consult-ing, avoiding surprises, and team decision making rather than one-man decisions that are prone to result in misjudgments. By establishing these principles and including them in your comprehensive opening statement, you can refer to them whenever they seem likely to be violated.

Establishing team and individual composure should take priority. This will make it easier for the team leader and members to adopt suitable patterns of behavior. But do so with a caveat: Remain good friends with the Chinese.

The leader

- Never respond to challenges until you have discussed the matter carefully with your team. Use silence when necessary.

- Make no response when the other party attacks the team or makes propos-als that leave you stunned. Remain calm and noncommittal and request a break to discuss the matter with your team.

- Take it slowly, patiently; be economical with words. If you are the spokes-person and an unreformed talker, you should realize that you will make the team much more powerful by switching to a laconic or silent-dominant role.

- Use other people as excuses for being unable to decide matters unilater-ally. Even if you are the CEO, you can conjure up the chairman or the board of directors as ultimate powers to whom you have to refer. Remem-ber that this is also a Chinese stratagem.

- Wait until circumstances favor you. If you are rushing to get answers to all your questions, you probably should not be your team's negotiation leader.

- Work for better circumstances, such as negotiations on your home territory.

- Defer key items for discussion on home territory.

- Never surrender agenda making; try to have your agenda accepted by the Chinese, with the items in the order that suits you best. If necessary, negotiate the entire agenda, and at least jointly manage it.

- Be prepared to tell the Chinese what you cannot do, such as make unilateral decisions. Explain that others also have input.

Team members

- Remain poker-faced regardless of the bombshells dropped. From the Chinese perspective, one of the greatest weaknesses of many foreigners is that they show their emotions and reactions easily. That could turn out to provide them with useful information on your bottom-line thinking.

- Unobtrusively observe and study the Chinese team, so that you can later discuss its psychology and group dynamics with your team.

- Be ready to learn from the Chinese. Take losses philosophically and seek to outdo them at their own games without appearing to be a game player.

- Show no unduly excited reaction to inducements or temptations, such as beautiful women, banquets, flattery, and other blandishments. Be polite and understanding, but do not succumb.

- Give minimal concessions, and no tip-offs. If they ask you questions informally, do the unexpected—answer their question with a question of your own. Say you will have to discuss the matter with your colleagues and suggest some possible reasons they might be asking the question.

- Always ask the Chinese party, and try to work out for yourself, what they are really saying to you. When asked a question, do not give them an immediate reply, but ask yourself what is it they really want to know. You might also tell them that you are not sure why they are asking that question, or ask them to rephrase the question so you may better understand.

- Make it a habit to pause and put yourself in their shoes.

- Work to allay any suspicions and doubts they might have about you.

With the negotiating style resulting from these changes, you ought to earn the respect and friendship of the Chinese over time. Together with an ample budget of time and money, you can expect to win much more often, although you will inevitably lose sometimes.

In the end, you will find yourself doing some things that they do, and they will do things that you do. You will be teaching each other to be more professional. Most important of all, your newly acquired negotiating style will take a load off your shoulders by making you smarter and less flustered. Be worried if these things don't happen.

❏ Foreigners in business meetings with the Chinese are generally more ill at ease, uncomfortable, and awkward than their Chinese counterparts.

❏ The Chinese are often introverted in the presence of strangers and foreigners, and they are not great talkers. Yet, in contrast to many foreigners, they do not lose their composure, alertness, or powers of observation.

❏ To enhance one's composure at meetings with Chinese, one should breathe smoothly and deeply through the nose and from the diaphragm. One thus avoids becoming fearful, annoyed, or stressed.

❏ Team and individual composure should be the number-one goal. They allow you to handle the unexpected.

❏ Being subjected to stratagems that one has never faced before can make it hard to remain composed. One should keep essential counterstrategies in the forefront of the mind: for instance, never respond to challenges without first carefully deliberating with one's team.

❏ When one's team is attacked or a proposal is made that leaves one stunned, one should make no response, remain poker-faced, and request a break to discuss the matter with team members.

CHAPTER
14

BUILDING STRATEGIC
FRIENDSHIPS

A Few Last Pointers

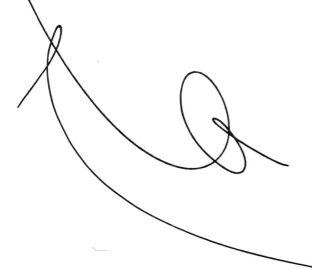

E very year, some fifty thousand foreign businesspeople go on their first business trip to China. It is interesting to ponder how these individuals are chosen; how well prepared they are for the business that awaits them; what challenges they face; how many of them feel sufficiently at home to be motivated, when it comes to learning what China is really like; how many might lead China negotiating teams in the future; and, of those, how many might succeed and end up living and working in China.

While dealing and working with the Chinese is challenging, it can also be stimulating and satisfying. What happens during interactions and the sense one makes of encounters depend in large part on how open minded and willing to learn one is. This book provides a roadmap, and this chapter points out a few more dangers and roadblocks along the way.

BEWARE OF FORMULAS: OPT FOR GENUINE UNDERSTANDING

There are no all-encompassing formulas for success in China. We believe that the best approach is one of selective naïveté (a variant of stratagem 27, Feign Ignorance and Hide One's Intentions), in which you allow the Chinese to educate you by answering your questions. We also know, from experience, that it is dangerous to blindly follow formulas and not adapt them to the situation at hand.

Some years ago, I trained some U.S. managers, who had already received Chinese cultural training, to negotiate with Chinese businessmen. Believing the trainees would be at home with China's formal behavior, I asked them to come out, two at a time, to role-play the first meeting between a Chinese and a U.S. businessman.

Their role-playing shocked both the senior company manager supervising the training and me. The trainees, supposedly playing themselves, behaved like nervous robots. Their bodies were stiff and awkward, their faces tense and unsmiling, and their demeanor ill at ease. Obviously preoccupied with not making mistakes, each fumbled for their business card and sought to present it as they had been taught: holding it in both hands, with the English text facing so that the Chinese recipient could read it.

After running all the trainees through this simple exercise and debriefing them regarding what they had just done, we discovered that the Chinese lady who had previously trained them had placed all her emphasis on the need to be proper with a hypothetical Chinese who was assumed to be critical and judgmental. The price of being proper, they realized after discussion, was the loss of spontaneity and friendly openness—characteristics that Chinese not only liked about Americans, but secretly envied.

The moral of this exercise is that reliance on a cure-all formula could have been a recipe for disaster. Being natural, friendly, and yourself are key to starting relationships off well with the Chinese, as they are with anyone else. Of course, good manners and appropriate etiquette are as much part of the equation as are showing that you enjoy what you are doing; like being with your counterparts; know your business thoroughly; are well prepared; know how to open and run meetings; can handle silence well; and sense when to move on or terminate discussion.

These personal characteristics ensure good atmosphere management, which is particularly important during initial meetings, and lead to good long-term business and personal relationships. The more trusting and familylike a relationship becomes, the more conventional meeting behavior gives way to friendly, informal, and cozy behavior. Commitment to a relationship usually comes only after a great deal of mutual sharing and discussion and trust has been established—or it may not come until joint projects have begun, or at the interdependence stage.

From joint ventures that mutually satisfy, there may develop opportunities for different projects with business friends of either party that may turn into significant strategic alliances. They, in turn, will require further learning. Once again, one's ability to make concessions or commitments to the other party without signatures on contracts may only emerge well into a relationship—months or perhaps years after the relationship has become familylike.

Social skills are needed at every stage but may develop naturally and become less formal and more intimate as individuals on each side grow more comfortable and open with one another and learn how to be kinder to and more thoughtful about their partners. For the attentive negotiator, reading the other party's mind comes with familiarity and experience.

In many cases, if the representative of your Chinese partner changes, you will have to learn to deal with a new person, and most likely the personal chemistry will be very different. Cross-cultural negotiations are delicate at best, and a new Chinese manager, himself finding it challenging to fit into a new job, may be touchy about what he has to learn and your role in informing him.

The more you practice and prepare, the better a communicator you will become. Review your progress every step of the way and learn from your mistakes. Everyone in your team should be encouraged to give feedback and opinions about recent meetings and progress—or lack thereof.

BEWARE OF GENERALIZATIONS

There is a huge variation in behavioral styles in China, and Chinese society is changing rapidly. There is a popular view among many foreigners that the Chinese will always bargain and haggle. However, we would do better to think that bargaining or haggling are intense when one deals with a generally available commodity, but less so when the product is a highly differentiated one. Whether one haggles depends on both the distinctiveness of the product and whether the market is a seller's or a buyer's.

The Chinese trader of fresh seafood in a wet market typifies the world of the haggler. One cannot make generalizations about market trends since, were there an oversupply of seafood, for instance, it would be a buyer's market. Similarly, in the international metals markets, because the spot markets can at any time experience oversupply or undersupply, one cannot generalize about those markets.

When thinking about China, rather than seeing it as a homogeneous haggling society, it is better to think of it as a diverse, pluralistic, stratified one, with a variety of attitudes regarding buying and selling.

As mentioned earlier, the Chinese understand that giving a discount the moment agreement is reached in a negotiation gives the buyer face. Most Chinese retailers today will offer you a final discount once you decide to buy a big-ticket item.

At all costs, you should avoid going into negotiations with the Chinese with thinly veiled hostility or on the defensive because of some shaky generalizations—which may well be untrue.

WHICH PEOPLE ARE BEST IN CHINESE POSTINGS?

When expatriates get together in the bars or clubs of Beijing and Shanghai, they have a lot to say about their experiences with the local businesspeople. Some expatriates, while proud of their knowledge of the local culture and people, are at the same time critical. They complain about the problems of dealing and communicating with the "locals," their lack of sophistication, and their shortcomings. They grumble about how difficult it is to make real friends among the Chinese. These are formidable issues.

In contrast, there is another type of expatriate who, also knowing the local people and their culture, has many friends among them, is interested in learning more, and wishes to become a genuine, close friend of the Chinese. This type of expatriate tends to be uncomfortable with conversations that complain about the locals or their culture.

"Conceptuals" are typically people with knowledge of the general differences between peoples of different cultures. In contrast, "adaptives" make little of their knowledge of general characteristics, for what is important to them is the personal relationships and friendships they make with locals. Conceptuals can be thought of as analytical, conceptual, theoretical, and even withdrawn. Adaptives see themselves as constantly changing, whereas the conceptuals think of the world of foreigners as if it were composed of stable phenomena about which solid, unchanging data could be collected. Adaptives use stereotypes to pose questions about foreigners they are meeting for the first time. For instance, they could easily ask, "Is he a typical hardboiled Shanghainese?"—but discard that question as soon as they get to know the person better.

GETTING ON WITH CHINESE—A FINAL WORD

Many businesspeople, new to China, seek practical tips on how to behave and adapt to China and the Chinese. Giving or seeking tips, in our view, is hazardous for the newcomer if that is all he demands. It is the way of the conceptualizer rather than of the adaptive. There is no substitute for being adaptive—that is, analyzing and understanding the immediate and specific situation you are in. Judge for yourself. Use your instincts, the points discussed in this book, and an understanding developed over time from your own experience.

Generally, tips belong to the thinking of conceptualizing, not adaptive, managers. Many tips fall pray to oversimplification, and should not be accepted at face value; further research is always advisable. Our best tip is the one we have already given about selective naïveté. Make the Chinese your teachers. Tell them, sincerely, that you know nothing, and ask them for advice about what to do, how to behave, how to understand what they say, or whether you should take what they say at face value. The one caveat is that asking too many questions is not regarded very highly among the Chinese. Most of them learn bookishly or by observing. So make your questions count, and ask them of someone with whom you have already begun to develop a friendship. Authentic naïveté, with its concomitant attitude of earnest learner/student, is culturally familiar to the Chinese. It can be a classic feigning stratagem (as we discussed earlier), but it might not be. Whatever, it will also do something very important socially in China—give the Chinese face.

Generally, the Chinese are as honest as any businesspeople in the world, and, provided that they believe that you authentically and sincerely desire "education," they will help you. The more Chinese you bring into your circle of learning, the better for you, as long as you don't let on that you are feeding at other information troughs. The Chinese take quick offense in such cases.

❑ There are no all-encompassing formulas for success in China, but a good approach is to adopt selective naïveté (a variant of stratagem 27) and allow the Chinese to educate you by answering your questions. Following formulas without adapting to a particular situation is folly.

❑ Being natural, friendly, and yourself; having good manners and appropriate etiquette; and showing that you enjoy what you are doing ensure good atmosphere management. This is particularly important during initial meetings and leads to good long-term business and personal relationships.

❑ Commitment to a relationship usually comes only after a great deal of mutual sharing and discussion, and trust has been established—or it may not come until joint projects have begun, or at the interdependence stage.

❑ Communicating with the Chinese requires mastery, and relationships need to be deliberately managed and preparation good.

❑ Beware of generalizations. There is a huge variation in behavioral styles in China, and Chinese society is changing rapidly.

❑ There are two broad types of expatriates: adaptives and conceptuals. The adaptives are intuitive, empirical, relational, and immediate. They see themselves as constantly changing and focus on personal relationships and friendships they make with locals. The conceptuals are analytical, theoretical, and even withdrawn. They see the world as stable and its cultures like jigsaw puzzles.

CHAPTER
15

ZEROING IN ON SUCCESS

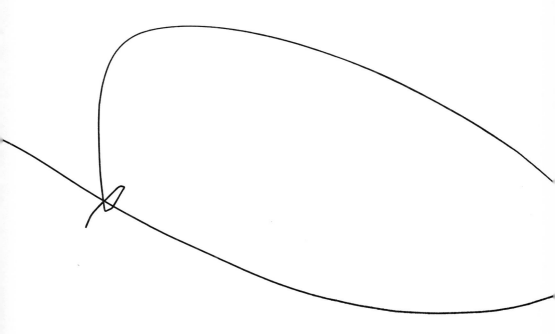

Watching negotiations involving Chinese and foreigners is intriguing. At that intersection of cultures, the parties feel neither completely at home nor quite sure how well they are relating to or communicating with their opposite number, and they constantly surprise each other.

This book is designed to provide the reader with cross-cultural reference points, offered as carefully selected case studies, a twelve-step process for planning negotiations (chapter 11), and a Strategic Negotiation Process (SNP, chapter 12). Used with care, the volume should help minimize mistakes and losses, maximize win-win outcomes, and cement long-term, profitable business friendships.

DOMESTIC VERSUS CROSS-CULTURAL NEGOTIATIONS

Many foreigners who are visiting China for the first time to negotiate are armed with skills honed at home. While that expertise will certainly be valuable, unless fortified with new perceptions, knowledge, and skills suited to the China arena, newcomers are likely to make many of the mistakes reported in these pages.

Even in their home country, business negotiators know that it is proper to warn amateurs that negotiations can be like a minefield, and that there is always the danger of an ambush by a wily foe. Thus it is only fair that China-bound foreign negotiators be made aware that China has many times more minefields than the home arena. It presents ambushes at almost every turn and is infinitely more dangerous for the foreign amateur.

In the context of China, amateur means someone sufficiently naïve to assume that China is not that different from home. A rude shock awaits such an individual, for they will have failed to do their homework on Chinese cultural, communication, strategic and tactical practices, and will have ignored the well-intentioned warnings of others.

DOES LOVING OR HATING CHINESE FOOD MATTER?

Don't laugh. Seemingly small factors can lead to failure, and a dislike of Chinese food is among them. We wonder how many foreigners have left China early because they cannot cope with Chinese food. As mentioned in chapter 3, foreign negotiators left China in the early stages of negotiation because, among other things, they couldn't adjust to Chinese cuisine. This suggests that managers should avoid sending personnel to China who dislike food or other things that are Chinese. Their cuisine, culture, and traditions are sources of pride for the Chinese, so anyone who is less than sympathetic should not be part of your team.

A TEAM CAN MAKE IT WORK

Team negotiation is the core of our twelve-step package, which takes into account the massive differences between the cultures of non-Chinese and China's culture. Presented in stark outline in these pages are China's negotiating and socializing styles, the use of tactics and stratagems, its culture-based adherence to firm protocols and formal behavior, and the problems arising from language differences and communication difficulties that frequently impact negatively on trust and/or provoke misunderstandings, misperceptions, and conflict.

One person alone in China (even a mercantile Einstein) who knows nothing will be utterly at sea. A smart team, composed of thoughtful people skillfully chosen, given an adequate budget, and allowed flexibility to vary plans and itineraries, however, has excellent chances of doing very well and establishing relationships for the long term.

CHOOSING THE RIGHT TEAM MEMBERS

The least-addressed question in the formation of cross-cultural negotiation teams is: How do we choose an effective leader and team, and do so without intermember conflict or rivalry? If you are very lucky, you can draw on people who are already experienced at working together. But either way, the truth is that no cross-cultural negotiating team develops naturally. Without a method of identifying viable team members, trial and error will be the only path to tread, and this will include the painful task of removing members who cannot fit in.

It is best to begin with a larger number of people than are needed, so that they can be screened against criteria such as those above and be submitted to tests of their negotiating skills in a team environment (such as observing and rating their performance in simulated negotiations). It is also advisable to see how different teams perform under different leaders.

Once the team members have been selected, further training in China-specific communication and cultural skills ought to be undertaken at a level appropriate to prior experience. After the team has established the leader's and each member's role, it should tackle the twelve-step process.

For a team to succeed, ideally it should include native mainland Chinese who know the cultures and languages of both parties, as well as a number of people who are motivated and experienced, have the needed professional skills and China-specific knowledge required by the team, fit well with one another, and include a leader or spokesperson accepted by the team.

The experienced or well-trained leader knows that, for China, it is best to decentralize the team, share leadership, organize the various contributions of each member, listen attentively, retain vision and insight, act prudently, be diplomatic, and facilitate good outcomes regardless of the time it takes (without lightly agreeing to any proposals). The leader should not monopolize leadership, not let the team members make foolish mistakes, nor either intimidate or offend the other side.

The best way to minimize mistakes is to conduct prenegotiation role-playing practice sessions of the forthcoming negotiations, with an opposing side to simulate the China team formed from other company personnel, preferably with past China experience, who have the mettle to play devils' advocates.

CAVEATS CONCERNING TEAM LEADERSHIP

Chapters 10, 11, and 12 present our approach to important aspects of the formation, leadership, and performance of a China team. What we have not included are caveats about the challenges of making teams successful.

Team negotiation is an acquired skill. Most teams, however bright their members might be, have much to learn. Those people with inquiring and analytical minds and willingness to listen and learn will develop the ability to eventually put together a team that can be successful.

APPOINTING A MEETING MANAGER

The negotiation leader ought not to be held entirely responsible for a team's performance. More often than not, the demands on a leader are heavy, so a capable meeting manager should be chosen to act as the leader's lieutenant. This individual would be a strong candidate for spokesperson at a later time, and so previous experience as a spokesperson, albeit in less ambitious negotiations, would be ideal.

The manager should be responsible for the following:

- Organizing prenegotiation meetings and negotiation rehearsals.

- Developing the agenda in advance of the first meeting.

- Making sure the team is cohesive and its members composed.

- Ensuring that team members understand their roles and do not allow any member's cultural baggage (prejudices, stereotyping, condescension, etc.) to cloud the atmosphere.

- Noting whether planned questions are asked and answered.

- Judging when breaks ought to be taken.

- Recording whether objectives are achieved.

- Seeing that agreements are put into writing and approved by the other side.

- Helping organize joint leisure activities.

SELF-PREPARATION

These days, many people are aware that negotiations usually fail as a result of a lack of preparation, yet they do not realize that preparation *must include self-preparation*. In addition to the twelve-step process for planning negotiations, self-preparation is crucial in cross-cultural situations. This includes training oneself to remain composed in unfamiliar situations as well as to concentrate on the role and the specific tasks one has been assigned. In fact, all recommended techniques for achieving composure are part of self-preparation.

We hope that our emphasis on composure will be recognized and fully understood. In our professional experience, lack of composure is well established as a pervasive negative factor that can gnaw at an individual's capacity to be masterful in China negotiations.

In many professions, self-preparation is critical. For actors and singers, this involves defining one's role, practicing composure, and memorizing one's part in all its subtleties. A team of well-prepared people is impressive in every way. It will come across as a pleasant and composed group of people who are at peace with one another and totally in charge of themselves and who radiate composure and a self-assurance that declares: "Not to be intimidated!"

In every well-promoted domestic course on negotiation in Western countries, preparation is considered important. These courses focus on negotiations conducted by individuals. Not one that we have come across recognizes that negotiations in China are typically conducted between teams—not individuals. Courses focused on individual skills-building certainly strengthen team-related negotiating skills, but then again only when one is negotiating with people of the same culture.

As many of our case studies have shown, with good training and leadership, international negotiating teams dealing with the Chinese and other societies can become professional and powerful. Those teams negotiating with the Chinese can become warriors who use the brush (persuasive words) and sword (strategies) with equal facility (*neng wen neng wu*). They will have the poise and composure of martial arts masters and be balanced beings, as they are termed in China.

OBSERVING THE OTHER SIDE

If you are entering what you expect to be a long-running negotiation, it will help you to analyze how the other party works—how the team members interact, and what particular members' agendas might be. This strategy is particularly necessary when dealing with very large corporations, since they assign many different people to negotiate at different times and on different topics. Should you be a senior decision maker who will be unable to attend every meeting, such analysis will be especially helpful.

PORTRAIT OF A MEETING

The meeting ran for eight hours, with four members of National Inventions Inc. (Nativent) of the United States who were always present, and eight members of Shanghai-based Zhendu Ltd. who were present at different times.

Below are selected excerpts from the notes written by Samuel Li, the ethnic Chinese business development manager of Nativent. Besides listing the name, business title and division, and time of arrival and departure of each attendee, he also summarized the attitude of each to the proposed business (to acquire new printing technology owned by Nativent).

NAME	TITLE AND GROUP	ATTITUDE
TW	VP Imaging	Waiting to be convinced of the advantages of Nativent's product and timeline for delivery.
BB	VP Corporate	Neutral. Attended to conduct brief corporate due diligence and to try to find a leverage point.
LZ	Director, Engineering	Waiting to be convinced of the advantages of Nativent's product and timeline for delivery.
ZZ	Director, Business and Development	Positive but needs to convince everyone of the benefits of the Nativent product.

The next part of the report was devoted to general impressions.

> Zhendu was poorly prepared for this meeting, which no one seemed to be driving. This was partly due to the time constraints on TW, BB, and ZZ. Toward the end of the meeting, they said that Zhendu was a very lean organization and that they had not spent as much time preparing as they might have. I believe they were referring to

> What Nativent CEO Morgan had said.
> The Nativent technology.

The opportunities for the technology.
The positioning of the product.

Early in the meeting, the Zhendu people were reluctant to accept Morgan's ideas, but they came around later and asked for his input. Eventually, when Zhendu could find no weaknesses in Nativent's financial or corporate structure, it was pleased with the prospects of obtaining the new technology.

The business and development people—from ZZ down—were excited by the opportunities the new technology offers. ZZ said he had already presented Nativent's ideas to his CEO.

The next section of Li's report comprised a summary of the agenda, detailed notes on each item, the outcome of each discussion, and a list of next steps.

The report included a comprehensive introduction to the issues discussed, as well as the personalities and their attitudes. Nativent had sent most of its key decision makers to the meeting, and they were pleased with the comprehensive report. Morgan said Li's report covered all the issues that they had to work on for the next meeting.

We believe that a detailed, written report is always desirable, however complex or simple the negotiations. Such reports chart the progress of negotiations, serve as invaluable tools for reviewing materials and planning the next steps, are windows on success and failure, and provide archives for study by junior managers, researchers, the legal team, and members of senior management who do not attend negotiations.

COACHING FOR SUCCESS

In large corporations, where team members can be chosen from a large number of people, selecting the right people who can work well together is not a random process; selecting the wrong people could result in heavy financial losses for the company. Certainly coaches and trainers can set up ways to choose those team members best able to work well together, and then choose one or more of their number to be effective and acceptable leaders—ideally, at least two leaders skilled to lead the team to success.

For companies that are inexperienced in China, having the assistance of a China negotiation coach might be critical to negotiating success. Senior managers sometimes assign personnel to a team without understanding their impact on team dynamics.

Some team members act as lone wolves, keep important information to themselves, offend the Chinese with their manner, are unreliable in their performance, and/or compete with the team leader by seeking to upstage him or put him down with superior knowledge or insights about the Chinese. Foreign teams need authentic experts, such as China-born-and-raised people, rather than dogmatic know-it-alls.

Team members need the challenge to become professional in dealing with the Chinese. Like other professionals, they must keep focused on the task and on their role in achieving it. Lose focus, and you are no longer professional. Some negotiators are balanced at home, but abroad, for one reason or another, they fall apart.

❏ For first-timers in China, negotiating skills honed at home need reforging. In the beginning, many mistakes are made. Negotiating is a minefield even at home, and China has many times more traps and ambushes.

❏ One person alone in China, who knows little about it, will be utterly at sea. However, a smart team of clever people skillfully chosen, with an adequate budget and the flexibility to adapt plans and itineraries, has excellent chances of doing well and establishing long-term relationships.

❏ Cross-cultural negotiating teams do not develop naturally. Once team members have been selected, training in China-specific communication and cultural skills should be undertaken.

❏ The best way to minimize mistakes is to conduct prenegotiation role-playing practice sessions.

❏ Prenegotiation role-play helps minimize team mistakes.

❏ Team negotiation is an acquired skill.

❏ Self-preparation is part of team, personal, technical, and interpersonal skills preparation. Composure is critical.

❏ Observing the dynamics of the Chinese team—interaction, agendas— and reporting on each meeting is a valuable intelligence-collecting activity.

Appendix

Managing Translators and Interpreters

Interpreters are a key part of your negotiating team, but few people have either experience or skills in managing interpreters or translators. We therefore encourage you to learn enough about the craft of both interpreting and translating documents to ensure that you feel in charge. There are some simple rules:

- It is essential to be adept at managing interpreters. Never go into negotiations feeling at their mercy.

- Prepare interpreters thoroughly. They should be briefed on your business and technical language; underlying issues; any information you might require, such as guesses about what the Chinese could be thinking but are not expressing or what their hidden agenda could be. Since this requires a smart interpreter, it is worth paying for top quality.

- Go slowly. Ask questions about the interpretation in terms of possible ambiguities in what the other side has said. Meet with your team members often and take breaks for private discussions.

- Study the art of interpreting and the potential pitfalls and problem areas, bearing in mind that the meaning is often lost if one attempts to interpret literally what is said or translate literally what is written.

How to achieve appropriate communication is the greatest challenge during cross-cultural negotiations, and one should always assume that misunderstandings will easily arise. Thus, even should the Chinese gentleman sound fluent in English, it is wise to be skeptical. Work on the basis that, at best, he understands eighty percent of what is being said, and rephrase important statements. It is often the case that the other party has not understood after all, despite the nodding and smiling. And when there is no nodding and smiling, this is even more likely.

It helps greatly to ask the other party for suggestions regarding how to make communication more effective. One could propose, for example, that key statements be put in writing or that an agenda be written up on a whiteboard where it can be seen by all.

One should keep asking questions of the other party and the interpreters. By making them your teachers and, thus, placing a huge responsibility on them, you are putting yourself in a position of strength.

Dogmatic statements and generalizations about cultures should be avoided. Generalizations all too easily lead to stereotyping, and that to dogma. A narrow mind impedes the understanding of individuals and prevents people from becoming friends on a one-on-one basis.

Keep your mind open and never assume that reticence or silence means lack of comprehension, because unlike in other cultures, to the Chinese words mean relatively little. It is wise to assume that the taciturn Chinese are in fact very, very smart.

BASIC GUIDELINES FOR USING INTERPRETERS

The Basics

- Brief interpreters in advance about the subject and provide a copy of the presentation for study and discussion.

- Speak loudly, clearly, and slowly.

- Maintain a pleasant attitude.

- Avoid little-known words.

- Avoid using slang.

- Avoid long sentences, double negatives, and the use of negatives when a positive form could be used.

Pacing and Clarity

- Explain each major idea in two or three different ways, as the point may be lost if discussed only once.

- Avoid superfluous words. Your point may be lost if wrapped up in generalities.

- Do not talk more than a minute or two without giving the interpreter time to speak. Be concerned if the interpreter is not making notes while the speaker is talking.

- While speaking, allow time for the interpreter to make notes of what is being said.

- Permit the interpreter to spend as much time as is necessary to clarify points not immediately grasped.

- Try to be as expressive as possible, using your hands, eyes, lips, shoulders, and head to supplement your words. The less physically expressive you are, the more difficult you are to understand.

- Do not expect an interpreter to work for more than an hour or two without a rest period. The work is exhausting.

- Consider using two interpreters should the need for interpreting last a whole day or run into the evening, so that when one tires the other can take over.

Give the Interpreter Breathing Room

- Do not interrupt someone while they are interpreting. To do so can cause misunderstandings, leave the overseas visitor only half-informed, and give the Chinese party a feeling that the foreigners are incompetent or ill prepared.

- Do not lose confidence if interpreters use a dictionary. No one is likely to have a vocabulary of some 40,000 words in each of two languages, and a dictionary is often essential.

- Do not jump to conclusions. Chinese ways of doing things are often different from what you expect. Listen *without* interrupting. You can always ask questions later, at the appropriate time.

- Do not be suspicious if a speaker talks for five minutes and the interpreter covers what was said in one minute. The speaker may have been wordy.

- Be understanding should the interpreter make a mistake. It is almost impossible to avoid making some errors, because Chinese and most other languages are so dissimilar.

Double-Checking during and after Meetings

■ During meetings, write out the main points discussed. This allows both parties to double-check their understanding.

■ After meetings, confirm in writing what has been agreed.

■ Assume that all numbers over 10,000 may be mistranslated. Repeat them carefully and write them down for all to see. In China, the system for expressing large sums differs from that used in other countries, often resulting in errors occurring. The unit billion should be avoided, as it means: 1,000,000,000,000 (one million million) in Europe and 1,000,000,000 (one thousand million) in the United States.

GUIDELINES FOR USING TRANSLATORS AND INTERPRETERS

Interpreting and translating provide challenges for the managers of specialists in these fields, especially when those managers do not know the target language. Those who are bilingual as well as managers should take a proactive approach involving a lot of questioning and checking of meanings, and a healthy skepticism about what one is being told. With translations, one should ask how confident a translator is that something can be translated only as has been done. And with interpreters, it is wise to check whether, even if the interpretation was a fair rendition of what was said, there had been any nonverbal cues on the part of the speaker that might cause one to doubt that the statement was unqualified.

You may wish to practice with machine translations (Google and other Web sites provide machine translations of retrieved items) and work with a native speaker of the target language to achieve an optimally lucid translation.

There is more than one way to express most ideas: "this is a pen," "a pen this is," and "this a pen is" could be acceptable translations, and which is best depends on context, grammar, and cultural determinants.

Remember that disagreement is never indicated by a statement of disagreement among the Chinese, vague answers being the norm. A direct response such as "I'll think about it" is one possible negative reply; and if in a personal conversation you were to ask, "How about dinner tonight?" the negative response could be, "Good idea, but I'll have to discuss it with my wife first." It is, thus, important that you instruct your interpreter to provide you with a cultural as well as a linguistic interpretation.

Interpreting can be successive or simultaneous. Most business interpreting is successive, as simultaneous interpreting usually requires the speaker to provide the interpreter with the script in advance or to speak only in small chunks before pausing for the interpreter.

Many business meetings include and allow interpreting, and all parties cooperate to ensure that communication is successful after each chunk of information before moving to the next.

It is generally better to use an outside, professional interpreter rather than one supplied by the other party. Doing so makes it easier to obtain more information about the cultural nuances of words or phrases and about body language. Such details are not likely to be forthcoming if the interpreter is a member of the other party.

Regarding translations, you should be proactive in discussing their meaning, paragraph by paragraph, sentence by sentence. You should always ask if there is any other way to translate the sentences and what other meanings—including covert meanings—particular words, phrases, and sentences might have.

Finally, it is best to regard your understanding of a controversial interpretation or translation as only provisional. So, should you want early closure and feel uncomfortable with delayed or provisional versions of what the other side has said, inform your colleagues that you are signing off on the meaning even though others might not.

Notes

1 Occasionally, we come across individuals who are masterful at negotiating with the Chinese. Invariably, they have special experience and skills, know China well and keep up to date, have a network of business friends, often have language fluency or use interpreters skillfully, and possess other well-developed knowledge or techniques. Other individuals simply fail, demonstrating that the team approach is, generally speaking, the only way to handle negotiations with the Chinese. Moreover, the best negotiating teams are those that have been coached (chapter 10).

2 Religion is not generally discussed among Chinese, many of whom are skeptical about something they believe breeds hypocrisy. Few Chinese in China understand religion and some question the Christian Bible for making no reference to China.

3 Chapter 9 treats this topic more fully.

4 Even if he seeks profit, an individual whose ways are virtuous will be respected and trusted. An individual who lacks virtue is considered inferior because he is untrustworthy and unscrupulous.

5 Li, or proper behavior, is not so important in business if one is virtuous.

6 Signs of a victim mentality abound in popular media. In the 1971 movie *Fists of Fury*, Bruce Lee is seen kicking down and destroying a sign that says: "No dogs or Chinese allowed." Legend has it that the English (others say the Japanese) put up similar signs in Shanghai parks in the 1930s. Be this fact or fiction, many Chinese today will say: "I saw Bruce Lee destroy that sign and, boy, did I feel good afterward! So it must be true."

7 Campaigns for good manners—such as drives to stop people from spitting in public places and to encourage people to help strangers—are being organized by the government.

8 $25,000 was spent on questionnaires and their analysis, and then on a first visit to China to discuss the results. Thereafter, there were three extended visits, with his team, on which they took three successive proposals. Each trip cost $100,000.

9 This is similar to a well-known Chinese saying, *Meiyo yongyuan de pengyou huo diren* (There are no lifetime friends or enemies).

10 All references in this book to Fang or Tony Fang denote Professor Tony Fang of the University of Stockholm, and author of the important book, *Chinese Business Negotiating Style*.

11 Also called *The Book of Changes*, the *I Ching* is an ancient Chinese manual based on a system of symbols known as the eight trigrams and sixty-four hexagrams that are symbolically interpreted in terms of the principles of yin and yang. Originally used for divination, the manual was later included as one of the five classics of Confucianism.

12 Adding to the complex of tactics and suspicions about people is the recent revival of a theory of personal power development called Thick Face, Black Heart. It comes from a book originally written in 1912 and counsels the development of secret tactical attitudes designed to help one win whatever one wishes to win (Chu 1992).

"The ideal practitioner of thick face, black heart, is one who has an inner image of himself so independent of his outward appearance or behaviors that he can be dominant or submissive as the situation calls for." Such an orientation to others creates a huge psychological distance that does not support friendship or honesty or personal integrity: one academic calls it "a travesty of the ancient wisdom of the East."

13 This was tested and refined from the mid-1980s through most of the 1990s, and eventually incorporated in an MBA graduate course, "Negotiating with the Chinese and Japanese," that began in 2001 at the University of New England, Australia. Most of the students were experienced businesspeople.

14 We believe that the Chinese are hardly better at reading the minds of Chinese from outside their region than non-Chinese. Intuitive and perceptive people should practice reading the Chinese and not be afraid of making mistakes.

Bibliography

Abramson, N., and J. X. Ai. 1996. "Performance Enhancing Strategies for China: Lessons for Japanese and American companies." Carnegie Bosch Institute, Working Paper 96 (1).

"Alliances to Hunt for Genetic Information." 2000. *Manufacturing Chemist* (February) 72 (2): 13.

Alston, Jon P., and Stephen He. 1997. *Business Guide to Modern China*. East Lansing, MI: Michigan State University Press.

Ambler, Tim, and Morgan Witzel. 2000. *Doing Business in China*. London: Routledge.

Argyle, Michael, and M. Henderson. 1985. *The Anatomy of Relationships*. London: Heinemann.

Bailey, E. K., and O. Shankar. "Management Education for International Joint Venture Managers." *Leadership & Organization Development Journal* 14 (3): 15–20.

Banthin, J., and L. Stelzer. 1988–1999. "'Opening' China: Negotiation Strategies When East Meets West." *The Mid-Atlantic Journal of Business* (December–January) 25 (2, 3): 1–14.

Barmé, Geremie R. 1999. *In the Red: On Contemporary Chinese Culture*. New York: Columbia University Press.

Bendlin, Heinz. 1986. "The Volkswagen China Experience." Chinese Culture & Management Seminar, Paris (23–24 January): 41.

Blackman, Carolyn. 1993. "Being Successful in China: The Pacific Dunlop Story." Typescript. Ballarat University College, Australia.

———. 1997. *Negotiating China*. St. Leonards, Australia: Allen and Unwin.

———. 2000. "An Insider Guide to Negotiating." *The China Business Review* (May/June) 27 (3): 44–48.

———. 2001. "Local Government and Foreign Business." *The China Business Review* (May/June) 28 (3): 26–31.

Bond, Michael H., ed. 1986. *The Psychology of the Chinese People*. Hong Kong: Oxford University Press.

Bond, Michael H. 1991. *Beyond The Chinese Face*. Hong Kong: Oxford University Press.

Brady, Anne-Marie. 2000. "Treat Insiders and Outsiders Differently: The Use and Control of Foreigners in PRC." *The China Quarterly* (December) 164: 943–96.

Brislin, Richard W. 1981. *Cross-Cultural Encounters*, New York: Pergamon Press.

Bruton, G. D., D. Ahlstrom, and E. S. Chan. 2000. "Foreign Firms in China: Foreign Human Resource Challenges in a Transitional Economy." *Advanced Management Journal*. Society for Advancement of Management (Autumn) 65 (4):4–11.

Burstein, Daniel, and Arne De Keijer. 1998. *Big Dragon: China's Future: What It Means for Business.* New York: Simon and Schuster.

Calantine, R. J., and Y. S. Zhao. 2001. "Joint Ventures in China: A Comparative Study of Japanese, Korean and U.S. Partners." *Journal of International Marketing* 9 (1): 1–23.

Casse, Pierre. 1982. *Training for The Multicultural Manager.* Washington, D.C.: Sietar International.

Casse, Pierre, and Surinder Deol. 1985. *Managing Intercultural Negotiations.* Washington, D.C.: Sietar International.

Chemical Market Reporter. 21 May, 2001: 3. "Celanese, China National Tobacco Explore Joint Expansion in China."

Chen, Min. 1995. *Asian Management Systems: Chinese, Japanese and Korean Styles of Business.* London: Routledge.

Chu Chin-Ning. 1992. *Thick Face, Black Heart.* St. Leonards, Australia: Allen and Unwin.

———. 1991. *The Asian Mind Game.* Toronto: Collier Macmillan Canada.

Clegg, Stewart R., and S. Gordon Redding, eds. 1990. *Capitalism in Contrasting Cultures.* Berlin: De Gruyter.

Cochran, Sherman. 2000. *Encountering Chinese Networks: Western, Japanese and Chinese Corporations in China.* Berkeley, CA: University of California Press.

Collins Associates. 1969. *Quotations From Chou En-Lai.* Melbourne: Flesch.

Davis, Deborah, ed. 2000. *The Consumer Revolution in Urban China.* Berkeley, CA: University of California Press.

Direct Investment and Joint Ventures in China: A Handbook for Corporate Negotiations. 1991. New York: Quorum Books.

Dunbar, R. L. M., and A. Bird. 1992. "Preparing Managers for Foreign Assignments: The Expatriate Profile Program." *Journal of Management Development* 11 (7): 58–66.

East Asia Analytic Unit Staff. 1996. *Overseas Chinese Business Networks in Asia.* Canberra: The Club.

Engholm, Christophe. 1994. *Doing Business in Asia's Booming China Triangle.* Englewood Cliffs, NJ: Prentice Hall.

Fang, Tony. 1996. "A Model of Chinese Negotiating Style." Paper presented at 6th Nordic Workshop on Interorganizational Research, Norwegian School of Management, Oslo (23–25 August).

———. 1997. "Chinese Business Negotiating Style: A Socio-Cultural Approach." Licentiate dissertation. Linkoping University, Sweden: Department of Industrial Marketing.

———. 1999. *Chinese Business Negotiating Style.* Thousand Oaks, CA: Sage.

———. 2001. "Culture as a Driving Force for Interfirm Adaptation: A Chinese Case." *Industrial Marketing Management* (January) 30 (1): 51–63.

Fang, Percy Jucheng, and Lucy Guinong J. Fang. 1986. *Zhou En-lai: A Profile.* Beijing: Foreign Languages Press.

Freeman, Duncan, ed. 1994. *The Life and Death of a Joint Venture in China.* Hong Kong: Asia Law and Practice.

Fukuyama, Francis. 1995. *Trust.* New York: Penguin.

Gao Yuan. 1991. *Lure the Tiger Out of the Mountains: The Thirty-Six Stratagems of Ancient China*. New York: Simon and Schuster.

Gibbons, Russell L. 1996. *Joint Ventures in China*. South Melbourne, Australia: MacMillian.

Giles, Lionel. 1988. *Sun Tzu and the Art of War*. Singapore: Graham Brash.

Godley, Michael R. 1981. *The Mandarin Capitalists from Nanyang*. New York: Routledge.

Goldenberg, Susan. 1988. *Hands Across the Ocean: Managing Joint Ventures with a Spotlight on China and Japan*. Boston: Harvard Business Press.

Greenblatt, Sidney L, Richard W. Wilson, and Amy Auerbacher (eds.). 1982. *Social Interaction in Chinese Society*. New York: Praeger.

Grow, Roy F. 1986. "Japanese and American Firms in China: Lessons of a New Market." *Columbia Journal of World Business* (Spring): 49–56.

Hakansson, Hakan, and Ivan Snehota. 1995. *Developing Relationships in Business Networks*. New York: Routledge.

Hammer, M. 1987. "Behavioral Dimensions of Intercultural Effectiveness." *International Journal of Intercultural Relations* 11: 65–88.

Harris, Philip T., and Robert T. Moran. 1979. *Managing Cultural Differences*. Houston, TX: Gulf Publishing Company.

Homans, George C. 1951. *The Human Group*. New York: Harcourt Brace.

Hu Wenzhong and Cornelius Grove. 1991. *Interacting with the Chinese: A Handbook for Americans in the PRC*. Yarmouth, ME: Intercultural Press.

Huang, Quanyu. 1994. *A Guide to Successful Business Relations with The Chinese*. New York: International Business Press.

Huang Quanyu, Joseph W. Leonard, and Tong Chen. 1997. *Business Decision Making in China*. Oxford, U.K.: International Business Press.

Inkpen, A. S. 1998. "Learning and Knowledge Acquisition through International Strategic Alliances." *The Academy of Management Executive* (November).

Isobe, T., S. Makino, and D. B. Montgomery. 2000. "Resource Commitment, Entry Timing, and Market Performance of Foreign Direct Investments in Emerging Economies: The Case of Japanese International Joint Ventures in China." *Academy of Management Journal* (June) 43 (3): 468–484.

Johanson, Jan, and J-E Vahlne. 1990. "The Mechanisms of Internationalisation." *International Marketing Review* 7: 11–24.

Kanter, R. M. 1994. "Collaborative Advantage." *Harvard Business Review* (July–August): 96–108.

Kanter, R. M., and R. I. Gow. 1994. "Do Cultural Differences Make a Business Difference?" *Journal of Management Development* 13 (2): 5–23.

Kapp, Robert A., ed. 1983. *Communicating with China*. Chicago: Intercultural Press.

Knutsson, J. 1986. "Chinese Commercial Negotiating Behaviour and Its Institutional Determinants." *Chinese Culture & Management*. Seminar Report. Paris: Euro-China Association for Management Development.

Krone, K. J., and L. Chen. 1997. "Approaches to Managerial Influence in the PRC." *The Journal of Business Communication* (July) 34 (3): 289–315.

Lee, K-H. 1996. "Moral Consideration and Strategic Management Moves: The Chinese Case." *Management Decision* 34 (9): 65–70.

Li, Z. S. 1994. *The Private Life of Chairman Mao.* New York: Random House.

Lin, Yutang. 1936. *My Country and My People.* London: Heinemann.

Lorange, Peter, and Johan Roos. 1991. "Why Some Strategic Alliances Succeed and Others Fail." *Journal of Business Strategy* (January/February): 25–30.

Luo, Yadong. 1997. "Performance Implications of International Strategy: An Empirical Study of Foreign Investment Enterprises in China." *Group & Organization Management* (March) 22 (1): 87–116.

———. 2000. *How to Enter China: Choices and Lessons.* Ann Arbor, MI: University of Michigan Press.

———. 2001. *Strategy, Structure, and Performance of MNCs in China.* Westport, CT: Quorum Books.

Mann, James. 1999. *About Face.* New York: Alfred A. Knopf.

March, Robert M. 1984. "The Development of International Men: Progress Report on a New Training Approach." *Aoyama Seikei Ronshu* 11.

———. 1989. *Ru he yu: Ribenren tanpan* (How the Japanese negotiate). Translated by Wang Hua. Nanjing: Jiangsu People's Press.

———. 1994. *Inscrutables Negotiating with Inscrutables: Japanese Views on Negotiating with the Chinese.* University of Western Sydney. Nepean Working Paper no. 46 (12).

———. 1995. *Asia-Literacy and Australian-Asian Business Relationships.* University of Western Sydney. *Nepean Working Paper no. 2.*

———. 1996. *The Inter/Manage Project—First Stage.* University of Western Sydney. Nepean Working Paper no. 6.

———. 1996. *The Internationalisation of the Manager.* Copenhagen Business School Working Paper no. 3.

———. 1997. *Managing Business Relationships with East Asia: Building and Testing a Model of Long-Term Asia/Western Business Relationships.* University of Western Sydney. Nepean Working Paper no. 3.

———. 2003. *Business Relationships with the Chinese: Professional Skills for Developing Relationships of Understanding, Trust, Friendship and Family-like Feeling with Chinese Partners.* Sydney, Australia: IMDC.

McGregor, James. 2005. *One Billion Customers: Lessons from the Front Lines of Doing Business in China.* New York: Free Press.

Moran, Robert Y., and William G. Stripp. 1991. *Dynamics of Successful International Negotiations.* Oxford: Butterworth-Heinemann.

Naumann, E. 1992. "A Conceptual Model of Expatriate Turnover." *Journal of International Business Studies* 23 (3): 499–531.

Newman, William H. 1992. "Focused Joint Ventures in Transforming Economies." *The Executive* (February) 6 (1): 67–70.

———. 1992. "Launching a Viable Joint Venture." *California Management Review* (fall) 35 (1): 68–73.

———. 1995. "Stages in Cross Collaboration." *Journal of Asian Business* 11 (4): 69–94.

Osland, G. E. 1990. "Business Encounters Troubles in Shanghai." *China Market* 2: 15–17.

———. 1990. "Doing Business in China: A Framework for Cross-Cultural Understanding." *Marketing Intelligence & Planning* 8 (4): 4–14.

———. 1994. "Successful Operating Strategies in the Performance of U.S.-China Joint Ventures." *Journal of International Marketing* 2 (4): 53–78.

Porter, Robin, and Mandi Robinson. 1994. *The China Business Guide.* Keele: Ryburn Publishing.

Powers, Patrick. 2001. "Distribution in China: The End of the Beginning." *The China Business Review* 28 (4): 8–12.

Pye, Lucian W. 1982. *Chinese Commercial Negotiating Style.* Santa Monica, CA: Rand Corporation.

———. 1986. "The China Trade: Making the Deal." *Harvard Business Review* (July–August): 74–84.

Redding, Gordon. 1990. *The Spirit of Chinese Capitalism.* Berlin: De Gruyter.

Rittenberg, Sidney, and Amanda Bennett. 1993. *The Man Who Stayed Behind.* New York: Simon and Schuster.

Roloff, Michael E., and Gerald L. Miller, eds. 1987. *Interpersonal Processes: New Directions in Communications Research.* Newbury Park, CA: Sage.

Saari, J. L. 1982. "Breaking the Hold of Tradition: The Self-Group Interface in Transitional China." In Sidney L. Greenblatt, Richard W. Wilson, and Amy Auerbacher (eds.), *Social Interaction in Chinese Society.* New York: Praeger.

Sanyal, R. N., and T. Guvenli. 2001. "American Firms in China: Issues in Managing Operations." *Multinational Business Review* (fall) 9 (2): 40–46.

Sarason, I. G., and B. R. Sarason. 1995. "Social and Personal Relationships: Current Issues, Future Directions." *Journal of Social & Personal Relationships* 12 (4): 613–619.

Scarborough, Jack. 1998. "Comparing Chinese and Western Cultural Roots: Why 'East Is East'…." *Business Horizons* (November/December) 41 (6): 15.

Seagrave, Sterling. 1995. *Lords of the Rim.* New York: Putnam's Sons.

Von Senger, Harro. 1993. *The Book of Stratagems: Tactics for Triumph and Survival.* Reprint ed. New York: Viking/Penguin.

Sheer, Vivian C. 2002. "Negotiator Expectancy and Credibility in the Eyes of the Counterparts: Findings from Sino-Western Business Negotiations." Paper presented to the National Communication Association, Seattle, U.S.A.

Sheer, Vivian C., and L. Chen. 2003. "Successful Sino-Western Business Negotiations— Participants' Accounts of National and Professional Cultures." *The Journal of Business Communication* (January) 40 (1): 50–85.

Sims, T. L., and J. J. Sims. 2000. "The Great Western Development Strategy." *The China Business Review* (November/December), 27 (6): 44–49.

Situ Tan. 1998. *Best Chinese Idioms.* Vol. 1 and 2 (bilingual). Hong Kong: Haifeng Publishing Company.

Solomon, Richard H. 1995. *Chinese Political Negotiating Behavior, 1967–1984.* Santa Monica, CA: Rand Corporation.

Studwell, Joe. 2002. *The China Dream: The Quest for the Last Great Untapped Market on Earth.* New York: Atlantic Monthly Press.

Stuttard, John. 2000. *The New Silk Road: Secrets of Business Success in China Today.* New York: John Wiley.

Sun Haichen. 1991. *The Wiles of War: 36 Military Strategies from Ancient China.* Beijing: Foreign Languages Press.

Supachai Panitchpakdi and Mark Clifford. 2002. *China and the WTO.* New York: Wiley.

Tenev, Stoyan, and Chunlin Zhang, with Loup Brefort. 2002. *Corporate Governance and Enterprise Reform in China: Building the Institutions of Modern Markets.* Washington, D.C.: World Bank.

Thomas, Timothy L. 2003. "New Developments in Chinese Strategic Psychological Warfare." *Special Warfare* (April) 16 (1): 2–11.

———. 2004. *Dragon Bytes: Chinese Information—War Theory and Practice.* Kansas: Foreign Military Studies Office, Fort Leavenworth, KS.

Tiessan, J. H., and J. D. Linton. 2000. "The JV Dilemma: Cooperating and Competing in Joint Ventures." *Canadian Journal of Administrative Science* (September) 17 (3): 203–216.

Trompenaars, Fons, and Charles Hampden-Turner. 1997. *Riding the Waves of Culture.* Ithaca, NY: Irwin.

Walker, Tony, Denis Levett, and Roger Flanagan. 1998. *China: Building for Joint Ventures.* 2nd edition. Hong Kong: Hongkong University Press.

Whyte, Martin King. 1974. *Small Groups and Political Rituals in China.* Berkeley, CA: University of California Press.

Wong, Y. H., and Thomas Leung. 2001. *Guanxi: Relationship Marketing in a Chinese Context.* New York: International Business Press.

Woo, H. S., and C. Prud'homme. "Cultural Characteristics Prevalent in the Chinese Negotiation Process." *European Business Review* 99 (5): 313–322.

Wu, Annie S. C. 1989. "One Must Dare to Take Risks in Doing Business with China." *China Market* no. 3: 22–24.

Yadong, Luo, and Min Chen. 1997. "Does Guanxi Influence Firm Performance?" *Asia Pacific Journal of Management* vol. 14: 1–16.

Yan, A., and B. Gray. 1994. "Bargaining Power, Management Control and Performance in U.S.-China Joint Ventures." *Academy of Management Journal* (December) 37 (6): 1478–1517.

Yan, Yu Xiang. 1996. *The Flow of Gifts.* Stanford, CA: Stanford University Press.

Yang, K. S. 1992. "Do Traditional Values Coexist in a Modern Chinese Society?" *Proceedings of the Conference on Chinese Perspectives on Values,* 117–158. Taipei: Center for Sinological Studies.

Yang, Mayfair Mei-hui. 1994. *Gifts, Favors, and Banquets.* Ithaca, NY: Cornell University Press.

Zapalska, A. M., and W. Edwards. 2001. "Chinese Entrepreneurship in a Cultural and Economic Perspective." *Journal of Small Business Management* (July) 39 (3): 286–292.

Zhao, J. T. 2000. "The Chinese Approach to International Business Negotiation." *The Journal of Business Communication* 37 (3): 209–237.

Acknowledgments

Many people whose paths we crossed over the years that we were developing this book gave us invaluable assistance. The China-connected businesspeople and professionals who contributed to our thinking include Dr. Dan Sun, Jennifer Chen, Jonathan Yan, Wang Hua, Piao Xijing, Li Qianxin, Martin Zhou, Sun Bei, Chanel Tong, Xu Feihu, Jack Hsiang, Yang Jing, Chen Ping, Xu Yan, Constant Cheng, and Chen Jianfu.

Businesspeople with experience in China also contributed ideas to this volume. We wish to thank James Blakeney, Eva Chen, Lawrence Fong, Andrena Gothard, Grace Pang, Joseph Tuma, David Wang, Jan Waszczuk, Rod Zamanek, and David Zhou.

Professionals in the field of Chinese or Asian business or negotiation who offered thoughts and information in the early stages of the book's development include: China negotiation specialist and author, Professor Tony Fang, University of Stockholm (tony.fang@fek.su.se); Professor Michael Blaker, University of Southern California; Professor Soo May Chen, University of Macau; Professor Gregory Clark, vice-president, Akita International University, Japan; former Australian Ambassador to Seoul Mack Williams; Professor Vic Wright, former director of the Graduate School of Business at the University of New England, Australia; Professor Huang Zhenhua, UIBE Beijing; and, in the more distant past, author Carolyn Blackman.

Many of the international business people enrolled in March's online course, "Business Negotiation with the Chinese and Japanese" (MBA School, University of New England), contributed case studies and anecdotes based on their experiences negotiating in China. They include Samantha Evans (who contributed the original version of "How Giving Face Can Brew Success," chapter 3), Stephen Ashmore, Gary Dawson, Rod Hanson, Ken M'Leod, Anne Normoyle, David Osborne, Durai Ratnam, Richard Zin, Peter Stavroff, Geoff Hussey, Andrea Gothard, Mark McClelland, James Salmon, Caven Tootall, and Attila Tottszer. We thank them sincerely.

Among the others who have helped with the development of our thinking on negotiating with the Chinese, we should like to mention the following individuals: John Pegler, CEO of Ensham Coal Resources, a rare CEO who takes responsibility for the small print of negotiation and whose trenchant thinking helped us both to revise and reshape our twelve-step process for planning negotiations and the Strategic Negotiation Process (SNP). In addition, gratitude goes to senior international manager John Mackay, for his intelligent mastery of the twelve-step planning process; the multilingual Dilip Khatri, who contributed ideas for our earlier training handouts that became the appendix, on how to manage interpreters and translators; and not least to our good personal and professional friend, Calum Coburn, Managing Director of the Negotiation Institute, who also provided important strategic assistance in putting this book to bed.

We undertook negotiation consulting in Southern China for Janette Lee, of Lee Ellison, for Brian Keough in Beijing, and others whose cases have been disguised for publication here. Ron Gosbee, formerly of AWA Aerospace, taught us a great deal about what it takes for a foreigner to develop genuine guanxi business relationships with the Chinese.

We are very grateful to our old friend Professor Huang Zhenhua of UIBE for his thorough reading of a late draft of the book and correcting a number of errors. We also owe a big professional and personal debt to Calum Coburn, Managing Director of the Negotiation Institute (calum.coburn@negotiationtraining.com.au), both for his professional cooperation and friendship at all times, and in particular for his assistance in the last stages of putting this book together.

Robert Thomas, Donald Westmore, and others read an early draft of the book and contributed valuable feedback that helped to rid the manuscript of many redundancies and structural defects. Thank you, too, Barry Lancet of Kodansha International in Tokyo (which has now published four of our books), an old friend who believed in our ideas from the beginning.

A Final Note from the Authors

The Chinese Negotiator was in incubation for ten years, while we led our lives as China-Japan businesspeople, consultants, seminar leaders, and lecturers. Then the manuscript underwent development for three years. The initial stimulus to write this volume had come from my earlier book, *The Japanese Negotiator* (Kodansha International, and still in print).

Those who teach and write about doing business with China would agree that successful negotiation outcomes and long-term relationships with the Chinese flourish on the seedbed of well-stocked minds, a love of inquiry, and tenacious curiosity. The necessary stimulus comes from two learning characteristics: range and power.

By **range** we mean that you should read as widely as possible. A good start is with wide-ranging introductory books on China, such as Ambler and Witzel's *Doing Business in China*, or Joe Studwell's epic *The China Dream: The Quest for the Last Great Untapped Market on Earth.*

Power means that you should delve into, immerse yourself in, and become knowledgeable about specific subjects. An important and powerful book is Mayfair Yang's *Gifts, Favors, and Banquets: The Art of Social Relationships in China.* It is the definitive work on *guanxi*—social relationships—among the Chinese. Informative and powerful, it sheds light on the bad as well as the good side of guanxi relationships between Chinese in all walks of life. We believe you cannot understand modern China without reading this book.

We have been involved in training China negotiators, consulting, and carrying out research projects since 1996, with special focus on the stages that business relationships go through as they develop between Chinese and Westerners.

Naturally, final responsibility for the quality of the book is ours.

(英文版) チャイニーズ・ネゴシエイター
The Chinese Negotiator

2006年10月30日　第1刷発行

著　者　ロバート・マーチ、スーファ・ウ
発行者　富田 充
発行所　講談社インターナショナル株式会社
　　　　〒112-8652　東京都文京区音羽 1-17-14
　　　　電話　03-3944-6493（編集部）
　　　　　　　03-3944-6492（マーケティング部・業務部）
　　　　ホームページ　www.kodansha-intl.com

印刷・製本所　大日本印刷株式会社

© ロバート・マーチ、スーファ・ウ 2006
Printed in Japan
ISBN 4-7700-3028-2